Brief Contents

W9-APE-041

Contents

Professionalism
Skills for Workplace Success

Custom Second Edition

Taken from:

Professionalism: Skills for Workplace Success, Second Edition
by Lydia E. Anderson and Sandra B. Bolt

The Job Searcher's Handbook, Third Edition
by Carolyn R. Robbins

PEARSON

ISBN 10: 1-256-50393-2
ISBN 13: 978-1-256-50393-4

Workplace Basics

Module 3 Relationships

Career Planning Tools

Module 4

Material in this book has been taken from the following Pearson sources:

Chapters 1-16 taken from *Professionalism: Skills for Workplace Success*, Second Edition, by Lydia E. Anderson and Sandra B. Bolt (chapters 1-16).

Appendix B taken from *The Job Searcher's Handbook*, Third Edition, by Carolyn R. Robbins (chapter 4).

Video Case Study Index

College educators continue to be bombarded with employer concerns regarding recent graduates' lack of ability to demonstrate appropriate workplace behavior. Few students are able to make the connection between self-esteem, personal financial management, and workplace performance. Many are unaware of the expectations regarding business etiquette, appropriate use of technology, and proper attire. In today's challenging economy and increasingly competitive work environment, it is imperative that students know how to appropriately communicate and deal with conflict, teamwork, and accountability in a fair and ethical manner. Educators have an obligation to employers to teach students these soft but vital skills regarding workplace behavior. This second edition text addresses these issues and provides readers with the current and practical skills necessary to maintain success on the job. Information is complete, yet presented in a concise, easy-to-read format.

Professionalism Skills for Workplace Success, is written to address employer concerns and provides employees with basic skills for success on the job. This text prepares students for their first professional workplace experience. However, the content is applicable to any individual who works within a traditional business environment. The book is designed not as a textbook, but as a workbook that can be kept and referred to throughout one's career.

Unique Approach

Presented in a simple, highly interactive format, the text assists individuals in understanding the foundation of effective workplace relationships and how to appropriately manage these relationships. Based on the basic business principle that workplace performance affects success and profitability, readers are able to integrate soft skills within the framework of a formal business structure. The topics and principles presented will benefit every individual, no matter their career goal. Utilizing a gender-neutral character named Cory, individuals will gain valuable insights based upon Cory's real workplace dilemmas presented as case studies. Additionally, throughout the text are exercises, web quizzes, student discussion topics, and activities designed to improve the reader's written and oral communication skills.

This book is written for professors, instructors, teachers, and workshop trainers to motivate individuals toward success in the workplace. Attitude, communication, and human relations are the keys to surviving in today's ever-changing workplace. This book teaches realistic survival skills and motivates individuals toward improving both their personal and professional performance.

Organization

The text is divided into four modules and sixteen chapters that are arranged to accommodate quarter-, half-, or full-semester courses. Module and chapter topics include:

Module 1: Self-Management

Attitude and Personality
Goal Setting and Life Management
Personal Financial Management
Time and Stress Management/Organization Skills

Module 2: Workplace Basics

Ethics, Politics, and Diversity
Etiquette/Dress
Customer Service/Quality
Human Resource Management

Module 3: Relationships

Communication
Accountability and Workplace Relationships
Teamwork, Motivation, and Leadership
Conflict and Negotiation

Module 4: Career Planning Tools

Job Search Planning
Resumé Package
Interview Techniques
Career and Life Changes

New to This Edition

Integrating feedback from instructors, students, and business leaders, this second edition text provides readers with current and necessary tools for both job search and career success. The custom edition has been heavily revised to incorporate a consistent professional tone and increased use of key terms, definitions, and examples for clarification. New chapter features include:

· **Web Quiz** directs students to online topic-related assessments.
· **Talk It Out** features focus on important discussion topics to stimulate lively in-class discussion.
· **Learn More** sections have been added to the end-of-chapter materials, recommending additional courses for students to take to encourage continuous learning.

Reflecting recent changes in the technological, economic, and employment environments, the following changes have been incorporated into this edition:

The **Self-Management** module includes:

- updated personal finance material to reflect the current U.S. economic challenges.
- cash management tips to address the appropriate use of debit and ATM cards.
- an updated discussion on the wise use of credit, FICO scores, free credit report information, and updated information regarding identify theft.
- a more concise stress management discussion that links stress to workplace performance.
- updated organization tips, including the use of current technological tools for organization.

The **Workplace Basics** module includes:

- Ethics and Politics (formerly Chapter 5) merged with Diversity (formerly Chapter 7) to create the new Chapter 5: Ethics, Politics, and Diversity.
- an expanded diversity discussion addressing individuals with physical and mental disabilities.
- a greatly expanded Chapter 7: Etiquette/Dress.
- an expanded dress code discussion, including its influence on safety and security issues.
- a greatly enhanced and updated section on technology etiquette regarding mobile communication devices such as PDAs, iPods, and wireless computers.
- a new section on the etiquette of texting.
- an expanded phone etiquette discussion.
- a new section on the appropriate use of speaker phones.
- a new section on the importance of employees knowing and practicing computer basics, including backing up files, conducting routine virus scans, and basic troubleshooting.
- clarification on the difference between goods and services.
- a new section on creativity and innovation.
- simplified human resources discussion on unions.

The **Relationships** module includes:

- the technological influences of sending formal communications via e-mail attachments.
- expanded discussion on documentation for business and billing purposes.
- a new section on effective presentations, including presentation types, preparation, handouts, and other issues guiding the student toward success and confidence in presentations.
- a new section addressing communication devices in work situations, including texting.
- a new section on text slang and foul language in a work environment.
- expanded discussion on personal accountability, including the appropriate times to call in sick and the importance of performing your job.
- an added section addressing appropriate behavior in shared work areas, including cubicles.
- a new section on meetings, including types of meetings, preparation, conference calls, etiquette, and an introduction to Robert's Rules of Order.
- a new section on team presentations and leadership styles.

The **Career Planning Tools** Module includes:

- individual chapters dedicated to job search planning, creating a resumé package, and the mastery of interview techniques.
- assessments, samples and examples, and hands-on, in-chapter activities that walk students through the process of creating and using the appropriate career planning tools.

A **Job Search** chapter, including:

- a new section on self-discovery.
- a new activity: Accomplishments Worksheet.
- a new section on career assessments.
- a new section on the development of a career objective and personal profile.
- industry research.
- targeted job searches.
- a new section on the importance of maintaining a clean electronic image.
- expanded job search portfolio information.
- a new section on employment applications.
- an expanded section on personal references and recommendations.
- expanded sources of job leads.
- a new section on pros and cons of social networking in a job search.
- expanded discussion on networking.
- a new section on job search privacy issues.
- a new section on keeping the right attitude during a job search.

A **Resumé Package** chapter, including:

- a unique walk-through of the process of creating a resumé in five steps.
- a new section on various resumé formats, including ASCII (scannable) resumés.
- increased sample resumés for student reference.
- an expanded section on cover letters, including increased samples for student reference.
- expanded discussion on tailoring a resumé.
- a new section of tips for ex-offenders.
- a new section on the complete resumé package, guiding the student through the process of reading a job announcement and adapting a resumé and cover letter to the sample job announcement.

An **Interview Techniques** chapter, including:

- important interview issues, including a targeted job search.
- expanded discussion on the importance of conducting company-specific research.
- a new section on the personal commercial.
- expanded discussion on the interview process.
- expanded discussion on the creation and appropriate use of the interview portfolio.
- updated discussion and samples of practice interview questions.
- updated discussion on pre-interview practice.
- a new section on interview methods and types of interview questions.

- discrimination and employee rights.
- a new section addressing tough interview questions, including employment gaps.
- a new section on negotiation tools.
- a new section addressing phone interviews.
- a new section addressing pre-employment screenings and medical exams.

The final chapter, **Career and Life Changes**, including:

- a new title to better reflect changes employees can make in their careers.
- a new section on entrepreneurship to reflect a common career change and career option.
- new Appendices.

New! Professionalism Video Cases

We are particularly excited about the new video case studies that are integrated into the textbook. These videos focus on key challenges students face in getting a job, and maintaining and prospering in that job. Topics include making ethical choices, workplace etiquette, proper dress and deportment, customer service orientation, conflict management, sexual harassment, meeting management, preparing for the job search, writing effective resumés and cover letters, interviewing technique, and how to behave in a performance evaluation. For a complete listing of the videos, consult the video index on page ix, following the table of contents.

These videos are available on DVD for use in the classroom to facilitate discussion and are accessible by students via the CD-ROM packaged with this text.

Resources for Students

Professionalism, Second Edition, Download Website www.pearsonhighered.com/anderson

From this location, students can download all documents, templates, and forms needed to complete textbook assignments.

NOTE: The above link accesses the download website for the 2nd edition of *Professionalism*. This custom edition contains additional appendices, templates and media. However, the student resources are identical to the regular 2nd edition, and should be obtained through the above link.

Resources for Instructors

Instructor's Resource Guide

This resource provides instructors an easy-to-follow teaching format for each chapter. Each chapter guide contains an outline of the chapter, suggestions for potential guest speakers and field studies, comprehensive writing activities, and answers to textbook exercises and activities.

Test Generator

The electronic test bank is presented chapter by chapter with true/false, multiple choice, and short-answer questions.

PowerPoint Lecture Presentation Package

Detailed PowerPoint lecture presentation slides are available.

The Instructor's Resource Guide, Test Generator, and PowerPoint Package can be downloaded at any time from the Instructor's Resource Center. To access supplementary materials online, instructors need to request an instructor access code. Go to **www.pearsonhighered.com/irc**, where you can register for an instructor access code. Within 48 hours of registering you will receive a confirming e-mail, including an instructor access code. Once you have received your code, locate your text in the online catalog and click on the Instructor Resources button on the left side of the catalog product page. Select a supplement and a log-in page will appear. Once you have logged in, you can access instructor material for all Pearson textbooks.

Professionalism Video Cases on DVD

All video cases presented in the textbook are available free of charge to adopters of the textbook on the Professionalism Video Cases DVD. Please contact your local representative for more information.

Acknowledgments

The success of our first edition exceeded our wildest dreams and we are tremendously thankful. Integrating feedback from the many business leaders and educators who have openly shared their expertise and concerns regarding necessary workplace skills, our hope is that this second edition continues to prepare students for real-world success. Updates in this second edition reflect the ever-changing and challenging business environment. We remain committed to providing readers a competitive advantage in successfully realizing and achieving their career goals, and we believe this updated edition does just that.

We are thankful for Prentice Hall and its wonderful staff who continue to provide us incredible support.

Our grateful appreciation goes to the reviewers of this text for their valued insight:

Bob Boutel, National College of Business and Technology
Shannon Cianelli, Kaplan University
Laura C. Gilliam, Western Piedmont Community College
Bonnie, Heimlich, Fox Valley Technical College
Julia Janssen, Ridgewater College
Arlyn J Melcher, Southern Illinois University
Nancy Poretto, Kathrine Gibbs School
Renee Trammell, Spartanburg Community College

In addition, we want to thank Mindy Shirey and Autumn Bell, Fresno City College coworkers, for their input toward the second edition.

Author Profiles

Lydia E. Anderson has a Masters in Business Administration with an emphasis in marketing. In addition to years of corporate marketing and strategic planning experience, she has been teaching for over twelve years in a community college setting. She is currently a tenured faculty member and past Chair of the Business Administration and Marketing Department at Fresno City College in Fresno, California, and also an adjunct professor at California State University, Fresno. Her teaching areas of expertise include human relations in business, management/supervision, human resources management, and marketing. Ms. Anderson regularly consults with corporations on business topics relating to management and marketing.

Sandra B. Bolt has a Masters in Business Administration with an emphasis in human resource management. She has been teaching in the college setting for over twenty years. She is currently a tenured faculty member and past Chair of the Business and Technology Department at Fresno City College in Fresno, California. Her teaching areas of expertise include workplace relationships, office occupations, office technology, resumé/interview, and document formatting. She is currently the Secretary/Treasurer of the college district union. She has extensive secretarial and leadership experience, and has served as a computer applications trainer. She is a certified Crown Financial Leader and Trainer and has led many personal financial management sessions for community groups. She has been a volunteer guest speaker at professional conferences and high school career fairs, in addition to her involvement with committees and student functions at Fresno City College.

Both authors have used their professional, educational, and personal experiences to provide readers with realistic stories and challenges experienced in a typical workplace.

To Carol, Dianne, and Sue, for your wisdom and treasured friendship. To my four peeps, for your laughter and for keeping me focused on the things that really matter in life. To my son, Tim, who makes me happy and proud. To my husband, Randy, I can't imagine life without you. And finally, to my awesome God, who continues to give me blessings beyond measure. —Lydia E. Anderson

To my husband, Bret, and my son, Brandon, who are my lifelines. They have been supportive, patient, and loving throughout the time it took to write this second edition. To the memory of my parents, who helped me through a rough time in my life and set me on the right path to my successful teaching career and to the writing of this text. And, of course, to God, for giving me the blessings and strength I have in my life. —Sandra B. Bolt

Your Attitude and Personality

chapter 1

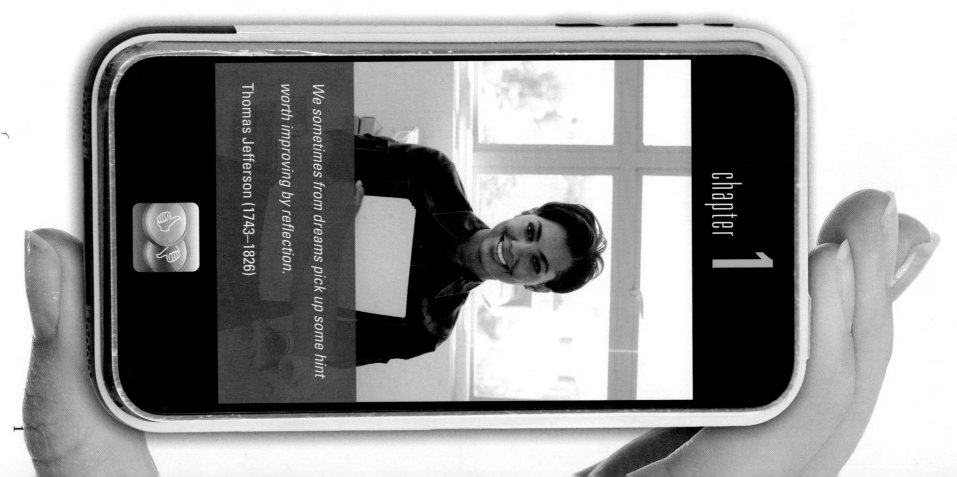

We sometimes from dreams pick up some hint worth improving by reflection.

Thomas Jefferson (1743–1826)

Objectives

- Define and describe *personality* and *attitude* and their influence in the workplace

- Identify individual personality traits and *values*

- State the difference between *self-esteem* and *self-image*

- Identify and develop a strategy to deal with past, negative experiences

- Define *locus of control*

- Identify your primary and secondary *learning styles*

- Create a personal handbook

All About You

Congratulations! Whether you know it or not, this is a book about you. And because this text is about you, we need you to first perform a simple exercise. Look in a mirror and write the first three words that immediately come to your mind.

1. _____

2. _____

3. _____

These three words are your "mirror words." Mirror words describe the foundation of how you view yourself, how you view others, and how you will perform in the workplace.

Reading this text is the first step toward experiencing a more fulfilling and productive career. The secret to healthy relationships at work is to first understand you. Once you understand your personal needs, motivators, and irritants, it becomes easier to begin to understand and successfully work with others. This is why chapter 1 focuses on you, including your personality, your values, and your self-esteem.

Personality and attitude dictate how one responds to conflict, crisis, and other typical workplace situations. Each of these typical workplace situations involves working with and through people. Understanding your own personality and attitude makes it much easier to understand your reactions to others' personalities and attitudes.

The workplace is comprised of people. **Human relations** are the interactions that occur with and through people. These interactions create relationships. You will have a relationship with anyone you come in contact with in an organization. For an organization to be profitable, its employees must be productive. It is difficult to be productive if you cannot work with your colleagues. Workplace productivity is a result of positive workplace interactions and relationships.

Because your personality is a result of influences, it is important to note that there are many outside influences that affect workplace relationships. These influences may include immediate family, friends, extended family, religious affiliation, and even society as a whole. This means that your experiences and influences outside of work affect your professional behavior. It also means the inverse: your experiences and influences at work affect your personal life. Therefore, to understand workplace relationships, you must first understand yourself.

Personality and Values

Your behavior is a reflection of your personality. **Personality** is a stable set of traits that assist in explaining and predicting an individual's behavior. For example, if you are typically organized at work and suddenly become disorganized, others may believe something is wrong. This is because your disorganized behavior was not in sync with your typical stable set of organized traits. In the total person approach, an individual's personality is shaped by many variables including past experience, family, friends, religion, and society influences. Perhaps a family member was incredibly organized and passed this trait on to you. Maybe someone in your sphere of influence was incredibly unorganized, which influenced you to be very organized. These experiences (positive or not) shape your values. **Values** are ideas that are important to you as an individual. Note that your values are good or bad based upon your personal experiences and influences. These influences include religion, family, and societal issues such as marriage, wealth, and materialism. For example, one individual may not value money because he or she has been told "money is the root of all evil." Contrast this with an individual who values money because he or she has been taught that it is a valuable resource used to ensure a safe, secure future. Since values are ideas that are important to you, they will directly affect your personality. For example, if you have been taught that money is a valuable resource you may be very careful in your spending. Your personality trait will be that of a diligent, hard-working person that spends cautiously.

Here is an example of how one's past experience shapes one's values. Cory has worked hard to secure a new job. None of Cory's friends attended college, and many have a hard time securing and/or maintaining employment. For this reason, Cory gets no support from friends regarding earning a degree and securing employment. Unfortunately, as long as Cory maintains the same set of friends, it will be difficult to achieve success at work because the influences from these friends heavily impact Cory's values and beliefs in the ability to perform successfully at work.

Attitudes

As explained in the preceding example, Cory's lifestyle and behavior are heavily influenced by a close peer group (family and friends). If not careful, over time, Cory may develop the same attitude regarding education.

An **attitude** is a strong belief toward people, things, and situations. For example, you can either be caring or uncaring about how your classmates feel about you. Your past success and failures affect your attitude. Your attitude is related to your values and personality. Using the previous money example, if you value money then your attitude will be positive toward work because you value what you get in return—your paycheck. Attitude affects performance. An individual's performance significantly influences a group's performance. A group's performance, in turn, impacts an organization's performance. Think about a barrel of juicy, red apples. Place one bad apple in the barrel of good apples, and, over time, the entire barrel will be spoiled. That is why it is so important to evaluate your personal influences. That barrel reflects your personal goals and your workplace behavior. Your attitude affects not only your performance but also the performance of those with whom you come in contact.

Does this mean you avoid anyone you believe is a bad influence? Not necessarily. You cannot avoid certain individuals such as relatives and coworkers. However, you should be aware of the impact individuals have on your life. If certain individuals have a negative influence, avoid or limit your exposure to the negative influence (bad apple). If you continue to expose yourself to negative influences, you lose sight of goals, which may result in a poor attitude.

Talk It Out

What cartoon character best reflects you?

Self-Esteem, Self-Image, and Projection

Let us review your "mirror words" from the beginning of this chapter. What did you see? Are your words positive or negative? Whatever you are feeling is a result of your **self-esteem**. Self-esteem is how you view yourself. Thoughts regarding your intelligence, attractiveness, or ability to achieve a dream are examples of self-esteem. **Self-image** is your belief of how others view you. If your self-esteem is positive and strong, you will reflect confidence and not worry about how others view your actions. If you are insecure, you will rely heavily on what others think of you; hence, you will rely heavily on creating a favorable self-image. While it is important to show concern for what others think of you, it is more important to have a positive self-concept—not conceited but self-confident. People are drawn to individuals who display a good attitude, are confident, and are consistently positive. If you believe in yourself, a positive self-image will follow without effort. It is easy to see the tremendous impact both personality and attitude have in the development of your self-esteem and self-image. The way you feel about yourself and your environment is reflected in how you treat others. This is called **projection**.

Envision a hand mirror. The handle of the mirror (the foundation) is your personality. The frame of the mirror is your personal values. The mirror itself is your attitude, which is reflected for you and the world to see. The way you view yourself is your self-esteem; the way others see you is your self-image.

Dealing with Negative "Baggage"

Many individuals have had past experiences that have been traumatic and painful. These past experiences may include rape, incest, an unplanned pregnancy, a criminal offense, or a poor choice. Unfortunately, these experiences are the ones that most heavily impact your personality, values, and self-esteem.

Consider the following example concerning Cory. In high school, Cory made a poor choice and got in trouble with the law. Cory paid the dues, yet is still embarrassed and feels unworthy of a brighter future. Cory is trying to climb the mountain of success carrying a hundred-pound suitcase. The suitcase is filled with previous poor choices and embarrassment. From others' perspective, Cory does not need to carry this unnecessary baggage. In fact, most friends and acquaintances are unaware of Cory's past mistake.

Exercise 1-1   All About You

Describe yourself.

Personality Traits	Your Personal Values	Your Attitude Toward Working Full-Time
1.	1.	1.
2.	2.	2.
3.	3.	3.

If you are one of these individuals who has had a painful experience, recognize the impact your past has on your future. Although you cannot change yesterday, you can most certainly improve your today and your future. Begin taking these steps toward a more productive future:

1. *Confront your past.* Whatever skeleton is in your past, admit that it occurred. Do not try to hide or deny that it happened. There is no need to share the episode with everyone with whom you come in contact, but it may help to confidentially share the experience with one individual (close friend, family member, religious leader, or trained professional) who had no involvement with the negative experience. Verbally talking through your feelings is the first step toward healing.

2. *Practice forgiveness.* Past negative experiences create hurt. A process in healing is to forgive whoever hurt you. This does not justify that what was done was acceptable. The act of forgiveness does, however, reconcile in your heart that you are dealing with the experience and are beginning to heal. Identify who needs forgiveness. Maybe it was a family member, perhaps it was a friend or neighbor, or maybe it was you. Your act of forgiveness may involve a conversation with someone, or it may just involve a conversation with yourself. Practice forgiveness. In doing so, you will begin to feel a huge burden being lifted.

3. *Move forward.* Let go of the guilt and/or embarrassment. Once you have begun dealing with your past, move forward. Do not keep dwelling on the past and using it as an excuse or barrier toward achieving your goals. If you are caught in this step, physically write the experience down on a piece of paper and the words "I forgive Joe" (replace the name with the individual who harmed you). Then take the paper and destroy it. This physical act puts you in control and allows you to visualize the negative experience being diminished. As you become more confident with yourself, your negative experience becomes enveloped with the rest of your past and frees you to create a positive future.

This sometimes painful process is necessary if your goal is to become the best individual you can be. It is not something that happens overnight. As mentioned previously, some individuals may need professional assistance to help them through the process. There is no shame in seeking help. In fact, there is great freedom when you have finally let go of the "baggage" and are able to climb to the top of the mountain unencumbered.

LOCUS of Control

The reality is that you will not be 100 percent surrounded by positive influences. You cannot control everything that happens in your life. Your attitude is affected by who you believe has control over situations that occur in your life.

Exercise 1-2   Letting Go

How should Cory deal with the negative baggage?

The **locus of control** identifies who you believe controls your future. An individual with an *internal* locus of control believes that he or she controls his or her own future. An individual with an *external* locus of control believes that others control his or her future.

Extremes on either end of the locus of control are not healthy. Realize that individual effort and a belief in the ability to perform well translate to individual success. However, external factors also influence your ability to achieve personal goals. Take responsibility for your actions and try your best. You cannot totally control the environment and future. Power, politics, and other factors discussed later in the text play an important part in the attainment of goals.

Learning Styles

Another element of your personality is your **learning style.** Learning styles define the method of how you best take in information and/or learn new ideas. There are three primary learning styles: visual, auditory, and tactile/kinesthetic.

To determine what your dominant learning style is, perform this common exercise: Imagine you are lost and need directions. Do you:

a. want to see a map,
b. want someone to tell you the directions, or
c. need to draw or write down the directions yourself?

If you prefer answer *a*, you are a visual learner. You prefer learning by seeing. If you selected *b*, you are an auditory learner. This means you learn best by hearing. If you selected *c*, you are a tactile/kinesthetic learner, which means you learn best by feeling, touching, or holding. No one learning style is better than the other. However, it is important to recognize your primary and secondary learning styles so that you can get the most out of your world (in and out of the classroom or on the job). As a visual learner, you may digest material best by reading and researching. Auditory learners pay close attention to course lectures and class discussions. Tactile/kinesthetic learners will learn best by performing application exercises and physically writing down course notes. Recognize what works best for you and implement that method to maximize your learning experience. Also recognize that not everyone learns the same way you do. With that recognition, you can become a better classmate, team member, and coworker.

Your Personal Handbook

Many new terms and concepts are defined in this chapter. The main idea of this discussion is that your personality and attitude affect your performance both personally and professionally. If you can say with confidence that you have no doubts regarding your external influences (friends and family) *and* your internal confidence and attitude, congratulations. You have just crossed the first big hurdle toward workplace success. If you are like the majority of the population and need a little improvement with either your internal or external influences, a bigger

Web Quiz

Take the online quiz to identify your learning style.

http://www.petersons.com/ education_planner/ discovering_article.asp? sponsor=2859&articleName =Learning_Styles_Quiz

congratulation is extended to you. Identifying areas for improvement is by far one of the most difficult hurdles to jump but certainly the most rewarding.

This book, which is about you, is designed to be a personal handbook. This handbook is going to take you on an exciting path toward creating both personal and career plans and developing a respect and understanding for personal financial management. Self-management skills including time, stress, and organization will be addressed, as well as professional etiquette and dress. Workplace politics, their implications on performance, and how to successfully use these politics in your favor will be discussed, as will your rights as an employee. These newfound workplace skills will improve your ability to lead, motivate, and successfully work with others in a team setting. Finally, you will learn how to handle conflict and work with difficult coworkers.

As we move through key concepts in this text, begin developing a positive attitude; believe in yourself and your abilities. Equally as important is that you learn from your past. Little by little, you will make lifestyle changes that will make you a better individual, which will make you an even better employee. It all translates to success at work and success in life.

Workplace Dos and Don'ts

Do realize the impact your personality has on overall workplace performance	*Don't* assume that everyone thinks and behaves like you
Do believe that you are a talented, capable human being. Project self-confidence	*Don't* become obsessed with how others view you. Be and do your best
Do let go of past baggage	*Don't* keep telling everyone about a past negative experience

Concept Review and Application

Summary of Key Concepts

- How you view yourself dictates how you treat others and what type of employee you will be
- Your views of yourself, your environment, and your past experiences comprise your personality, values, attitude, and self-esteem

- Negative past experiences create unnecessary baggage that either delays or prevents you from reaching your goals. Acknowledge and begin dealing with these negative experiences
- There are three primary learning styles: visual, auditory, and tactile/kinesthetic (sight, sound, and touch). Individuals must recognize how they best learn and also be aware that others may or may not share their same learning style

Key Terms

attitude
locus of control
self-esteem

human relations
personality
self-image

learning style
projection
values

If You Were the Boss

1. How would you deal with an employee who displays poor self-esteem?
2. How would recognizing different learning styles help you be a better boss?

Learn More

To learn more about subjects addressed in this chapter take an Introduction to Psychology course

Web Links

http://www.humanmetrics.com/cgi-win/JTypes1.htm
http://www.colorquiz.com
http://personality-project.org/personality.html
http://www.ncrel.org/sdrs/areas/issues/students/learning/lr2locus.htm

Reference

Rotter, J. B. "Generalized Expectancies for Internal versus External Control of Reinforcement." *Psychological Monographs* 80, (1966).

Activity 1–1

Apply the learning styles discussed in this chapter and complete the following statements.

In the classroom, I learn best by

_____

In the classroom, I have difficulty learning when

_____

How will you use this information to perform better?

_____

Activity 1–2

Write down four words to describe your ideal self-image.

1. _____

2. _____

3. _____

4. _____

What steps are necessary to make your ideal self-image a reality?

_____

_____

Activity 1–3

What outside experiences and influences affect your educational behavior?

Outside Experiences	Outside Influences
1.	1.
2.	2.
3.	3.
4.	4.

Activity 1–4

Tell us about yourself.

1. What is your name?

_____

2. Where were you born?

_____

3. What is your major (if you don't have one, what interests are you pursuing at school)?

_____

4. What is your favorite color?

_____

5. What is your favorite thing about attending school?

_____

6. If you could be any animal what would it be and why?

_____

7. What else would you like us to know about you?

_____

Sample Exam Questions

1. The _____ identifies who you believe controls your future.

2. _____ is an individual's perception of how he or she views himself or herself, while _____ is one's belief of how others view him or her.

3. When one understands his or her own _____ and _____, it is much easier to understand reactions to others' actions.

4. A/An _____ affects group performance, which, in turn, impacts organizational performance.

5. Dealing with negative baggage involves _____ your past, _____, and moving _____.

6. Past influences shape our _____.

Goal Setting and Life Management

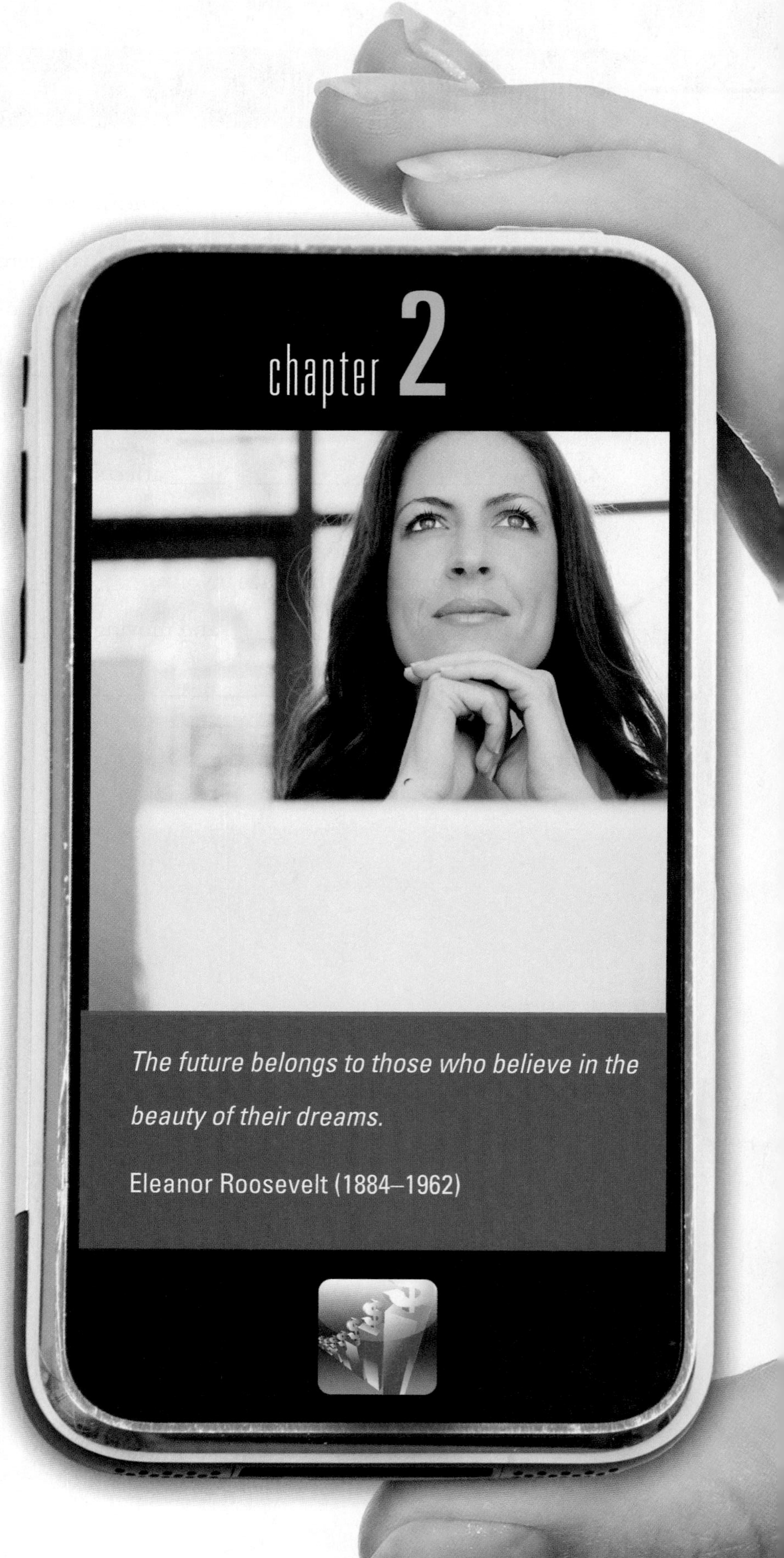
chapter 2
The future belongs to those who believe in the beauty of their dreams.
Eleanor Roosevelt (1884–1962)

Objectives

- Describe the importance of goal setting
- Identify the impact setting *goals* and *objectives* will have on your life plan
- Set realistic goals to help you reach your full potential in life
- Define goal-setting techniques
- Create *short-term* and *long-term goals*
- Describe the importance of setting *priorities*
- State the advantages of having a *mentor*

The Importance of Personal Goal Setting

To realize the importance of a goal, you must first know what a goal is. A **goal** is a long-term target. Think of a goal as a reward at the top of a ladder. To reach that reward, you need to progress up each step of the ladder. The degree of your goal will determine how long it will take to get there. Each step on your ladder has to contribute to your achievement of the final reward and support your personal values.

Goals will help you become more focused; help you increase your self-esteem; and help you overcome procrastination, fear, and failure. Setting goals will help you become more successful in your career. By setting and focusing on goals, your career plans will become more clear and meaningful.

Influences of Goals

Goals help you keep focused on where you want to be in your future. They keep you motivated to continue working to improve yourself. Goals help you achieve, not just hope for, what you want in life.

Take a look at Cory. When twenty-two years old, Cory had only a high-school education. After working as a service clerk since graduating from high school, Cory decided to go to college to become a Certified Public Accountant (CPA). Cory's long-term goal is to finish college in five years. Self-supporting and having to work, Cory set a realistic goal to obtain an associate degree in accounting within three years. After achieving that goal, Cory has found a good job, has a good income, and has more self-confidence. Still committed to becoming a CPA, Cory needs to earn a bachelor's degree and has set a goal to do that within two years. This is motivating Cory to perform well.

In the example with Cory, as one goal is reached, you will be motivated and self-confident enough to set a higher goal. You will continually strive for improvement.

Goals can and should be set in major areas of your life including personal, career, financial, educational, physical, social, and psychological. Goals help you maintain a positive outlook in all aspects of your life. They also help you maintain a more positive perception of yourself and will result in improved human relations with others. If you perceive yourself as doing well and being positive, others will feel your positive attitude.

How to Set Goals

Achieving short- and long-term goals is like climbing a ladder. Imagine that there is a major prize (what you value most) at the top of the ladder. The prize can be considered your long-term goal, and each step on the ladder is a progressive short-term goal that helps you reach the major prize.

Set short-term and long-term goals, and put them into writing. **Long-term goals** are anywhere from five to ten years, although you should reevaluate your goals each year.

To set goals think of what you want to accomplish in your life. Write down everything you can think of, including personal, career, and educational dreams. Then review the list and choose what items you most value. In reviewing your list, ask yourself where you want to be in five to ten years. These are your long-term goals. Make sure that each goal is realistic and something that you want. Each goal should be challenging enough that you will work toward it, but it should also be attainable. There must be a reason to reach this goal. Identify why each long-term goal is important to you. This is a key step because you are setting yourself up for success. Identify both opportunities and potential barriers toward reaching your goals. For example, remember Cory's goal to be a CPA? Cory has a reason to become a CPA: it represents success. It is important to Cory, and it is a realistic goal that can be reached.

Exercise 2-1   Long-Term Career Goal

Fill in the star with your long-term career goal. Identify where you want to be in your career in five years.

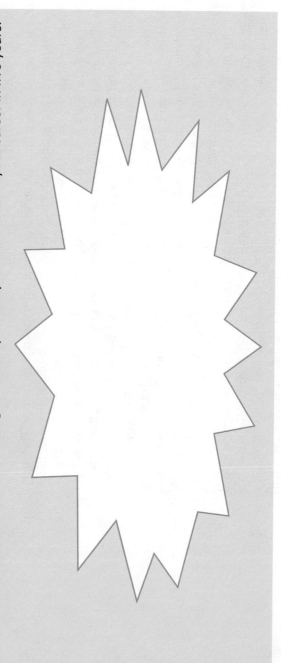

Short-term goals are goals that can be reached within a year's time. Short-term goals are set to help reach long-term goals. Businesses often refer to short-term goals as **objectives** because they are short-term, measurable, and have specific time lines. When creating personal goals, several short-term goals need to be set. These goals can be achieved in one day, a week, a month, or even several months. However, they should be achieved within a year's time and support a long-term goal.

Short-term goals/objectives must be realistic, achievable, and important to you. They need to be measurable so you know that you actually have reached them.

Another example of a long-term goal for Cory is to buy a car in one year after graduation. Cory has set several short-term goals, one being to save a specific amount of money each month. Another supporting goal is to work a specific number of hours each week. Cory also needs to be specific about the type of car, whether to buy used or new, and whether Cory needs to take out a loan. The answers to these questions will determine if the time frame is realistic and how much Cory needs to save per month.

Exercise 2-2 Short-Term Goals

Using your long-term career goal from Exercise 2-1, identify short-term goals (objectives) for each step on the ladder.

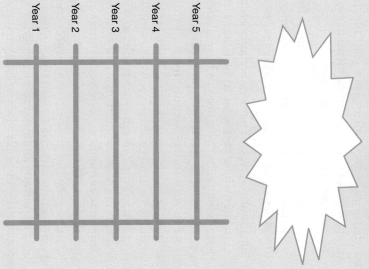

Year 1

Year 2

Year 3

Year 4

Year 5

Now that you have a list of goals, there are a few more important aspects of goal setting to consider. These include owning the goals, being in control of the goals, making the goals measurable, and setting a time frame to achieve these goals.

Owning the goal is important for successfully reaching a goal. Make sure the goal belongs to you. You should be the one to decide your goals, not your parents, spouse, significant other, friends, relatives, or anyone else who may have influence over you. For example, if Cory goes to college because it is a personal dream of being a CPA, it will be accomplished. However, if Cory goes to college to become a CPA because it was Cory's parents' idea for Cory to be a CPA, this would not be Cory's goal, and it could be hard to accomplish this goal.

Know who is in *control of the goal*. Make sure you have the right information to create these goals. This means knowing what resources and constraints are involved. Drawing on the concept of locus of control from chapter 1, not every factor is within your control. Therefore, be flexible and maintain a realistic control of your goal.

Set a time frame for reaching the goal. A time frame makes your goal measurable so you will know when you have reached your goal. Write down details. For example, instead of writing "I will become a manager in the future," write "I will become a manager with a top Accounting Firm by the beginning of the year 2014."

Write goals positively and in detail. Include: what you want, when you want to accomplish it, where you will be when you reach the goal, who is involved in helping you reach the goal, and how you will get there. Identify what it will take to meet goals in regard to finances, education, and other matters. Keep your goals realistic so they are achievable.

Talk It Out

Discuss one goal that can be set for this class.

Web Quiz

Take the online goal-setting quiz to see if you are making the most of your career potential.

http://www.achievebalance.com/data/articles/goalsetting.htm

Creating a Life Plan

Creating goals will help you with your life plan. A life plan is a written document that identifies goals in all areas of your life, including personal, career, and education. Some of your goals may blend in two or more of these areas.

Consider the following life issues:

- *Social and spiritual*: Marriage, family, friends, religion.
- *Financial*: Home ownership, car ownership, investments.
- *Activities*: Travel, hobbies, life experiences.

Think about the type of personal relationships you want in the future.

Consider where you want to be financially. Many people dream of becoming a millionaire, but you need to be realistic. Think about what kind of house you want to live in and what type of car you want to drive. If a spouse and children are in your future, account for their financial needs as well. Also, identify what outside activities you enjoy. Your personal financial plan will determine your ability to achieve these goals. This will be discussed in more detail in the next chapter. Think about what results and rewards will come from achieving your goals. Look at both intrinsic and extrinsic rewards.

Intrinsic rewards include such things as self-satisfaction and pride of accomplishment. These come from within you. **Extrinsic rewards** include such things as money and praise. These rewards come from external sources. Intrinsic and extrinsic rewards are needed to achieve satisfaction in your future. Both are equally important and need to be recognized. They motivate and can help you keep a positive outlook when working toward goals.

Planning a career is equally as important as planning your personal life. When planning your career consider:

- Why your selected career is important.
- What resources are needed to achieve your career goals.
- How you will know you have achieved career success.

Choosing the right career is important. People choose careers for different reasons, including earning power, status, intellect, and self-satisfaction. If there is a career center available at your college, take time to visit and see what it offers. Talk to friends and family members about what you do well. There are several personality and career interest tests you can take that will help you determine your potential career. These career assessments are offered at many college career centers or online. They will help you identify interests, abilities, and personality traits to determine what career will suit you best. Use all resources available and gather information to help you make the best career decision. Conduct Internet searches and interview people who are already working in your field of interest.

To be successful in your career, it is important to enjoy what you do. Select a career that supports your short-term and long-term goals.

Education is an important key to achieving your life plan. Just as your personal life goals and career goals are important, education is another contributing factor toward reaching your life plan. Consider:

- Degrees/certificates needed
- Time frame
- Financial resources
- Support network

Talk It Out

Share common rewards that are important to you. Identify these rewards as intrinsic or extrinsic.

No one can ever take your knowledge away from you. Make college course choices based upon your desired educational goals. Choose courses that will benefit you and help you explore new concepts.

Take a trip to your college career center or talk to a counselor. An excellent method to use to explore potential careers is through volunteering, job shadowing, and internships.

Priorities

Priorities determine what needs to be done and in what order. Juggling priorities is the key to reaching goals. Not only is it important in your personal life, but it will be necessary at work as well.

You may need to adjust priorities to reach your goals. Before priorities can be put in order, you need to determine what they are. Sometimes your first priority is not necessarily what is most important in life; it is just that a particular activity demands the most attention at a specific point in time. For example, if Cory has a young child, that child will be most important to Cory. However, if Cory is attending college to become a CPA and needs an evening to study for a big exam, the priority will be to study for that test. That does not mean the exam is more important than the child. However, the test is a step to a better future for Cory and the child.

Cory's decision is called a **trade-off**. A trade-off means giving up one thing to do something else. Another example involving Cory is the decision to purchase a car in one year; Cory needs to save a certain amount of money each month. In order to do this, Cory may have to give up going to the coffeehouse each morning and, instead, make coffee at home in order to save enough money to meet the savings goal to purchase the car.

Be prepared to be flexible in all areas of your life plan. When working toward goals, flexibility is important. Times change, technology changes, and your priorities may change. Reevaluate your goals at least once a year. At times, you may need to update or revise your goals and/or time lines; do not just give them up.

Mentoring

Another opportunity to improve your job skills and increase your potential for career advancement is to find a mentor. A **mentor** is someone who can help you learn more about your present position, provide support, and help you to grow in your career. In addition, the mentor will help you learn about the culture of the company. The **corporate culture** includes the values, expectations, and behaviors of people at work. Knowing the culture of the company will help you succeed. By understanding a company's corporate culture you will learn about the politics, policies, and how people expect you to act on the job.

A mentor is different than a coach. Although a mentor can be a coach, a coach is not a mentor. A mentor is someone who will help you focus and work toward your career goals. A coach is someone who serves as an advisor that focuses on improving personal performance.

Finding a mentor can be a formal or informal process. Some companies have a formal mentor program. In this instance, you will be assigned a mentor

Talk It Out

Identify priorities and trade-offs for successfully completing this course.

who is able to help you succeed on the job. In addition, he or she will be able to help you to identify and reach your career goals. This mentor may be paid by the company to help you. This allows more time for the mentor to work with you.

If your company does not offer a formal mentor program, try to establish a mentoring relationship with someone who can help you while you are learning about your new job and career. This person may choose you, or you may choose that person. Your mentor should be someone who you can trust, someone who knows the company and industry, and someone who is willing to spend time to help you succeed.

Exercise 2-3   Finding a Mentor

Name at least three qualities you would look for in a person that you would want to be a mentor to you.

1. _____

2. _____

3. _____

What would you say to that person (how would you ask that person to be your mentor)?

_____

_____

_____

Workplace Dos and Don'ts

Do set goals in writing	*Don't* set goals that are difficult to reach
Do set long-term and short-term goals	*Don't* give up on goals
Do make your goals attainable	*Don't* wait to create goals
Do have measurable goals	*Don't* create unrealistic goals
Do set priorities. Include trade-offs and flexibility when setting goals	*Don't* give up when working to reach your goals
Do try to establish a mentor relationship	*Don't* try to learn about the company culture on your own

Concept Review and Application

Summary of Key Concepts

- Goal setting is important in helping you keep focused. It will increase your self-esteem and help you become more successful in all areas of your life
- As goals are reached, motivation and self-confidence will increase
- Goals need to be put into writing. They need to be realistic and measurable. Know who owns the goals and who controls the goals. A time frame is needed to know when you plan on reaching these goals
- Long-term goals are set to be achieved in five to ten years
- Short-term goals are achieved within a year's time and are needed to reach long-term goals
- When creating a life plan, consider all aspects of your life, including personal, career, and education
- Flexibility and juggling priorities are needed to achieve goals
- As you begin your new job, establish a relationship with a mentor
- A good mentor will help you learn more about your position and the company

Key Terms

corporate culture	extrinsic rewards	goal
intrinsic rewards	long-term goals	mentor
objectives	priorities	short-term goals
trade-off		

If You Were the Boss

1. Why does an employer need to set goals?
2. Why is it important that an employer ensure that employees set personal and career goals?
3. Why would you establish a mentoring program for your employees? What specific advantages would it provide your company?

Learn More

To learn more about subjects addressed in this chapter take an Introduction to Psychology course

Web Links

http://www.mindtools.com/pages/article/newHTE_06.htm
http://www.topachievement.com/goalsetting.html
http://www.mygoals.com/helpGoalsettingTips.html
http://www.gems4friends.com/goals/index.html
http://www.management-mentors.com

Activity 2-1

List three personal, career, and educational dreams you want to accomplish in your life.

Personal	Career	Education
1.	1.	1.
2.	2.	2.
3.	3.	3.

Activity 2-2

From your Activity 2–1 list, create three long-term goals in each section. Make sure they are realistic.

Personal	Career	Education
1.	1.	1.
2.	2.	2.
3.	3.	3.

Activity 2-3

From Activity 2–2, prioritize the goals you set.

Personal	Career	Education
1.	1.	1.
2.	2.	2.
3.	3.	3.

Activity 2-4

Using the previous activities in this chapter, set long- and short-term goals. The star is your long-term goal. The steps are your short-term goals. Write positively and in detail. Set one personal goal and one career goal. Keep goals specific, measurable, and realistic. Include what (the goal), when (specific time you plan to achieve it), and how to get there (be specific). *Hint:* Refer back to Cory's goal to obtain a car.

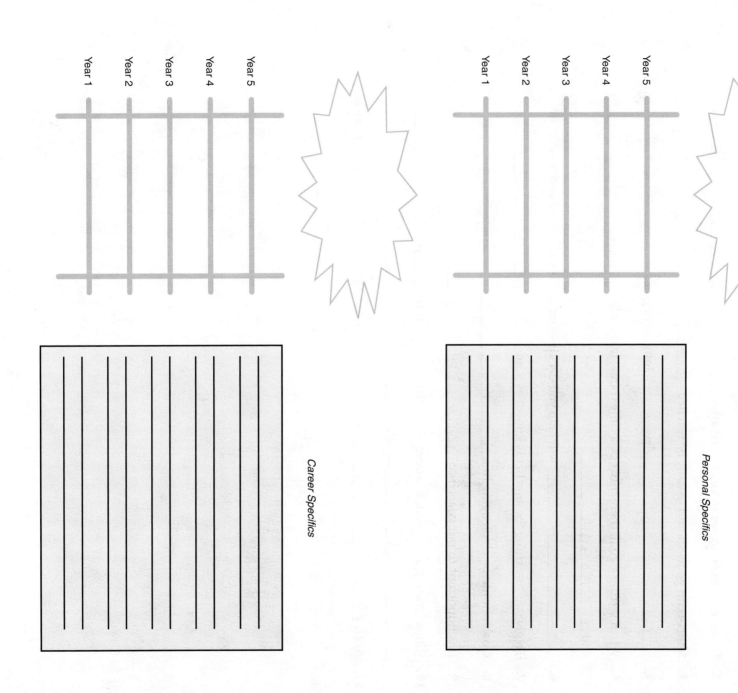

Year 1
Year 2
Year 3
Year 4
Year 5

Year 1
Year 2
Year 3
Year 4
Year 5

Career Specifics

Personal Specifics

Sample Exam Questions

1. Goals need to be set so you can become _____.

2. Long-term goals are set to be reached after _____.

3. Short-term goals should usually be reached _____.

4. _____ help you reach long-term goals.

5. When setting a goal, there must be a time frame; it must be _____ and _____.

6. _____ will help you decide what needs to be done and in what order.

7. To give up one thing for another is known as a/an _____.

8. Goals should be challenging but _____.

9. It is important to put goals into _____.

10. When creating a life plan, consider the following three areas: _____, _____, and _____.

11. A/An _____ is someone who can help you to develop in your career.

This writing assignment guides you through the process of creating goals. Remember that these goals must be realistic, attainable, important to you, and measurable. Be as specific as possible in every paragraph.

Ten-Year Goal

Paragraph 1	*In ten years, I want to be . . .* Identify and write your ten-year career goal here. Be specific: Identify what kind of job and what title you want, in what city you want to work, whom you want to work for, and why you chose this goal.

Five-Year Goal

Paragraph 2	*In five years, I want to be . . .* Identify and write your five-year career goal here. Be specific: Identify what kind of job and what title you want, in what city you want to work, whom you want to work for, and why you chose this goal.

One-Year Goal(s)

Paragraph 3	*In order to reach my five-year goal, I need to set the following short-term goals . . .* Identify necessary steps to reach your five-year goal. Be specific with activities, resources, and time frames.
Paragraph 4	*I am currently . . .* What are you currently doing to reach these short-term goals? Be specific with activities, resources, and time frames.
Paragraph 5	*I will know I have reached these goals when . . . .* Goals must be measurable. How will you know when you have reached each short-term goal? Be specific with activities, resources, and time frames.
Paragraph 6	*I need the following resources to reach my goal . . . .* Identify physical, financial, emotional, and social resources and where they will come from.
Paragraph 7	*My priorities for reaching my goals are . . . My priorities include . . . . I must be flexible . . . .* Have priorities set for reaching your goals. Include your trade-offs and the areas where you may need to be flexible.

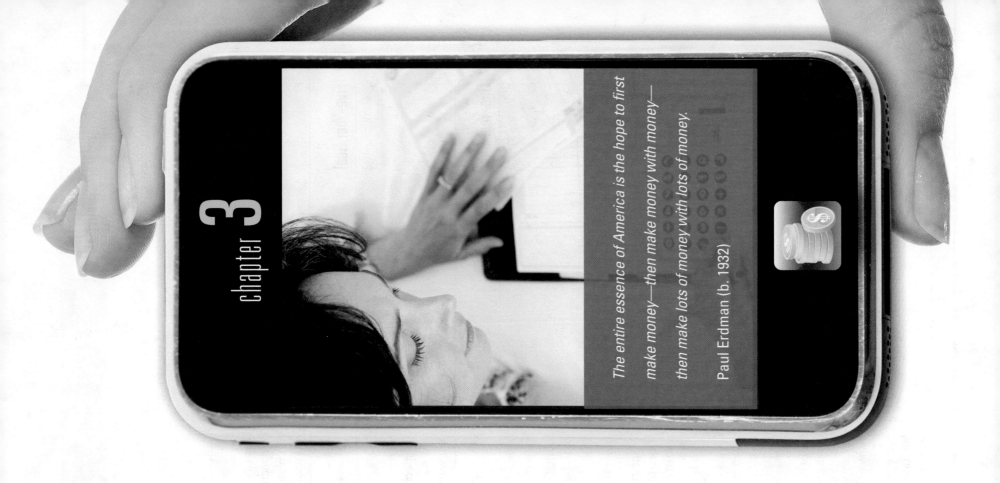

chapter 3

The entire essence of America is the hope to first make money—then make money with money—then make lots of money with lots of money.

Paul Erdman (b. 1932)

Personal Financial Management

Objectives

- Describe the importance of *personal financial management*

- Identify the significance of money management and budgeting

- Identify the difference between *gross income* and *net income*

- Create a personal *budget*

- Recognize *money wasters*

- Identify *debt* and debt management resources

- Identify wise use of credit

- Describe the importance of savings and investments

- Protect yourself from identity theft

Financial Management

Personal financial management is the process of controlling your income and your expenses. Your **income** is money coming in. This money may come from your parents, grants, student loans, and/or a job. While you are a student, your income may be minimal. However, after finishing college, you will start your new career and your income will increase. Although you need to be careful handling your money presently, this becomes even more important later in your career.

An **expense** is money going out. This is money being spent. Examples of expenses associated with being a student include tuition, textbooks, school supplies, housing, and transportation. Expenses you have because of life needs include food, shelter, and clothes. Then there are other expenses such as hobbies, entertainment, and miscellaneous activities.

As you achieve your career goal and your income increases, your expenses will also increase. This is where personal financial management becomes extremely important. Practice healthy financial management by creating good spending and saving habits.

Personal Financial Management Affects Work Performance

Be aware of how finances impact all areas of your life. Finances are important in helping you reach the goals that you identified in chapter 2. Personal financial management does not have to restrict your activities. Instead, it is a way to make your financial resources help you reach goals while ensuring a healthy financial future. Now is the time to start making your money work for you. This is done through money management.

Manage your money and keep debt under control. Maintain a positive credit report by using credit wisely and begin savings and investment plans now. In addition, be aware of how to protect yourself from identity theft.

You are probably wondering how personal financial management can affect your work situation. If you are not properly managing your finances, you will eventually have difficulty making purchases and paying your bills. You will also experience considerable strain and stress. In turn, this stress will flow into the workplace and your performance will start to deteriorate. This will then cause stress within the workplace. Many employers now require that you submit references and/or agree to a credit check prior to hiring, especially if your job requires working with money. Employers rationalize that if you cannot manage your personal finances, you may not be a responsible employee.

For example, a coworker has been asking to borrow money for lunch from Cory. Cory has noticed that this coworker comes into work with a specialty coffee each morning and buys lunch every day. This is causing a strain on the relationship between Cory and this coworker. Cory has been on a strict budget since starting this job. Cory brings lunch from home instead of buying it and only goes to the coffeehouse on special occasions. After loaning money to the coworker several times, Cory decided to confront the coworker. Cory shared with the coworker the importance of budgeting and helped the coworker to create a budget of her own. The coworker stopped asking Cory and others for money. The coworker started bringing lunch from home and treated herself to a specialty coffee only once in a while. A few months later this coworker thanked Cory because now she is beginning to save money.

Your Paycheck

Like most students, you have probably been struggling to keep up with your expenses. Although you may currently have or had a job, your wages may have not been very high. Perhaps you have been low on cash and have had just enough money to get through school. Once you graduate and begin a job in your desired field, your wages will most likely increase. With the pay increase, you will have extra cash. While it may be tempting to increase spending on treats that you could not afford in the past, now is the time to start managing your money.

Chapter 2 explained how to create goals. These goals are supported by finances. Work with your finances and create a budget to reach the goals you created in chapter 2. Many goals take time and money to achieve. Therefore, it is important to create both long-term and short-term financial goals. Cory has a goal to buy a car after working for one year. Cory has to stay on a budget and put away a specific amount of money to get that car when planned. It is important to start that budget as soon as possible. Sometimes it is tempting to go and spend money just because you have it. Do not give in to that temptation. Financial success begins with discipline and planning.

Money Management

The best way to manage your money and still be able to buy some of the extras you want is to create a budget. A **budget** is a detailed financial plan used to allocate money for a specific time period. A budget reflects your goals and specifies where your money goes in order to reach these goals. Control and prioritize your spending to match these goals. Be as precise and honest as you can when you are creating and working with a budget.

Cash management is the key to good budgeting. Carry only a small amount of cash. It is too easy to use cash and you will usually spend more cash if you have it readily available. A good cash management practice is to track every single transaction. Keeping a mental record of how much money you have in your account results in inaccurate accounting. Many individuals forget how much money has been spent and where it has gone. Physically record all deposits and withdraws made with your ATM card, debit card, or your checking account when they occur. Reduce your trips to the ATM as well. Prior to spending money, take time to seriously think about where your money is going and if the expense is a necessary expense or if it's an impulse purchase.

These cash management tips will help you realize when and where you are spending your money.

The first step in creating a budget is to identify goals. That is why in chapter 2 you were taught how to create goals and started identifying goals for the future. Remember, effective goals must be in writing and should provide direction for creating your budget. You should have some of these goals identified from chapter 2. Next attach financial goals to these personal goals. Exercises throughout this chapter will assist you in developing your financial goals.

The next step in creating a budget is to determine your income and expenses. Remember, income is money coming in and an expense is money going out. It is best to set up a budget on a month-to-month basis.

Determine your income by including all money that you receive on an annual (yearly) basis. Then divide by 12 to determine your monthly income. Technically, when creating a budget, use your **gross income** and then deduct your taxes and/or other deductions. Gross income is the amount of money on your paycheck before taxes or other deductions are made. However, to make it easier to set up the budget, you only need to know your **net income**. The net income from your paycheck is the amount you have after your employer takes out all taxes and deductions.

Exercise 3-1 Determine Your Annual Income

Fill in the following information the best you can.

Salary(s)/wage(s) per year $ _____

(Make sure you use net income—after taxes.)

Interest income per year   _____

(Savings, checking, other)

Other income per year   _____

Total annual income   _____

Total monthly income   _____

(Divide annual income by 12 to get total monthly income.)

After you have identified your monthly income, it is time to determine your expenses. Exercise 3-2 lists categories with common expenses. Estimate how much you spend every month in each category. If you spend money in an area that is not listed, add another category to the list. Do not overuse the miscellaneous category. The idea is to track exactly where your money is being spent. Ideally, you need to track all of your expenses over the next few months. Make sure to track every penny. Doing so will give you a true picture of where you really spend your money in each specific category. At the end of this chapter, you will find additional activities designed to assist you in determining your exact expenses.

Fixed expenses are more easily identified. These are expenses that do not change from month to month, such as your monthly mortgage or rent payment. **Flexible expenses** are those that change from month to month, such as food or utilities. It is better to average flexible expenses than to try to determine which months may be more or less.

Exercise 3-2   Determine Your Annual Expenses

Complete the following information as accurately as you can. Determine what amount goes in each category. This will be an estimate. Over time, identify and update actual amounts as you become aware of them.

Category	Annual	Monthly (Divide Annual by 12)
Housing	$	$
Food		
Transportation		
Education		
Health		
Clothing		
Entertainment		
Loans (debts)		
Utilities		
Daycare		
Investments/savings		
Insurance		
Donations		
Miscellaneous		
Total	$	$

First budgets are not perfect. Adjust your personal budget monthly as you identify specific income and expenses. Activity 3-4 provides you the opportunity to create a personal budget.

The following is an example of a partial budget.

	Estimated (what you have been receiving and paying or what you think you will receive and pay for the month)	**Actual** (this is the actual amount you received or spent)	**Difference** (this is actual amount minus estimated amount)	**Balance** (income minus all expenses—what you have left to spend and save)
INCOME				
1. Net Income	$1,600	$1,760	$160	$1,760
EXPENSES				
2. Housing	500	510	10	1,250
3. Food	200	240	140	1,010

1. Your previous net income (take home pay) has been $19,200 for the last year. To find your ESTIMATED monthly you calculate $19,200 ÷ 12 (months in a year) = $1,600 per month. However, assume this month you got a raise (assume you did not know about the raise) to make your yearly net salary $21,120. Your new monthly salary would be $1,760. That would be your ACTUAL net income. The DIFFERENCE would be $1,760 − $1,600 = + $160. The BALANCE is income minus expenses. The income for this month was $1,760.

2. Your rent has been $500 a month (estimated). This month your rent went up to $510 (actual). The difference would be $510 − $500 = + $10. The balance is $1,760 − $510 = $1,250.

3. Your food usually costs about $200 a month (estimated). This month you ate out more and you spent $240 on food (actual). The difference is + $40. The balance is $1,010.

Your budget will identify where you are spending unnecessary money and will allow you to modify your spending while developing good personal financial management. You will be able to determine **money wasters**, which are those small expenditures that you do not realize are actually using up a portion of your income.

Here is a common example of a money waster: Think about how many times you have gone to a coffeehouse. On average, a specialty cup of coffee is about $3 (depending on where you go). If you buy a cup of coffee five days a week, over a year's time you have spent $780 ($3 × 5 days × 52 weeks) on coffee. You may have been buying coffee because you do not have a coffeemaker and think you cannot afford to purchase one. Assume a coffeemaker costs about $25 and, on average, flavored coffee runs about $8.99 a pound. This will last one person about two to three months. So the total spent for coffee for the year would be under $100 ($8.99 × 5 + $25). If you purchased the supplies and made your own coffee, you could save $680. Just think about what you could do with an extra $680.

Exercise 3-3 Determine Money Wasters

Working with a partner, list at least three ways people waste money on small expenditures. What is the estimated cost? What can be done to save that money? Refer to the coffee example.

Small Expenditure Waste (Money Wasters)	Estimated Cost	Behavior Change
1.	$	
2.		
3.		

Wise Use of Credit

The best way to stay out of a debt hole is to manage your credit. As you begin your career, you may receive offers from credit card companies. You should not accept every offer. Although credit can buy you a lot of things, do not abuse the privilege of credit. As experienced in our nation's most recent and historical economic downturn, many individuals received credit and made purchases they ultimately could not afford. It is important to build credit and maintain that credit. Good credit aids in purchasing large items such as a car or home at a lower interest rate. If you have a credit card, use it as a tool for establishing good credit. Spend wisely and pay off the balance each month. This will assure good credit and keep you out of debt. If you know you cannot pay the balance each month, do not use a credit card. Only use the credit card for items you can afford. Always make credit payments on time.

If you find yourself in a credit hole, do not get in the habit of only making a minimum payment. Pay as much of the balance as you can. Do not skip a payment, and do not make a late payment as this will show on your credit report. Try to stay away from taking out loans. The only exception to this rule is for reliable transportation, education, and a home. Use the loan money wisely and do not overspend on these items. When you purchase a home make sure it is one you can afford.

When applying for credit, lenders consider your character, capacity, collateral, and condition. Your character reflects your past attitude toward any previous credit and/or that you pay your bills on time. This is displayed in your credit history, thus telling the lender if you will repay the loan. Capacity is your ability to repay the loan; your salary will play an important role in this matter. Collateral is used by comparing your assets and liabilities to determine your net worth, which also shows your ability to repay the loan. Other issues to be aware of when applying for a loan are interest rates, hidden costs, the purpose of the loan or credit card, what your payments will be, and how long you will be paying on the loan. Always read and understand the fine print of loan documents prior to signing the loan agreement. Loan documents outline the lenders right to change the terms and conditions of a loan. Once you agree to the loan, you are legally obligated to abide by these terms and conditions.

Talk It Out

Identify potential terms and conditions that you should consider before getting credit from a lender.

For example, Cory has been receiving preapproved credit cards and is undecided what to do. Cory knows credit cards can be dangerous and can cause financial trouble. However, Cory also realizes that good credit is needed in order to get a car loan. Cory decided that getting a credit card would not be a bad idea as long as it was not used on frivolous items. Cory read all the details on each credit card application, including annual fees, minimum payments, and annual percentage rates. After researching the fine print on the credit offers, Cory identified all hidden fees. Cory secured a good credit card but uses it only for establishing credit. Cory rarely uses the credit card, and each time it is used it is paid in full each month.

Debt Management

Debt is money you owe. What is the difference between an *expense* and *debt*? An expense is money going out. A common expense is a bill. A **loan** is a large debt that is paid in smaller amounts over a period of time and has interest added to the payment. **Interest** is the cost of borrowing money; it is extra money you pay a lender. Debt includes all types of loans (car, home, school) and credit cards. You may already have some debt such as a student loan or a credit card.

With the ease of credit card availability and use, it is no wonder so many people are in deep debt. Many end up filing bankruptcy, which causes long-term bad credit. Do not let yourself fall into the debt trap. The best way to avoid this is to purchase only what you can afford.

Keep your net worth positive. Your **net worth** is the amount of money that is yours after paying off debt. This is determined by comparing your assets and liabilities. Although your net worth may not be high now, in the future as you practice sound money management it will increase. You increase your net worth by decreasing your liabilities and increasing your assets.

Total assets − total liabilities = *total net worth*.

Personal **assets** are what you own. These are tangible items that are worth money—for example, a car, home, and furniture. A **liability** is what you owe. If you have a car loan, it is a liability.

If you are in debt, now is the time to begin getting yourself out of debt. Seek advice and support from a parent, school counselor, or financial counselor. Talk with your creditor; you may be able to work out a reduced payment or lower interest rate. Cancel and destroy the credit card. There are some national, non-profit credit counseling services that can help such as *The National Foundation for Consumer Credit* or *Myvesta Foundation*.

The following are general steps to get out of debt:

1. Do not create additional debt. Avoid using an existing credit card (cut it up if necessary) or taking on additional debt.
2. Prioritize your debt. Pay off the smallest amount or the amount with the largest interest first.
3. After you have paid off one loan, apply the extra cash to the next debt on your priority list.

Talk It Out

What are warning signs that you may be getting into debt?

Exercise 3-4   Debt Repayment Goals

If you have debt, write down each loan you currently have. Then put the amount you pay each each month and the total amount you owe. Include the amount of interest you pay annually. Identify which creditor should be paid first.

Creditor (Whom You Have the Loan With)	Amount Paid per Month	Total Amount Still Owed	Interest Percentage	Order of Payoff
1.	$	$	%	
2.				
3.				
4.				

Credit Reports

A **credit report** is a detailed credit history on an individual. Creditors look at this report before deciding if you are a good candidate for credit. A credit report details balances and payments on current and past credit cards and loans. It shows if you have paid these debts on time or if you don't pay them at all. Credit reports are summarized in the form of a credit score. Your credit score is a credit scoring system that evaluates the risk of lending you money based upon your credit history. The most common credit rating is known as a FICO score. The higher your FICO score, the better candidate you are for getting a loan at a lower interest rate. If you have a low FICO score, you have a bad credit rating.

The credit report will include personal identification information. This includes any previous names, addresses, and employers. Liens, foreclosures, and bankruptcies will appear on this report. If you are denied credit because of information on your credit report, the institution is required by law to provide you a copy of your credit report.

There are three credit reporting agencies. They are Equifax, Experian, and TransUnion. Your FICO score is a combination of Equifax and TransUnion's agency ratings. Under federal law, you are entitled to a free copy of your credit report from these agencies once every twelve months. For details, please visit www.annualcreditreport.com. While there are many other websites that offer free credit reports, this is the only site that is sponsored by the three national credit reporting agencies and is affiliated with the national free credit report program. Take advantage of this free benefit and regularly monitor your credit. Because you can receive one free report from each agency every year, it is recommended you request a free copy from each reporting agency at different times throughout the year. For example, request a copy from Equifax in January and a copy from TransUnion in June. Doing so allows you to monitor your credit for free throughout the year. If you find an error on any of these reports, immediately notify the credit reporting company.

Savings and Investments

Do not wait until you have acquired your career job to start a savings plan. Now is the time to start saving. A good rule of thumb is to have at least five months' income saved for emergencies or major expenses that you did not expect. How do you save this amount? You spend less than you earn. Make a commitment to take a certain percentage, about 5 percent, from your paycheck and put it in the bank. You will need to sacrifice spending so you have extra money for saving. When you complete your budget, determine what you can realistically sacrifice.

Keep your savings in a bank so you can earn interest. You can take the money to the bank each payday or have an **automatic deduction plan.** If your company provides this service, the automatic deduction plan usually works best because the funds are automatically deducted from your paycheck and placed into your savings account so you do not get the opportunity to spend the money.

When saving money, decide if you need the money to be readily available or if it can be left untouched for a specified period of time. This will help you determine if you should place your money in a traditional savings account or place it in a certificate of deposit (CD). A traditional savings account typically pays a lower interest rate than a CD. However, you can add and take out funds at any time from a traditional savings account. A CD pays a higher rate than a traditional savings account, but the funds are locked in for a specified time period. You are not allowed to add funds to the amount during the specified time period. If funds are withdrawn before the maturity date you will pay a penalty.

There is a difference between saving and investing. Saving money means that you are putting away funds for short-term goals and/or emergencies. Investing provides a greater opportunity to increase the value of your money and generally is a long-term endeavor. Typical investments include stocks, mutual funds, and real estate. However, investing involves risk. It is recommended that individuals first establish a traditional savings account for emergencies. Once an emergency fund is established, funds can be directed to an investment account.

Investments for the future are important to start now. If invested properly, money grows over time. There are many ways to invest money, all of which you should research to decide what level of risk you want to take. Remember, do not invest all of your money and do not invest it all in one place. You still need to keep an emergency fund available, so investments should be in addition to your savings.

Identity Theft

Protecting yourself from identity theft has become increasingly important over the last few years. Identity theft is when another individual uses your personal information to obtain credit in your name. To prevent this from happening to you dispose of junk mail properly, including credit card offers. Make sure anything thrown in the garbage does not have personal information listed. This includes your social security number, date of birth, credit card numbers, and mother's maiden name. Cut up or shred junk mail. Keep track of all your credit card numbers and other important information. Make a copy of your license, social security number, and all credit information. Keep it in a safe place. Do not share your social security number, birthplace, birthday, or mother's maiden name unless you have verified that this individual works for the company from whom you want to secure credit. This private information is used to verify your identity and credit history. If this information gets in the wrong hands, it can give someone access to your identity.

The following are tips to remember:

- Do not share your social security number over the telephone or Internet without verifying the authenticity of the company and individual requesting the information.
- Document all important numbers, such as license, credit cards, savings account, and others, and keep them in a private and safe place.
- Practice good personal financial management by routinely reviewing details on your credit card bills, bank statements, credit reports, and other financial documents.
- Delete your name from credit card lists and marketing lists.
- Monitor your credit and bank accounts regularly.
- If you receive a call from a collection agency and do not have poor credit, do not ignore the call. Someone may have taken credit in your name and made you a victim of identity theft.

If you become a victim of identity theft, the first thing you need to do is file a police report. Immediately contact your bank, all credit card companies, and your cell phone provider. Do not change your social security number, but do call the Social Security Administration Fraud Department and all of the three credit report agency fraud lines. Document, in writing, everyone you talk to and everything you do.

Important Telephone Numbers and Websites

The following is a list of important resources to assist you with credit and fraud issues.

Consumer Counseling Services

- The National Foundation for Consumer Credit: 1-800-388-2227 or http://www.nfcc.org
- Myvesta Foundation: http://www.myvesta.org
- Social Security Administration Fraud Department: 1-877-438-4338 or http://www.ssa.gov/oig/ifyou.htm

Credit Report Agencies and Resources

- Equifax credit report: 1-800-685-1111; fraud: 1-800-525-6285
- Experian credit report: 1-800-397-3742; fraud: 1-800-397-3742
- TransUnion credit report: 1-800-916-8800; fraud: 1-800-680-7289
- Free Credit Reports: 1-877-322-8228; www.annualcreditreport.com

Workplace Dos and Don'ts

Do	Don't
Do create good financial goals	*Don't* use credit cards unwisely
Do keep a budget	*Don't* waste money
Do start saving and investing now	*Don't* ignore credit reports
Do learn to protect yourself from identity theft	*Don't* use cash for all spending

Concept Review and Application

Summary of Key Concepts

- Personal financial management is the process of controlling your income and expenses
- Income is money coming in
- Expense is money going out
- A budget is a detailed plan for finances
- The first step to creating a budget is to identify goals
- Debt (liability) is the money you owe
- Net worth is assets minus liabilities
- A credit report is a detailed credit history
- Identity theft is when another individual uses your personal information

Key Terms

assets	automatic deduction plan	budget
credit report	debt	expense
fixed expenses	flexible expenses	gross income
income	interest	liability
money wasters	net income	net worth
personal financial		
management		

If You Were the Boss

1. You need to hire a receptionist that will be handling cash. What steps would you take to make sure you hire the right person?

2. Why should you teach your employees the importance of personal financial management? What are some creative ways of doing this?

Learn More

To learn more about subjects addressed in this chapter take a course in Personal Financial Management.

Video Case Study: Healthy Personal Financial Management

This video presents a financial professional providing expert advice on how to practice healthy personal financial management. Refer to the CD that accompanies your text, watch this video, and answer the following questions.

1. What specific steps can you take to improve your spending habits?

2. Share two specific pieces of advice the financial expert shared regarding saving and investing.

3. Name four methods of using credit wisely.

Web Links

http://www.betterbudgeting.com
http://www.personal-budget-planning-saving-money.com
http://financialplan.about.com/cs/budgeting/a/Budgeting101.htm
http://www.moneyadvise.com

References

Fair Isaac Corporation, Minneapolis, MN. www.myfico.com
Federal Reserve Bank, Washington, DC. www.federalreserve.gov
Annual Credit Report Request Service, Atlanta, GA. www.annualcreditreport.com

Activity 3-1

Create a personal financial statement. Put the net worth of all your *assets* (what they would be worth today if you sold them). Under *liabilities*, put the total amount you owe (not just monthly payments) to any creditors. For your *net worth*, take your total amount of assets minus your total amount of liabilities.

Assets	Amount
(Present Value)	
Cash (savings/checking)	$
Investments	
Life insurance	
House	
Automobile	
Furniture	
Jewelry	
Other assets	
Total assets	$
Liabilities	
Home loan	$
Automobile loan	
Credit card debt	
Educational loan	
Other Loans	
Total liabilities	$
Net Worth (Total Assets Minus Liabilities)	$

Activity 3-2

Create financial goals and a budget to support these goals. Write the specific goal you want to reach. Identify the amount of money needed to reach that goal. In the last column, identify when you want to reach that goal.

Goals	Amount	Time
Debt payoffs	$	
Education		
Personal (car, home)		
Miscellaneous		
Savings		
Starting a business		

Activity 3-3

Use these sheets to record all income and spending for two weeks to identify where you are spending your money. Record all spending. Even minor expenses (every penny) should be recorded. Include the date, amount spent, what you bought (service or product), and how you paid for the item (means).

SPENDING RECORD SHEET WEEK 1

Date	Amount Spent	Item Bought	Payment Method (Cash, Credit Card, Debit Card, Check)
	$		

SPENDING RECORD SHEET WEEK 2

Date	Amount Spent	Item Bought	Payment Method (Cash, Credit Card, Debit Card, Check)
	$		

Activity 3-4

Create a personal budget. Refer to page 29 for an example.

BUDGET FOR MONTH OF _____

Monthly Payment Category	Estimated Budget	Actual Budget	Difference + OR –	Balanced Budget
Net spendable income per month	$	$	$	$
Housing				
Food				
Insurance				
Debts				
Clothing				
Medical				
Donations				
Entertainment				
Miscellaneous				
Investments				

Sample Exam Questions

1. _____ is the process of controlling your income and your expenses.

2. A/An _____ is a detailed plan for a specific time period for specifying your financial goals.

3. The small expenditures that add up to larger amounts are referred to as _____.

4. When considering applications for credit, lenders consider _____, _____, and _____.

5. _____ is money you owe.

6. Your _____ is the amount of money that is yours after paying off debts.

7. A detailed credit history on an individual is called a/an _____.

Time and Stress Management/ Organization Skills

chapter 4

Objectives

- Describe how stress impacts workplace performance

- Identify the causes of stress and name methods of dealing with stress

- Apply *time management* techniques in the workplace

- Define the importance of organizing for optimal performance

- Apply organizational techniques in the workplace

We must use time as a tool, not as a crutch.

John F. Kennedy (1917–1963)

The Impact of Stress on Performance

Employers need employees who are healthy, relaxed, and well organized. Healthy employees are able to perform at their highest levels, have decreased absenteeism, and have fewer health claims than their unhealthy counterparts. Stress can impact workplace productivity including self-care issues such as diet and exercise and organizational issues like time management.

Stress is the body's reaction to tense situations. Stress can cause more than just a bad day. Constant stress can result in permanent mental and/or physical harm.

Although some forms of stress are beneficial and keep you mentally challenged, continued stress will eventually harm you in one way or another. It may start to affect your work performance and will most likely carry on to your personal life. It is important to maintain a low and controlled stress level. Stress-related losses are high and are costing organizations billions of dollars annually.

This chapter addresses the many areas where stress can impact workplace productivity including time management, being organized, working with others, and managing common workplace stressors. Personal stress can harm your performance at work. Take the ideas learned in this chapter and make a commitment to begin to applying them to both your work environment and your personal life.

Talk It Out

How can stress from school impact other areas of your life?

Types of Stress

Stress is a part of life. What is important is that you recognize when you are stressed and deal with the stress appropriately. There is positive and negative stress. You will experience stress at work; there is no avoiding it. However, how you react and deal with stress determines how it will affect you. Some stress is minor and affects you at a specific time. This can be **positive stress**. Positive stress is a productive stress that provides the strength to accomplish a task. However, even positive stress can become negative if it continues and becomes problematic. For example, if you have a rushed deadline for a special project, your adrenalin will increase giving you the mental and/or physical strength to finish the project on time. However, if you consistently have rushed deadlines, your stress level could increase and will eventually start working negatively on your mind and body.

Any stress can become **negative stress.** Becoming emotional or illogical or starting to lose control of your temper is a sign that you are experiencing unproductive or negative stress. This stress is continuous and may affect your mental and/or physical health. Negative stress commonly results in anger, depression, and/or distrust. Other signs of negative stress may include frequent headaches, fatigue, diminished or increased appetite, and physical weakness. Negative stress can ultimately result in ulcers, heart disease, or mental disturbances.

Cory has been noticing that a coworker, Tammy, has been short-tempered and moody lately. Because Tammy is normally very pleasant to work with, Cory decides to ask her if something is wrong. Visiting with Tammy, Cory finds out that Tammy is being harassed by someone at work. She tells Cory how stressful this has been and that it is affecting her work and personal life. Cory encourages Tammy to take steps to stop this harassment (as presented in chapter 12). Cory also gives Tammy some tips to help deal with the stress. After a few weeks, Cory notices there is a positive change in Tammy. Dealing with the problem, along with using stress relievers, is helping to get Tammy back to her pleasant self.

The key is to become aware of what is causing stress. Ignoring stress does not make it go away. Your body responds to stress. By being aware of what causes your stress, you can change how it will affect you.

Exercise 4-1   Recognize Your Stress

List at least three significant things that have happened to you in the last year that have caused you stress. Next to the stressor, include what happened to you mentally and/or physically.

Stressor	Symptoms of the Stressor (How You Respond Mentally and/or Physically)
1.	
2.	
3.	

Dealing with Stress

Learning to deal with stress will reduce its negative effects. Identify key stressors in your life; Be aware of these stressors and how they affect your attitude and behavior. Life is not stress free. The following steps will assist you in not allowing stressful situations to get the best of you:

1. Identify the stressor. Find out what is causing you to be stressed.
2. Recognize why and how you are reacting to that stressor.
3. Take steps to better deal with the stress by visualizing and setting a goal to respond in a positive manner.
4. Practice positive stress relief.

The following are some ways to relieve stress:

- Find an outlet to release tension. This could include daily exercise, a hobby, or some other healthy activity.
- Diminish (or ideally eliminate) the use of alcohol and/or drugs. These stimulants will cause mood swings that typically make matters worse.
- Do not become emotional. Becoming emotional means you are losing control and may become illogical in your response to the stress.
- Get organized. Take control of your work space by eliminating unwanted clutter and prioritizing projects.
- Make time for yourself and learn to relax.
- Eat a balanced diet and get plenty of sleep.

One common way to help manage stress is to control your diet. Your nutritional intake should be balanced. A healthy physical body leads to a healthy mental body. Consistently eat a balanced diet including breakfast, lunch, and dinner. At these meals, balance protein, carbohydrates, vegetables, and fruit. Do not skip meals, especially breakfast.

Along with a balanced diet, exercise is a must. This does not mean you have to join a gym or lift weights; it just means you need to have a consistent exercise

Talk It Out

What are common negative stressors students face and what are positive responses?

plan. Exercising is a good way to clear your mind of troubles and increase your creativity. There are other ways to increase your physical activity. Walk up stairs instead of taking the elevator or park your car a little farther away from a building to increase your walking distance.

Exercise 4-2   What Have You Eaten in the Last Twenty-Four Hours?

A nutritious diet can make a difference in how you perform throughout the day and how you react to stressful situations. List what you have eaten in the last twenty-four hours. Decide whether or not it was nutritional.

What Have You Eaten?	Is It Nutritional?
1.	
2.	
3.	
4.	
5.	
6.	
7.	
8.	
9.	
10.	

You can relieve stress in many other ways. You probably do some of these things without realizing that they relieve stress. A few other methods to relieve stress follow:

· Develop realistic goals
· Maintain relationships with people you can talk to and trust
· Have some leisure time
· Listen to music
· Relax
· Get enough sleep
· Do some deep breathing exercises
· Use positive visualization
· Meditate

Recognize what situations cause stress. If you recognize these situations, you can better control them. The more organized you are, the better prepared you will be, thus reducing stress.

Talk It Out

What are ways you relieve stress?

When at work, if you cannot surround yourself with positive people, then create a personal space. Find a private place where you can take a few minutes each day for yourself to relax. Realize that people are not always going to agree with you at the workplace. There may be annoying people, and there may be people with whom you may not have a positive relationship. You may find yourself in situations that become very stressful. Use the stress relief tools mentioned earlier in this chapter and make the best of the situation. As we discussed in chapter 2, only you can control you attitude and your response to situations.

Take time outside of work to relax. Do not bring your work troubles home with you. When you recognize your stressors and take care of yourself, you can reduce and/or eliminate the harm stress can do to you both at work and at home.

If you feel you cannot control your stress see if your company has an employee assistance program and use it to get professional help. Typical employee assistance programs offer help with financial, legal, and psychological issues. Additional information on employee assistance programs is provided in chapter 8.

Time Management Tips and Tricks

Time management is how you manage your time. Sometimes it seems like there are never enough hours in the day. You want to get out of work on time, but you have not completed what needs to be done. It takes time to get organized enough to use your time wisely. Taking time to organize your life will be time well spent.

You may get stressed at work because you do not have enough time to complete a project. However, many of your projects will probably be similar. Prior to starting a project, take time to make a plan. Set priorities and get organized and do not wait until the last minute. If you have similar projects, take time to create a template so you are not starting over with each project. Rushing through a job typically results in errors that will only take more time to redo. Take a little extra time to complete a job right the first time.

In business, time is money. The ability to use time wisely is a skill in itself. This skill is needed in the workplace. By using your time efficiently, your tasks will be completed on time. Focus on tasks at hand and pay attention to details needed to do the job right. If you are being more efficient and paying attention, your employer sees that you care about your job and are organized. In turn, this may lead to higher pay and/or a promotion.

Without proper time management skills, you may spend more time than needed on a project or you may forget to complete an important task or lose an important project. Make the effort to get organized and control your time. Activity 4-1 is a time log to help identify how you spend your time. The following tips will help you organize and control your time:

1. *Keep a calendar handy at all times.* Your personal calendar should list all appointments, meetings, and tasks for each day. This can be a regular paper calendar or an electronic calendar (handheld or computer application).

2. Make a list of tasks for each day and prioritize that list; this is commonly referred to as a to-do list.

3. *Organize your work area.* Use file folders and in-boxes to organize and prioritize your projects.

4. *Avoid time wasters.* Time wasters are small activities that take up only a small amount of time but are done more frequently than you may realize. These include unnecessary visiting and unproductive activities.

5. *Practice a one-touch policy.* After you have looked at a project, letter, memo, or other item, file it, put it into a priority pile, pass it on, or throw it away. Do not keep piling papers on your desk.

6. Set time aside each day to address all correspondence at once.

7. Do not be afraid to ask for help.

Cory has learned to save time by answering some memos in a unique way. When Cory receives a memo that only requires a short response, instead of creating a new memo, Cory writes a response on the original memo. After writing the answer and making a copy for record, Cory sends the memo back. This has saved Cory time.

Talk It Out

How can you apply what you just learned regarding time management to your school performance?

Exercise 4-3   Avoid Time Wasters

List time wasters you have experienced in the last few weeks. How did these time wasters affect your productivity? What can you do to improve this?

Time Waster	How Did It Affect Productivity?	What Will You Improve?
1.		
2.		
3.		

Organizing and Performance

Getting yourself organized for optimal performance is not difficult. Being organized will not only optimize your performance but will also help you use your time more efficiently and reduce stress. There are many tools for getting organized in the workplace (which can be used at home as well). Technology has made it easier to get organized with electronic devices (handheld or computer). However, there are other common organization tools to use including shredders, utilizing desk space appropriately, and filing.

One of the easiest ways to get organized is the use of a calendar. There are many calendaring options including a computerized calendar, a mobile calendar, and of course, a traditional paper calendar. For efficiency purposes, businesses prefer an electronic calendar for networking purposes. It is common to have both a computerized information manager and communications program on a computer and a mobile device. Determine which type of calendar works best for your work situation. Once you have determined which option is best for you, make a commitment to record all meetings and important deadlines, both work related and personal. If your personal information manager and communications program is electronic, store telephone numbers, e-mail addresses, and other important messaging data for easy access. Tasks and notes can also be monitored and updated. Keep your data current by immediately recording changes. If you use multiple organization tools, transfer information on a daily basis. For maximum efficiency, customize applications to suit your needs.

Other ways to help you keep organized and improve performance are to return phone messages at one time; answer e-mails at one time; and break large tasks into simpler, smaller tasks. It is inefficient to return each phone message or e-mail as it comes in. Check and answer your phone messages and e-mails at regular intervals. The only exception to this is if there is an important message or e-mail that needs to be answered immediately. When you break down tasks, you can space out projects. This enables you to organize the time needed to complete each task before starting the next. Again, the exception to this would be if you have a priority task that needs to be completed immediately.

Keep your work space/environment and desk clean and clutter free. No more than two personal items on a desk will maintain a professional look. All work tools should be easily accessible. These include a stapler, tape, notepad, pens, pencils, correction fluid, paper clips, scissors, ruler, calculator, highlighters, and a computer storage device. In addition, the use of a small bulletin/white board for posting important reminders will help you keep track of important tasks and appointments. Have a trash can close to your desk, and throw away supplies that have been used or do not work anymore.

A shredder is often a shared piece of office equipment that is used to dispose of confidential materials. Shred confidential materials at least once a day.

Maintain paper files properly in a file cabinet and keep the files neatly arranged in clearly labeled file folders. Keep dated documents in chronological order (most recent first). Other files can be arranged by subject or alphabetically. Be consistent in your filing method. Routinely used files should be easily accessible. Keep files updated, and be sure to dispose of old files properly. Any unnecessary files with personal information or identification numbers are considered confidential and should be shredded. If files are not important and do not have identification, they may be thrown in the trash.

Effective organization includes the proper handling of paper mail. Your job may include sorting and/or opening mail for your department. Use a letter opener to open all mail at one time. After opening the mail, sort it into piles. Throw away or shred junk mail immediately after opening. Respond to the sender of the mail if needed, file the document, or forward the mail to the appropriate party within the company. Do not open mail that is marked confidential unless instructed to do so. Mail should be kept private and not shared with coworkers. If you encounter a piece of mail that should be confidential, place it in a separate envelope and mark it confidential. Company letterhead or postage is not for personal mail.

Workplace Dos and Don'ts

Do recognize your stressors	*Don't* let stress go until you get mentally or physically sick
Do deal with stress appropriately	*Don't* think that stress will just go away
Do eat a balanced diet and have an exercise plan	*Don't* skip breakfast
Do manage your time by setting priorities and getting organized	*Don't* be afraid of asking for help when getting behind
Do take time to get organized	*Don't* give in to time wasters

Concept Review and Application

Summary of Key Concepts

- Stress is a physical, chemical, or emotional factor that causes bodily or mental tension
- Stress can be positive and/or negative
- Signs of stress include becoming emotional or illogical or losing control of your temper
- The first step in dealing with stress is to identify the stressor
- A balanced diet along with exercise will help you to better manage stress
- There are many ways to reduce stress, such as setting goals, relaxing, and getting enough sleep
- Good time management comes from being organized
- Being organized will optimize your performance and reduce stress

Key Terms

negative stress
stress

positive stress
time management

If You Were the Boss

1. You have noticed that an employee frequently is calling in sick and appears agitated when at work. What do you do?

2. You have just become the supervisor for a new department. What can you do to make the department and its employees more organized? Discuss appointment tools, necessary equipment, and software.

Learn More

To learn more about subjects addressed in this chapter, take a course in Health, Anatomy, Nutrition, and/or Physical Education

Video Case Study: Time Management and Organization Tips

This video presents expert advice on time management and workplace organization. Refer to the CD that accompanies your text, watch this video, and answer the following questions.

1. Name three reasons why time management and workplace organization is important.

2. Share three time management tools.

3. Share three organization tools you should practice in your personal work area.

4. Define time wasters and explain how to deal with them.

Web Links

http://www.mindtools.com/smpage.html
http://www.cdc.gov/niosh/topics/stress
http://www.effective-time-management-strategies.com
http://www.studygs.net/timman.htm

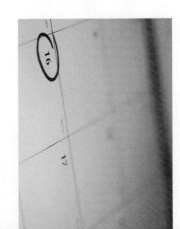

Activities

Activity 4-1

Visit the course website to download a time log and keep track of how you spend your time for the next 24 hours. Track exactly how your time was spent. At the end of the time period, identify specific time wasters.

Identify three time wasters from your time log.

1.

2.

3.

Activity 4-2

In addition to what was mentioned in the chapter, research physical responses generated by prolonged stress. List your findings.

1.	4.
2.	5.
3.	6.

Activity 4-3

Conduct additional research and identify tips for relieving work stress. List them and explain how they help relieve stress.

Tip for Relieving Stress at Work	How Does It Help?
1.	1.
2.	2.
3.	3.
4.	4.

Activity 4-4

Identify the workplace effects of good and bad time management.

Effects of *Good Time Management*	Effects of *Bad Time Management*
1.	1.
2.	2.
3.	3.
4.	4.
5.	5.

Sample Exam Questions

1. Stress is a physical, chemical, or emotional factor that causes tension and may be a factor in

   _____.

2. Stress can be positive and/or _____.

3. The first step in dealing with stress is to _____.

4. Some ways to relieve stress include (choose four):

   _____, _____, or

   _____, _____.

5. Realizing your stressors and taking care of yourself will reduce or eliminate

   _____.

6. Managing time when you do not seem to have enough hours in the day is

   _____.

7. Being organized can _____ your performance.

Ethics, Politics, and Diversity

chapter 5

I hope I shall possess firmness and virtue enough to maintain what I consider the most enviable of all titles, the character of an honest man.

George Washington (1732–1799)

Objectives

- Define *ethics* and its impact both personally and professionally

- Identify the importance of maintaining *confidentiality*

- Define and identify the appropriate use of *power* and power bases

- Understand the topics of *politics* and *reciprocity* and their appropriate use in the workplace

- Understand the importance of ethical decision making

- Define *workplace diversity* and realize its impact on performance

- State the basic employee rights and legal protection available for workplace diversity issues

- Recognize the negative impact *stereotypes* and *prejudice* have in the workplace and on performance

- Identify *cultural* differences and the positive and negative impact these differences have on business

Ethics Defined

Throughout our schooling, we are told to behave ethically. In education, ethics typically refers to not cheating on homework and exams. At work, cheating can occur in all areas of a job. From the time we clock in to the time we leave the office—and even extending into the weekend, we must behave in an ethical manner. Ethical behavior is a twenty-four-hour process. Behavior reflects ethical values. In turn, our ethical behavior reflects and represents our company.

Ethics is a moral standard of right and wrong. Although the definition of ethics is a simple statement, it is important to identify who and what determines what is morally right and wrong. Just as your personality is shaped by outside influences, so is your ethical makeup.

Ethical behavior is a reflection of the influences of coworkers, friends, family, religion, and society. For example, if you associate with people who shoplift, you most likely will not view shoplifting as an unethical act. As a result, you may shoplift without remorse. If your family routinely lies about a child's age to pay a lower admission fee to a movie theater or amusement park, the child is being taught to be dishonest. Common religions teach that lying, cheating, and stealing are wrong. Consider the influences our society and culture have on our ethical behavior. Corporate America has been bombarded with ethics-related scandals. Additionally, many of the marketing messages we receive on a daily basis influence ethical behavior.

Although the preceding factors all have an enormous influence on the makeup of one's ethics, it is important to note that ethical behavior starts with the individual. As we explore the concept of ethics at work, remember that ethics begins with you.

Talk It Out

Discuss recent corporate ethics-related scandals.

Influences on Ethics at Work

At work you will be confronted with ethical issues. Many issues must be kept **confidential,** meaning they are matters that should be kept private. These matters include client records, employee information, business reports, documentation, and files. Whether you are told or not told to keep work-related information confidential, you have an obligation to not share information with individuals with whom the business is of no concern. This is called **implied confidentiality.** An example of implied confidentiality would be not sharing customers' personal information with others. Sometimes, you may be tempted or even asked to share confidential information. Do not fall into that trap. If you are uncertain about sharing confidential information with someone, check with your boss. Doing so will demonstrate to your boss that you want to not only maintain the privacy of your department but also behave in a professional manner.

Your ethical behavior extends beyond the professionalism of how you deal with others. It is also reflected in your dependability and how you conduct yourself on company time. Remember that the company is paying you to work when you are on the job. Although at times it may be necessary to conduct personal business on company time, it is inappropriate to consistently spend your time on noncompany activities. The following activities should not be done during work time:

- Surfing the Internet for personal business
- Taking personal telephone calls
- Making personal telephone calls (including family, personal appointments)
- Routinely exceeding allotted break and lunch periods
- Playing computer games
- Using company supplies and equipment for nonbusiness purposes

If you must conduct personal business while at work, only do so during your break or lunch hour. Whenever possible, conduct the business before or after work hours and in a private manner.

Talk It Out

What activities done during class could be considered unethical?

Web Quiz

Test your business ethics.

http://resources.monster
.com/tools/quizzes/bizethics

Power and Ethics

Power is one's ability to influence another's behavior. Whether you recognize it or not, everyone at work has some form of power. Some people understand this ability to influence others' behavior and use it appropriately. Let us first review the different types of power, what they are, and how you can increase this use of power at work. There are seven bases of power: legitimate, coercive, reward, connection, charismatic, information, and expert.

Legitimate power is the power that is given to you by the company. It includes your title and any other formal authority that comes with your position at work. For example, a manager has legitimate power to assign schedules.

Coercive power is also power that is derived from your formal position. However, the difference between legitimate and coercive power is that coercive power uses threats and punishment. An example of coercive power is if your manager threatens to cut your hours. In contrast to coercive power is **reward power.** Reward power is the ability to influence someone with something of value. For example, a manager has offered you a bonus for meeting a goal. Those with legitimate power can reward others with promotions, pay increases, and other incentives. You do not have to have legitimate power to reward others in the workplace. **Connection power** is based on using someone else's legitimate power. Consider the department assistant that arranges meetings based on his boss's power. This is because the department assistant has a connection to an individual with authority.

The last three types of power come from within. They are often referred to as types of personal power. **Charismatic power** is a form of personal power that

Exercise 5-1   Identify What Power Can Do

Identify three ways employees without legitimate power can reward others.

1.

2.

3.

makes people attracted to you. We all know someone who walks into a room and immediately people are attracted to him or her. This is because the individual with charismatic power or charisma shows a sincere interest in others. **Information power** is based upon an individual's ability to obtain and share information. Doing so makes you more valuable to those with whom you interact. For example, a coworker is part of a committee and routinely shares information. **Expert power** is power that is earned by one's knowledge, experience, or expertise. Consider the company's computer repair technician. On the company's organization chart, he or she is not very high in the formal chain of command. However, this individual wields a lot of power because of his or her computer expertise.

Increasing Your Power Bases

As mentioned earlier, everyone possesses some form of workplace power. The trick is to recognize, utilize, and increase your power. The easiest way to increase your legitimate power is to make people aware of your title and responsibilities. Because coercive power utilizes threats and/or punishment, coercive power should only be used when an individual is breaking policy or behaving inappropriately.

Reward power can be used daily. Whenever possible, dispense a sincere word or note of appreciation to a coworker who has assisted you or has performed exceptionally well. Doing so will develop and enhance relationships not only within your department but also outside your department. Just remember to be sincere. Increase your connection power by strengthening your network. **Networking** means meeting and developing relationships with individuals outside your immediate work area. Network with individuals within and outside of your organization. A more in-depth discussion of the importance of networking is discussed in chapter 13.

Charismatic power is increased when you focus attention on others. Make eye contact, initiate conversation, and focus the conversation on the other individual instead of on yourself. Information power is developed by attending meetings, joining committees, and networking. Whenever possible and without over committing, join committees and attend meetings. Doing so exposes you to other people and issues throughout the company. You, in turn, not only learn more about what's going on within the organization but also increase your connection or network power. Increase your expert power by practicing continual learning. Read books and business-related articles, scan reputable and applicable Internet sites, attend workshops and conferences, and learn new technology when possible. Whenever you learn something new that can assist others at work, share this information. Coworkers will see you as the expert in the respective area.

Politics and Reciprocity

When you begin to obtain and utilize your power, you are practicing politics. **Politics** is obtaining and using power. People generally get a bad taste in their mouth when someone accuses them of being political, but this is not necessarily a bad thing. As mentioned, it is important to recognize, increase, and utilize the various power bases at work. It is when one expects reciprocity that politics at work gets dangerous. **Reciprocity** is when debts and obligations are created for doing something. Suppose you are on a time crunch and must get a report out in two hours but you need help. You ask a coworker to help you. He or she stops what she is doing and assists you with an hour to spare. You have just created a reciprocal relationship with the coworker. When he or she is in a crunch, he or she will not only ask you but expect you to help him or her out. The workplace is comprised of reciprocal relationships. Unfortunately, sometimes the phrase "you owe me" encroaches on our ability to behave ethically.

Cory has a coworker who helps Cory out with special projects when time is short. When the coworker tells Cory she needs help with something, Cory immediately responds, "Sure, no problem." Unfortunately, there is a problem. The coworker wants Cory to attend a meeting for her and tell people at the meeting that she is home sick when Cory knows she plans to take a trip with friends. Cory tells the coworker that it would be unethical to cover for her. "But you owe me!" says the coworker. Cory is unsure what to do. After some thought, Cory tells the coworker that Cory wants to repay the favor and appreciates all the help the coworker provides but Cory's ethics cannot be compromised. Cory should expect some tension between the two, but, in the long run, the worker will respect Cory.

Corporate Values/Culture

Each company has a corporate culture. A corporate culture is the way a company's employees behave. It is based upon the behavior of its leaders. This culture can be viewed from a corporate level and also from a departmental level. For example, if all the executives within the company are very laid-back and informal, most employees throughout the company will also be laid-back and informal. If a department supervisor is always stressed out and unprepared, the department members will most likely be stressed out and unprepared as well. This behavior also reflects an organization's ethical behavior. Companies that want to be proactive and decrease any type of unethical temptation will have and enforce an **ethics statement.** An ethics statement is a formal corporate policy that addresses the issues of ethical behavior and punishment should someone behave inappropriately. As Corporate America recovers from its scandals, more companies are placing great importance on ethics statements. Included in most corporate ethics policies will be a statement regarding **conflict of interest.** A conflict of interest occurs when you are in a position to influence a decision from which you could benefit directly or indirectly.

Cory's company needs a flower vendor for an upcoming company event. Cory's uncle owns a local flower shop, and getting this contract would be a big financial boost to his store. Cory wonders if it would be unethical to tell his uncle about the opportunity. After some thought, Cory decides to ask the boss about the dilemma. Cory's boss explains that there is no conflict of interest if Cory does not financially benefit from the contract and encourages Cory to contact the uncle.

If there is ever any possibility that someone could accuse you of a conflict of interest, excuse yourself from the decision-making process. If you are uncertain that there is a conflict, check with your boss or the respective committee. Explain the situation and ask for your boss's or committee's opinion. To avoid a conflict of interest, many companies have strict policies on gift giving and receiving. Many companies do not allow the acceptance of gifts or have a dollar limit on the value of a gift allowed.

Exercise 5-2   Receiving a Gift at Work

Your company has a strict policy on not accepting gifts valued over $15. A key vendor for your company sends you flowers on your birthday. The arrangement is quite large, so you know it clearly exceeds the $15 limit. What do you do?

_____

_____

_____

Making Ethical Choices

As you attempt to make ethical choices at work, use the three **levels of ethical decisions.** *The first level of ethics is the law.* When confronted with an ethical issue, first ask if the action is legal. If the action is illegal, it is unethical.

The second level of ethics is fairness. Your actions/behavior should be fair to all parties involved. If, when making a decision, someone is clearly going to be harmed or is unable to defend himself or herself, the decision is probably not ethical. Note that the concept of "fairness" does not mean that everyone is happy with the outcome. It only means that the decision has been made in an impartial and unbiased manner. Sometimes, a behavior is legal but may be considered unethical. Just because a behavior is legal does not mean it is right. Take the case of an individual who has a romantic relationship with someone who is married to someone else. There is no law that says having an extramarital affair is illegal. However, many consider this behavior unethical.

It is understandable that not everyone agrees on what is right and fair. This is where *the third level of ethics—one's conscience*—must be considered. This is also when an ethical decision gets personal. In the classic Disney movie, *Pinocchio,* there was a character named Jiminy Cricket. He was Pinocchio's conscience. He made Pinocchio feel bad when Pinocchio behaved inappropriately. Just like Pinocchio, each individual has a conscience. When one knowingly behaves inappropriately, most will eventually feel bad about his poor behavior. Some people take a bit longer to feel bad than others, but most everyone at some point feels bad when they have wronged another. Sometimes a behavior may be legal and it may be fair to others, but it still may make us feel guilty or bad. If it does, the behavior is probably unethical.

Cory is responsible for the department's petty cash box. Cory is planning on going to lunch with friends but does not have time to stop by the ATM until later in the afternoon. Cory struggles with the thought of temporarily borrowing $10 from the petty cash box and returning the money later in the day (after a visit to the ATM). No one would ever know. Technically, it is not stealing. It is just borrowing. Cory decides the behavior is unethical, does not take the petty cash, and skips going out to lunch with friends.

Exercise 5-3   Legal Behavior

Based on Cory's dilemma, is Cory borrowing money from the petty cash box legal?

Yes ☐ No ☐

Whom could it harm and why?

_____

_____

Is this behavior fair?

Yes ☐ No ☐

_____

_____

Exercise 5-4   Honesty: Part I

It is 9:00 P.M., it is raining, and you are hungry. You are on your way home from a long workday. You only have $5 in your wallet, so you decide to go to a fast-food drive-through restaurant to get dinner. You carefully order so as not to exceed your $5 limit. You hand the drive-through employee your $5, and he gives you change and your meal. You place it all in the passenger's seat and drive home. When you get home, you discover that the fast-food employee gave you change for $20. What do you do?

_____

_____

_____

_____

Review the scenario; apply the three levels of ethical decision making to the following questions. Is your behavior legal? Is it fair? How do you feel about keeping the money?

Is it legal to keep the money?

Yes ☐ No ☐

Is it fair to keep the money?

Yes ☐ No ☐

How do you feel about keeping the money?

_____

Exercise 5-5   Honesty: Part II

Typically, in the fast-food business, employees whose cash boxes are short or over more than once are at risk of being fired. If you initially were going to keep the money, but now you know the employee who gave you too much cash could get fired because you decided to keep the money, would you still keep the money?

_____

_____

When Others Are Not Ethical

The last section discussed how to behave ethically at work. But what should you do when others are not behaving ethically? Let us go back to the three levels of ethical decision making. Everyone must abide by the law. If someone at work is breaking the law, you have an obligation to inform your employer immediately. This can be done confidentially to either your supervisor or the human resource department. Whenever you accuse anyone of wrongdoing, have documented facts and solid evidence. Keep track of important dates, events, and copies of evidence. Your credibility is at stake. Remember, depending on the enormity of the situation, you, as an employee, have three choices: (1) alert outside officials if the offense is illegal and extreme; (2) if the offense is not extreme and is accepted by management, accept management's decision; or (3) if the inappropriate behavior is accepted by management and you are still bothered, decide whether you want to continue working for the company.

Cory finds out that a certain coworker received a laptop computer from a vendor for personal use. No other employee received a laptop. The coworker said the laptop was an incentive for the company's good standing with the vendor and, because he was the employee who made the purchases, it was his right to keep the laptop. Cory thinks this is not fair and is unethical. Cory politely checks with the human resource department, and they tell Cory that the coworker can keep the laptop. Cory must accept the company's policy. Although construed as being unethical in Cory's mind, the company found no conflict with its policies. Cory decides the offense is not extreme; and, because it was accepted by management, Cory accepts management's decision.

Another common ethical issue at work occurs in the area of company theft. Company theft is not always large items such as computers or equipment. More often, it is smaller items such as office supplies. Time can also be stolen from a company. If you use company time to surf the Internet, make personal calls, or take extra long breaks, you are stealing from the company. You may not realize that taking a pen or pencil home is stealing from your company. Office supplies should only be used for business purposes. Although it is heavily influenced by the company and how others view right behavior from wrong, ethical behavior starts with the individual.

Diversity Basics

This section addresses workplace diversity, cultural differences, and employee rights regarding these differences. Diversity comes in many forms. Although most people think of diversity as a race issue, the topic goes far beyond race. People are different in many aspects, ranging from ethnicity to the way we wear our hair. As we discuss these issues, it is important to note three primary messages regarding workplace diversity:

- No matter what our differences, treat everyone with respect and professionalism.
- Diversity should be used as an asset that utilizes our differences as ways to create, innovate, and compete.
- Workplace diversity should only be an issue when the diversity negatively affects performance.

The following is a common example of workplace diversity: One of Cory's new friends at work has a lifestyle that is not as conservative as Cory's. Although Cory's friend has never openly mentioned his lifestyle, he behaves in a feminine fashion and always talks about various parties he attends. Cory really enjoys the workplace friendship with this co-worker. He is older and watches out for and helps Cory; yet, Cory does not know how to behave around this friend. Cory thinks about talking to coworkers about the new friend and his lifestyle but ultimately decides that personal opinions on one's lifestyle should be kept private. Cory decides it is best to maintain a good working relationship with the new friend regardless of lifestyle differences.

Forms of Diversity

Workplace diversity means there are differences among coworkers. Whenever people address the issue of diversity at work, they primarily address cultural and racial differences. Diversity extends well beyond culture and race. We differ in age, gender, economic status, physical makeup, intelligence, religion, and sexual orientation, among other things.

The Equal Employment Opportunity Commission (EEOC) enforces laws that protect individuals from workplace discrimination in recruiting, hiring, wages, promotions, and unlawful termination. These laws are based upon Dr. Martin Luther King Jr.'s establishment of Title VII of the Civil Rights Act, which prohibits discrimination based on sex, religion, race or color, or national origin. Since that time, additional laws have been made to further protect individuals from discrimination in the area of age (over forty years), physical and mental disabilities, gender, sexual orientation, hate crimes, pregnancy, and military service. If you ever feel you are a victim of discrimination, first contact your human resource department. If you feel you are still experiencing discrimination, contact your state's *Department of Fair Employment and Housing* or the *Equal Employment Opportunity Commission.*

Exercise 5-6 What Do You See?

Look around the room and list at least three differences between you and your classmates.

1.

2.

3.

Race is defined as people with certain physical traits. Racial differences include various ethnicities including Hispanics, Asians, African Americans, Native Americans, and Anglo-Saxons. **Culture** is the different behavior patterns of people. Examples of various cultures may include where you live geographically, your age, your economic status, and your religious beliefs. As the workplace becomes more diverse, it is hard to imagine a workplace that does not include various races and cultures.

Web Quiz

How diverse is your thinking? Take the diversity quiz.

www.augsburg.edu/education/edc210/diversityquiz.html

As we understand how race and culture impact our workplace, we will begin to recognize how these differences influence our values and behavior. In chapter 1, we discussed that not everyone thinks and behaves like you do. Moreover, people look different and have different value systems. Although we may not like one's looks or agree with others' values or religious beliefs, we must respect everyone's differences and treat them professionally.

Digging deeper into the issue of culture, we need to appreciate the various generational differences and its impact on the workplace. Individuals entering the workforce (eighteen- to twenty-two-year-olds) have different needs than those preparing to retire (fifty-five and older). Moreover, these needs reflect priorities, values, and attitudes.

Stereotypes and Prejudice

In chapter 1, we discussed the differences in people's attitudes and how these attitudes form our personalities. Everyone is a product of past experience. Individuals use these past experiences to form perceptions about people and situations. A **perception** is one's understanding or interpretation of reality. If we had a positive previous experience, we will most likely have a positive perception of a person or circumstance. For example, if your boss calls you into his or her office, you will either have a positive or negative perception of the upcoming situation. If your boss is a good communicator and you frequently visit his or her office, you will have a positive perception of being called into the office. On the other hand, if your boss only calls you into his or her office for bad news, your perception of reality is that the boss's office only represents reprimands and punishment.

To make situations easier to understand or perceive, we often stereotype. **Stereotyping** is making a generalized image of a particular group or situation. We often take our perceptions and mold groups or situations. These images can be positive or negative, but we generally apply them to similar situations and groups. At work, this can include types of meetings (situations) or members of specific departments (groups). Using the preceding example of the boss and his or her office, one could stereotype that all bosses are good communicators.

It is important to not only know the definition of stereotyping but also to avoid applying stereotypes in a negative manner. Let us use the example of females with blonde hair. A common stereotype is that females with blonde hair are not intelligent. This is not true. Prior to responding to a situation, conduct an attitude check to ensure that you are not basing your reaction on a perception or stereotype rather than responding to the current facts and situation.

Using the previous example of attitudes toward females with blonde hair, if we assume that all females with blonde hair are unintelligent (stereotype), we have just demonstrated prejudice. **Prejudice** is a favorable or unfavorable judgment or opinion toward an individual or group based on one's perception (or understanding) of a group, individual, or situation. Typically, at work, prejudice is a negative attitude or opinion that results in discrimination. Therefore, if we do not hire females with blonde hair because we believe they are not intelligent, we are guilty of discrimination. **Workplace discrimination** is acting against someone based on race, age, gender, religion, disability, or any of the other areas we have discussed in this chapter.

Many people harbor some form of prejudice. Recognize what areas you may be harboring prejudice and begin understanding why. Once you recognize what areas need improvement, begin taking action to decrease your prejudice. One way is to learn about the individual, group, or situation that is causing the prejudice.

Talk It Out

What does the Cory story found in the Diversity Basics section have to do with stereotypes and prejudice?

What areas of prejudice do you see on campus?

_____

_____

_____

What areas of prejudice do you see in your community?

_____

_____

_____

Exercise 5–7 Look for Prejudice

Labeling is when we describe an individual or group of individuals based upon past actions. We attach positive or negative labels to groups or individuals, and we frequently have the group or individuals live up or down to these standards. We then watch for supporting behaviors to see if these behaviors live up to or dispel the labels we have attached. For example, if we label a coworker as being the smartest person we know, that person may live up to this expectation by behaving as the smartest person (regardless of if he or she really is intelligent). However, he or she may dispel the label by purposely behaving opposite of a smart person.

Assumptions sometimes are made at work based on people's language differences and accents. These assumptions may include economic status, intelligence, and social customs. In our melting pot society, it is common for individuals to speak a different language (bilingual) when at home. At work, speaking a second language can be a means of attracting and meeting customer needs. Therefore, being bilingual can be a workplace asset.

Do not make fun of people with different cultures or lifestyles or individuals with physical and mental disabilities. Even jokes that we believe are innocent may cause deep wounds. Moreover, they may not only be offensive but violate one's civil rights. Inappropriate comments can be construed as both workplace discrimination and harassment.

For example, Cory is invited to lunch with some new coworkers. During the meal, one of the coworkers tells a joke against a blind person of a certain ethnicity. Cory politely chuckles at the punch line but is actually offended. Cory wonders how to best handle the situation. Should Cory tell the joke teller that the joke was offensive? Should Cory tell the department supervisor? Cory clearly believes that this type of behavior is inappropriate. Cory decides to informally tell the joke teller that the joke was offensive. If Cory continues to see inappropriate or offensive behavior from this employee, Cory has decided to mention the behavior to the department supervisor and request diversity training for the department.

Companies are attempting to better address workplace diversity through several actions. First, they are developing **diversity statements.** These statements remind employees that diversity in the workplace is an asset and not a form of prejudice and stereotyping. Secondly, companies are providing **diversity training** to teach employees how to eliminate workplace discrimination and harassment. This training applies to all employees, customers, and vendors. Thirdly, they are eliminating the **glass ceiling** and **glass walls.** These are invisible barriers that frequently make executive positions (glass ceiling) and certain work areas such as a golf course (glass wall) off limits to females and minorities. A glass ceiling stops females and minorities from advancing up the corporate ladder through promotions. Glass walls are barriers that prevent females and minorities from certain situations. Finally, proactive companies offer formal mentoring programs to assist in identifying and training women and minorities for promotion opportunities. People should not receive special treatment because they are female or a minority, but they should be given an equal opportunity. The employer is responsible for hiring the most qualified candidate.

Cultural Differences

Our society is a mix of individuals from all over the world. For this reason, it is important to address cultural differences and its impact on the workplace. Cultural differences include, among other things, religious influences and the treatment of individuals based on age, gender, and family influences.

There are many different religions in the world. Although most major U.S. holidays are based around Christian holidays, not everyone who works in the United States is a Christian. Individuals who do not share your religious values are afforded the same rights as you. As mentioned earlier in this chapter, the Civil Rights Act protects individuals from discrimination based on religion. Everyone is entitled to observe his or her respective religious holidays and traditions. Once again, we must be respectful of everyone's individual religious beliefs and not condemn someone for his or her religious difference. Although an individual's religious beliefs may permeate every element of his or her life, as with other issues of diversity, if religion negatively impacts performance, the issue must be addressed.

Some countries have self-centered cultures, while other countries put what is best for society as a priority over personal needs. In some cultures, women and children are often not treated as equals to men. Although we may not agree with this treatment, we have to respect cultural differences. It is important to understand these differences so you do not offend others. For example, some hand gestures that are commonly used in the United States may be offensive to someone who has come from another country. If you feel you may have offended someone based upon a cultural difference, find out what behavior offended the other person, apologize if necessary, and make sure you do not repeat the offensive behavior.

Cultural differences have both a positive and negative impact on business. Learning about other cultures can provide insights into new markets and stimulate creativity. With so much diversity among employees and customers, knowing other cultures will result in improved relationships. Outcomes can be negative when companies do not properly train and address cultural differences; this is when opportunities for prejudice and discrimination may emerge.

Workplace Dos and Don'ts

Do always behave in an ethical manner	*Don't* behave one way at work and another around your friends
Do keep information confidential	*Don't* break the company's trust
Do recognize and increase your workplace power bases	*Don't* use your workplace power in a harmful or unethical manner
Do know your rights regarding workplace diversity	*Don't* accept defeat in discriminatory situations
Do learn to respect differences in others	*Don't* use your minority status to take advantage of situations
Do be proud of your culture and heritage	*Don't* show prejudice toward others
Do take responsibility for increasing awareness about workplace diversity issues	*Don't* label people

Concept Review and Application

Summary of Key Concepts

- Personal ethical behavior is a reflection of the influences of friends, family, religion, and society
- Do not share confidential information with individuals with whom the business is of no concern
- Power and power bases are effective tools to use in the workplace
- Be cautious to not use power and reciprocity in an unethical manner
- A conflict of interest occurs when you are in a position to influence a decision from which you could benefit directly or indirectly

- No matter what our differences, treat everyone with respect and professionalism
- Title VII of the Civil Rights Act prohibits discrimination based on sex, religion, race or color, or national origin
- Diversity should be used as an asset that utilizes our differences as ways to create, innovate, and compete
- Workplace diversity should only be an issue when the diversity negatively affects performance

Key Terms

charismatic power	coercive power	confidential
conflict of interest	connection power	culture
diversity statements	diversity training	ethics
ethics statement	expert power	glass ceiling
glass wall	implied confidentiality	information power
labeling	legitimate power	levels of ethical decisions
networking	perception	politics
power	prejudice	race
reciprocity	reward power	stereotyping
workplace discrimination	workplace diversity	

If You Were the Boss

1. You have just been promoted to boss. What are the first five things you should do?
2. What is the best method of dealing with an ethical decision regarding the performance of an employee?
3. What would you do if you noticed an employee treating another employee in a discriminatory manner?
4. What can you do to minimize workplace discrimination and harassment?

Learn More

To learn more about subjects addressed in this chapter take an Introduction to Sociology class and/or a Business Ethics class

Video Case Study: Making Ethical Choices

Two employees are having a conversation at work. This video shows two different ethical perspectives. Refer to the CD that accompanies your text, watch this video, and answer the following questions:

1. Are either of the characters in this video demonstrating unethical behavior? If so, what are the specific unethical behaviors?
2. Is Brian's ethical behavior Regina's business? Why or why not?
3. How does the ethics test apply to this scenario?
4. What should the company be doing to address the situation?

Web Links

http://www.discriminationattorney.com/eeocdfeh.shtml
http://www.managementhelp.org/ethics/ethics.htm
http://www.dol.gov
http://www.dol.gov/dol/topic/discrimination/index.htm
http://www.executiveplanet.com

References

Etzioni, Amitai. *Comparative Analysis of Complex Organizations*, 4–6. (New York: The Free Press), 1961, 4–6.

French, John R. P., and Bertram Raven. "The Bases of Social Power." In *Studies in Social Power*, (Ann Arbor: University of Michigan Press, 1959), 150–67.

Kotter, John P. "Power, Dependence and Effective Management." *Harvard Business Review* (July–August 1977): 131–36.

Peale, Norman V., and Kenneth Blanchard. *The Power of Ethical Management*, (New York: William Morrow, 1988).

Activities

Activity 5-1

Is it ever ethical to take paper clips, copy paper, and pens home from work?

Yes ☐   No ☐   Sometimes ☐

Support your answer.

_____

_____

Activity 5-2

Research a company's conflict of interest policy.

Name of company: _____

Policy: _____

_____

What would you add to the policy to make it better?

_____

What would you eliminate?

_____

What should you do if you work for a company that does not have a policy?

_____

_____

Activity 5-3

List a time when you overheard confidential information that should not have been shared—for example, sitting in a physician's office or overhearing a private conversation while shopping.

_____

_____

How should this situation have been better handled?

_____

_____

Activity 5-4

Identify at least three potential areas for employee theft on a small scale.

1. _____

2. _____

3. _____

4. _____

Identify at least two potential areas for employee theft on a large scale.

1. _____

2. _____

Activity 5-5

In the United States, the thumbs-up symbol communicates a job well done. Research and identify what the thumbs-up symbol communicates in at least two other countries. What did this activity teach you about various cultures and hand gestures?

Country	Meaning

Conclusion: What did you learn? _____

Activity 5-6

Identify a recent experience or observed act of prejudice. How would you have handled the situation differently?

Act of Prejudice	How You Would Handle the Situation?

Activity 5-7

With a partner, dialogue what you would say if someone offended you with a joke. Was this dialogue easy? Why or why not? Share your findings with your class.

_____

Sample Exam Questions

1. _____ is a moral standard of right and wrong.

2. _____ is your obligation to not share information with individuals with whom the business is of no concern.

3. Everyone at work has some _____. The difference is that some people understand this ability to _____ and use it appropriately.

4. _____ means creating debts and obligations for doing something.

5. A/An _____ occurs when you are in a position to influence a decision from which you could benefit directly or indirectly.

6. The first question for ethical decision making is: Is it _____?

7. The second question for ethical decision making is: Is it _____?

8. The third question for ethical decision making is: How does it _____?

9. Differences among coworkers are referred to as _____.

10. _____ is a group of individuals with certain physical traits, while _____ are different behavior patterns of various groups.

11. Companies provide _____ to teach employees how to eliminate workplace discrimination and harassment.

Etiquette/Dress

chapter 6

Winning is accomplished in the preparation phase, not the execution phase.

Anonymous

Objectives

- Describe and discuss the importance of professional behavior in your career

- State the impact dress can have on others' perception of you

- Demonstrate a professional and correct introduction and handshake

- Demonstrate appropriate professional behavior in business dining situations

- Recognize and apply the appropriate use of technology in business/social situations

- Utilize professional *etiquette* in appropriate business situations

Executive Presence

The way you look and behave is a reflection of the organization for which you work. **Executive presence** is defined as having the attitude of an executive. Projecting an executive presence is important because one of the biggest concerns employers have when hiring are new employees' lack of knowledge regarding basic workplace behavior.

The purpose of this chapter is to provide basics regarding expected professional behavior on topics including attire, social etiquette, dining, and the appropriate use of technology. There is a reminder of what many of our parents taught us early in life that some have forgotten, such as smiling and saying please and thank-you. You will encounter many of these social situations daily at work, while other situations may not be as common. Knowing how to behave in the social situations presented is important.

Some of this information may be new to you, and you may feel awkward when you first implement these positive behaviors. The purpose of this chapter is to prepare you for many of the social experiences you will face in the workplace. Practice makes perfect.

Influences of Dress in a Professional Environment

Both your maturity and the importance you place on your job are reflected in the way you behave and dress at work. Because impressions are often made in the first few minutes of meeting someone, individuals rarely have time to even speak before an impression is made. The majority of first impressions are made through your visual **appearance**, which is how you look. Coworkers, bosses, and customers form attitudes based on your appearance. Appearance has an impact on how you perform at work. If you dress professionally, you are more apt to act in a professional manner. The more casual you dress, the more casual you tend to behave. Think of your appearance as a frame. A frame is used to highlight a picture. You do not want the frame to be too fancy, because it will take away from the picture. You want a frame to complement the picture. This appearance frame highlights not only your physical features, including your face, but also your attitude, knowledge, and potential.

Exercise 6-1   Define Your "Frame"

What does your frame look like? Be honest with these answers.

Is it trendy, outdated, professional, or inconsistent?

_____

Does it complement your desired appearance as a professional?

_____

If your current frame is not yet professional, what changes need to occur?

_____

One of the toughest transitions to make when entering the workplace is appropriate dress. Dressing professionally does not have to conflict with current fashion trends. The trick is to know what is acceptable. A basic rule of thumb is to make it a habit to dress one position higher than your current position (i.e., dress like your boss). Doing so communicates that you are serious about your career and how you represent the company. Dressing professionally will assist you in projecting a favorable image at work and position you for advancement.

Know your workplace dress policies. One of the first steps to determining appropriate attire for work is to identify your company's **dress code**. A dress code is a policy that addresses issues such as required attire, uniforms, hairstyle, undergarments, jewelry, and shoes. Many organizations have policies regarding appropriate workplace attire for customer service, safety, and security reasons. Frequently, these policies are included in the employee handbook. If there is no policy, ask your boss if there is a formal dress code and secure a copy. An important cue to workplace attire is how managers dress. Suits are not always the preferred attire. In some situations, pants are acceptable for women, while in other situations they are not. Note that sweats (shirts and/or pants) are not appropriate for work.

Once you have identified what your organization considers proper attire, begin to create a **work wardrobe**. These are clothes that you primarily wear only to work and work-related functions. You need not invest a lot of money when building a work wardrobe. Start with basic pieces and think conservative. For women, this includes a simple, solid skirt or pantsuit in a dark color and a blazer. Skirts should not be above the knee. Pants should only be worn with a matching blazer. For most office environments, men should select dark slacks, a matching jacket, and a tie. Frequently, these items can be found inexpensively at thrift and discount stores. If these items are purchased at a thrift store, take them to the dry cleaners for cleaning and pressing. You will be surprised how professional these items will look after they are cleaned and pressed. Select items that are made of quality fabrics that will not wear out quickly. Purchase items that fit properly and are comfortable. As you begin to earn money, continue building your wardrobe and develop a style that conforms to both company policy and your taste.

Tips from Head to Toe

Regardless of the company's dress code, practice these basic hygiene rules:

- *Shower daily.*
  If needed, use deodorant. If you wear perfume, lotion, or cologne use it sparingly. Scent should not be overpowering.

- *Clothes should be clean and ironed, not torn or tattered, and they should fit properly.*

- *Hair should be clean, well kept, and a natural color.*
  Your hairstyle should reflect your profession. Fad hairstyles and unnatural color are inappropriate in many workplaces.

- *Hands and nails should be well groomed, clean, and trim.*
  Nails that are too long are inappropriate. Women, if you use polish, it should be neat and color/artwork conservative.

- *Jewelry should be kept to a minimum.*
  Jewelry should complement your outfit. Do not wear anything that is distracting or that makes noise.

Talk It Out

Name local places where you can buy professional attire at a low cost.

- *Shoes should be in good condition.*

  Keep your shoes polished and free of scuffs. Flip-flops are not appropriate for the workplace. Men, sock color should match shoe or pant color. Women, heels should be in good condition; if not, get them repaired or replaced. Heels should not be too high. Nylons should be free of runs and snags.

  A woman's outfit should be a reflection of her style and personality—within reason. When dressing for work, your goal is to appropriately frame yourself in a manner that draws attention to your face (i.e., your brains and inner beauty). Additional tips for women include the following:

- *Makeup should be for day wear.*

  Makeup is appropriate for work. Makeup that makes people think you are going to a bar after work is not. Do not wear heavy eyeliner, eye shadow in colors that draw attention, or lipstick in bold colors.

- *It is not acceptable to wear suggestive clothing.*

  This means no cleavage or bare midriffs. No matter the current fashion trends, undergarments (bras, panties, and thongs) should not be visible. Remember, skirts should not be above the knee.

  Just like a woman's outfit, a man's outfit should be a reflection of his style and personality. For some positions, a suit may not be appropriate. The biggest wardrobe blunder men make is wearing clothing that is not clean and/or pressed. After checking with your company's dress code, heed these unspoken rules regarding professional dress at work for men:

- *Shave and/or trim facial hair, including nose and ear hair.*
- *In an office environment, dress pants are the only pants that are professional.*

  With the exception of casual workdays, jeans are inappropriate. Baggy pants that reveal underwear are also inappropriate. Whenever possible, wear a neutral, plain belt that does not draw attention.

- *Shirts should be tucked in.*

  A polo shirt or a dress shirt with a tie is best. Shirts should not display excessive wear (check around the collar line). Shirts with inappropriate logos or offensive phrases should not be worn at work.

- *Hats should not be worn inside buildings except for religious purposes.*

Talk It Out

When or when not is it appropriate for a woman to be sleeveless in a professional setting?

Exercise 6-2   Professional Dress List

What do you have?

Take inventory of your current wardrobe.

_____

List clothing you own that you can use for your professional wardrobe.

_____

_____

List the necessities that you are missing.

_____

_____

Jewelry, Body Piercing, and Tattoos

Although body art, piercing, and body rings/jewelry appear to be current fads, they are offensive to some individuals. For this reason, it is important that you check with your company regarding its policies. However, in general:

- Nose rings, lip rings, and/or tongue rings are not professional and should not be worn in a professional setting.
- Any other body piercing/body jewelry should not be visible at work.
- More than two earrings worn on each ear is considered unprofessional.
- Earrings, chains, and other jewelry should not draw attention. This includes symbols or words that could be considered offensive to others. Do not wear clothing that is tattered, stained, or torn (even if it is considered stylish).
- Body art (tattoos) should not be visible at work. If you are thinking about getting a tattoo, consider the long-term consequences. They are painful and expensive to remove and are designed to last a lifetime.

Casual Workdays and Special Events

Many companies allow **casual workdays.** These are days when companies relax their dress code. Unfortunately, too many employees attempt to stretch the term *casual.* If your company has a casual workday, remember that you are still at work and should dress appropriately. Of course, you can wear jeans if jeans are the preferred attire; just adhere to the *head-to-toe tips* recently presented. Do not wear clothing that is tattered, stained, or torn (even if it is considered stylish). Avoid wearing shirts with sayings or graphics that may offend others.

Your company may also play host or invite you to attend a special function. Holiday parties and receptions are such examples. In these situations, instead of daily work attire, more formal attire may be required. Just as with casual workdays, stick with the basics provided in the *head-to-toe tips.* Women, if appropriate, should wear something in a more formal fabric. Although you have increased freedom and flexibility regarding style and length, this is still a work-related function, so remember to dress conservatively and not suggestively. Men, check ahead of time and see if tuxedos are preferred. Although seldom required these days, if a tuxedo is required, you may need to rent one. For most semi-formal occasions, a suit will suffice.

As a reward for winning Employee of the Month, Cory was invited to attend a one-day conference/luncheon with several managers from Cory's company. Cory had not attended a function like this before and was a little nervous about how to dress and behave in this new business situation. Cory did some preparation and found that dress and behavior are as important in public situations as they are at work. Cory checked with others who had attended these functions and decided dressing more formal would be most appropriate. Cory made sure to shower, clean and trim fingernails, wear polished shoes, and not wear inappropriate jewelry.

Business Etiquette

In a modern workplace, human interaction is unavoidable. Our society has a standard of social behavior that is called **etiquette.** Typically, when individuals think of etiquette, they think it only applies to the wealthy, high society. This is

---

Talk It Out

Identify people in class who are wearing something appropriate for a casual workday.

not true. Socially acceptable behavior should penetrate all demographic and economic groups. Individuals wanting to succeed in the workplace need to heed this protocol and consistently utilize it not only at work but in all areas of their life.

Before we study common areas of business etiquette, we need to define a few terms. Understanding these terms and integrating them into your daily routine will make it much easier to carry out the desired and appropriate workplace behavior. The first word is **courtesy.** When you display courtesy, you are exercising manners, respect, and consideration toward others. The second word is **respect.** Respect is defined as holding someone in high regard. This means putting others' needs before your own needs. Displaying both courtesy and respect toward others are the keys in becoming ladies and gentlemen at work.

Some of the first words parents teach young children are *please* and *thank-you.* Although they are not used as frequently as they should be, both are extremely powerful words that can actually create power for you at work. Think about it; when someone says "please" and "thank-you" to you, you are more likely to repeat a favor or gesture because your deed was acknowledged. When someone does something nice, verbally say "thank-you." Not doing so makes you appear selfish and unappreciative. When you express thanks, individuals will be more likely to continue performing kind acts for you.

Make it a habit to write a thank-you note when someone does something for you that takes more than five minutes or when someone gives you a gift. Do not wait more than three days to write the thank-you note. Write the note as soon as possible. Always send a thank-you note within twenty-four hours of completing a job interview, and remember to send thank-you notes to individuals who agree to be job references for you.

In addition to saying "please" and "thank-you," do not underestimate the value of a simple smile and eye contact. If you have a positive attitude, it will be reflected in your demeanor. When encountering people in the hallways, elevators, and/or meeting rooms, make eye contact, smile, and greet them.

At times, you will be with individuals who do not know each other. When you are with two people who do not know each other and you know both people, it is your responsibility to introduce the two individuals to each other. Politely introduce the least important person to the most important person. For example, "Roger, this is Tim Wilson, the president of our company." "Tim, this is Roger Hue, my next-door neighbor." Apply this introduction rule to all social situations including dining, meetings, receptions, and parties.

A daily function of business is making and keeping appointments. Sometimes you will be required to work with receptionists and/or administrative assistants to schedule these appointments. Be kind to the receptionist and/or administrative assistant. These individuals are the gatekeepers to their bosses; they control schedules and often wield great power in decisions. When scheduling an appointment, state your name, the purpose of the meeting, and the desired date and time. If possible, avoid scheduling appointments on Monday mornings. Many use Monday mornings to schedule their own week and are less likely to accommodate you. If you will be arriving late to an appointment, call and let the other party know you are running late. If you must cancel an appointment, do so immediately and apologize for any inconvenience. Do not just ignore an appointment. When keeping an appointment, arrive five minutes early. After you enter the office, greet the receptionist and politely introduce yourself. State whom you have an appointment with and

Talk It Out

Discuss ways you can be courteous and respectful in class.

the time of the meeting. When entering an office for a meeting, wait to be invited to sit down. After the meeting, extend a handshake and thank the individual for his or her time.

Handshakes

A good handshake conveys confidence. Make a habit of greeting others in business situations with a professional handshake and greeting. Approach the individual you are greeting and extend your right hand as you verbalize a greeting. For example, "Hello Ms. Jones, my name is Danielle. We met at last week's meeting. It's nice to see you again." Ms. Jones will extend her right hand. Your two hands should meet at the web (see Figure 6-1). Grip the other person's hand and gently squeeze and shake hands.

· Do not squeeze the other hand too firmly.
· Make certain you shake the entire hand and not just the other person's fingers. Doing so is insulting and implies that you feel you are better than the other person.
· Do not place your hand on top of the other person's hand or pat the hand. Doing so is insulting.
· If your palms are sweaty, discretely wipe your palm on the side of your hip prior to shaking.

Make eye contact and smile while extending your hand. A good handshake takes practice. As mentioned earlier, get into the habit of being the first to greet and introduce yourself to others. At first you may not feel comfortable, but practice makes perfect. The more frequently you initiate a good handshake, the more comfortable and confident you will become.

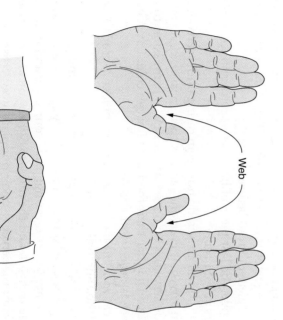

Web

Figure 6-1

Proper Handshake

Exercise 6-3   Shake Hands

Pair up with a classmate and practice initiating an introduction making sure to include a professional handshake. Rate the quality of the introduction and handshake on a scale of 1 to 5 with 5 being the best. Discuss what improvements should be made.

Dining

In business, you will encounter a variety of dining situations. Some dining experiences will be less formal than others. You will most likely encounter some form of the table setting illustrated in Figure 6-2. Take time to study and review a common place setting to help you understand proper use for utensils, plates, and cups. Apart from fast food, few college students are generally comfortable eating in a formal dining situation. Here are several rules of thumb regarding dining etiquette:

- As soon are you are seated, place your napkin on your lap. If you need to leave the table, place your napkin to the side of your plate instead of on your chair.

- Utensils are set to be used in order of necessity. As your courses are served, start with the outside utensil and work in, toward the plate. The utensils set at the top of the plate are for your dessert.

- When serving coffee, water, tea, or any other beverage available at the table, first offer and serve others at your table.

- Do not order anything expensive or messy.

- Do not order alcohol unless others at your table first order an alcoholic beverage. Abstaining from alcohol is the most desired behavior. If you choose to drink, limit consumption to one drink.

- When bread is available, first offer bread to others at your table before taking a piece.

- Place your bread on the bread plate (located at the top left corner of your dinner plate). Place your serving of butter on the bread plate. Do not butter the entire piece of bread at one time. Tear a piece of bread, and butter only that piece of bread before eating.

- Do not take the last piece of bread or appetizer unless it is first offered to others at your table.

- When your meal arrives, do not begin eating until everyone at your table has been served. If everyone receives their meals except you (you are the last to be served), give others at your table permission to begin eating without you so that their food does not get cold. Eat your meal at the same pace as others at the table.

- Do not eat your meal with your fingers unless your main course can be eaten without utensils.

- Burping and slurping are inappropriate while dining. If you accidentally burp or slurp, make sure you immediately apologize and say "excuse me."

- When you are finished eating, place your knife and fork together, with the blade facing in and the tines up. When you are only resting and you do not want the server to take your plate away, cross your utensils with the tines facing down.

- It is inappropriate to use a mobile communication device while dining. If you must take a call or text, excuse yourself from the table.

When Cory arrived at the conference, Cory was glad to be dressed professionally. Everyone there was dressed as a business professional. Cory was introduced to many business professionals. Cory was sure to make eye contact, smile, and properly shake hands when meeting new people. Cory was also careful to follow dining etiquette during lunch. At work the next day, Cory immediately wrote a thank-you note to the managers for being included in the event. At the end of the day, Cory's manager invited Cory into the office and let Cory know what a great impression Cory made at the conference. Several colleagues had mentioned to Cory's manager how impressed they were with Cory's professionalism. Cory realized that doing a little research and being professional was well worth the effort.

A major area of business involves attending social functions. Many invitations request an RSVP, which is French for *répondez s'il vous plaît* (i.e., please respond). As soon as you receive an invitation, send a reply—whether it is an acceptance to attend or a regret that you cannot attend. Not acknowledging the invitation and failing to respond is rude.

When you attend a social function, remember that you are attending the function to meet and network with other professionals, not to receive your last meal.

- Refrain from or limit the consumption of alcohol.
- Serve yourself a small plate of hors d'oeuvres and move away from the food table.
- Hold your hors d'oeuvres in your left hand, leaving your right hand free to shake hands and greet others.
- Do not talk with food in your mouth.

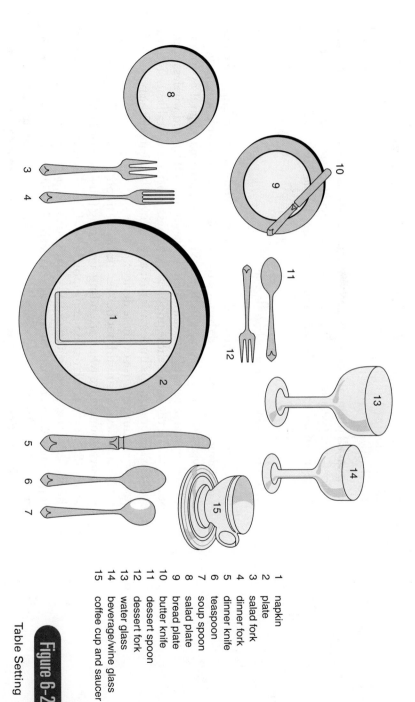

Figure 6-2

Table Setting

1   napkin
2   plate
3   salad fork
4   dinner fork
5   dinner knife
6   teaspoon
7   soup spoon
8   salad plate
9   bread plate
10 butter knife
11 dessert spoon
12 dessert fork
13 water glass
14 beverage/wine glass
15 coffee cup and saucer

Talk It Out

Share common dining and social situations that make you uncomfortable and identify how best to deal with these situations.

Web Quiz

Rate your workplace etiquette.

http://www.emilypost.com/business/business_ei_quiz.htm

Technology at Work

Texting, cell phone usage, messages, voice mail, e-mails, portable entertainment devices—it all gets so confusing! This section provides basic rules for the appropriate use of technology-based communications in the workplace.

Mobile (Portable) Communication Devices

Today's business environment relies on current technologies to improve communication. This is achieved through the use of mobile (portable) communication devices. Common devices include cell phones, personal digital assistants (PDAs), portable music/entertainment devices (e.g., iPODs), and wireless computers. While the use of these important business tools is acceptable in selected business situations, it is important that all employees be aware of the proper etiquette regarding the use of these devices.

Mobile devices should not be seen or heard in public. Therefore, turn off or silence your device when attending a meeting (business or nonbusiness related). If you are anticipating an important call/message, if possible, inform the leader of the meeting and explain that you are expecting an important call or message. When the call or message is received, quietly step out of the meeting to respond to the call/message. It is rude to use your communication device while dining or while attending meetings or performances. It is not polite to take calls in front of others. Doing so implies that the individuals you are with are not important. When taking a call, excuse yourself and step away for privacy. Finally, when interacting with others, it is inappropriate to use or display portable music/entertainment devices in the workplace unless the device provides quiet background music appropriate for a professional workplace.

Text messaging etiquette is equally as important when using portable communication devices. Many students utilize text slang, text shorthand, acronyms, and codes. The use of these styles is not appropriate for formal and informal business communications. In the workplace, texting should only be used for brief, informal communications, utilizing proper spelling. Just as with other portable communication devices, it is not appropriate and is considered rude behavior to view and send text messages while with others (including discreetly during meetings).

Phone Etiquette

The phone is clearly one of the most common workplace communication tools. Phone etiquette, whether land line or wireless, is one topic that every individual must practice to create and maintain a professional image for his or her company. Because the individual(s) on the other end of the phone cannot see you, it is important for you to communicate properly through the words you choose, your tone of voice, the pitch of your voice, and your rate of speech.

Convey a positive, friendly attitude when speaking on the phone. Smiling when you speak creates a friendly tone. Speak clearly and slowly, and do not speak too softly or too loudly.

Phone calls are for brief interactions. If you expect the discussion to be lengthy, ask the individual on the other end of the line if he or she has time to talk or if he or she prefer you call at a more convenient time. When you are having a phone conversation, do not eat or tend to personal matters.

Speakerphones are useful communication tools for specific situations and require proper etiquette. A speakerphone should only be used when you are on a conference call with other participants in the same room or when you require a handsfree device. Only use a speakerphone when you are in a private room where your call will not be distracting to others in your work area. When you use a speakerphone, ask individuals included in the call for permission to use the speakerphone. If all parties agree, alert those included in the call that others are in the room with you and make introductions. This ensures confidentiality and open communication between all parties. Those using a speakerphone should be aware that any small noise he or she makes may be heard and distracting to those on the other end of the line.

When answering a phone call, answer by the second ring. Taking a call in the presence of others implies that the individual in your presence is not important. When with others let the call go into voice mail. If you are expecting an important call and are in the presence of others, inform those you are with that you are expecting a call and will need to take it when it arrives. When the call is received, politely excuse yourself. If you are in your office, politely ask your office guest to excuse you for one moment while you quickly take the call. If you take a call and need to place the caller on hold, politely tell the individual on the phone that you are placing him or her on hold. If an individual is placed on hold for more than 1 minute, get back on the line and ask if you can return the call.

Voice mail messages are a routine part of conducting business. A voice mail impression is equally as important as how you answer in person. Keep voice mail messages brief. State your name, purpose of the call and return number at the beginning of the message. Speak slowly and clearly. After you have left your message, repeat your name and return number a second time at the end of the call. When you receive voice mail messages, it is proper and important to promptly return all messages left for you. Routinely check and empty your voice mail box.

On both portable and land-line phones, it is important that you keep your voice mail greeting professional. Cute voice mail greetings are not professional. Musical introductions or bad jokes do not form favorable impressions when employers or customers are attempting to contact you.

E-Mail and Computer Usage

In addition to all other workplace tools and equipment, your work computer is the property of the company. Therefore, only use it for company business. This includes Internet use and electronic messaging.

When composing or responding to e-mails, emoticons (faces made and embedded in e-mail messages) are inappropriate. Include the business subject in the subject line to let the receiver know your message is not junk e-mail or a virus. The subject "hello" or "hi" is not appropriate. Check all outgoing messages for spelling and grammar. Do not send e-mail messages with large and colorful letters or all capital letters. This is interpreted as yelling and is considered rude. Carefully proofread and think about a message before you press reply to ensure that it cannot be interpreted improperly.

Talk It Out

Do you agree with the technology communication rules of etiquette? Why or why not?

If you receive a work-related message that requires a reply, respond to the message. Ignoring a message is rude; it communicates to the sender that you do not care. You also run the risk of being excluded from future messages. Do not forward messages that do not involve work-related issues. Routinely clean and empty your e-mail box. Additional information on business-related e-mail is included in chapter 9.

Other Etiquette Basics

• *Knock before entering an office.*

Do not enter an office until you are invited. If the individual you want to see is with someone else, politely wait your turn. If the matter is urgent, apologize for interrupting.

• *Put others first.*

When you are with colleagues and you are taking turns (in line, to order, etc.), allow your colleagues to go first.

• *Interruptions.*

In today's society, we have so many inputs trying to attract our attention. As a result, we often get anxious to share our point of view in a conversation and fail to allow others in the conversation to complete their sentence. Show others respect by not interrupting conversations. If you accidentally interrupt someone, immediately apologize and ask him or her to continue his or her statement.

• *Apologies.*

Everyone is human. Therefore, everyone makes mistakes. When you realize that you may have said or done something hurtful to someone, apologize immediately. Apologizing is not a sign of weakness; it is a sign of strength and maturity. Even if you are not sure whether you have offended someone, apologize to avoid any potential misunderstandings. However, do not unnecessarily and continually apologize. Doing so not only gives you the appearance of being needy and insecure, more importantly you are not being assertive and possibly not standing up for your rights in an unoffending manner.

• *Profanity.*

This type of language does not belong in the workplace. Do not assume others are comfortable with profanity. Conversations should be professional and respectful.

• *Dominating a conversation.*

There is a key to carrying on a successful conversation. The key is listening. Listening means that you value the information the other individual is providing. Too frequently, individuals dominate a conversation with their own personal accounts. In general, this is not appropriate. This behavior becomes annoying to the listener when you turn the conversation to yourself. Next time you are in a conversation, listen to how many times you state the words *me, I,* and *my.* Try to minimize the use of these words in your conversation.

Workplace Dos and Don'ts

Do	Don't
Do wear professional clothes to work	*Don't* wear sweats, tennis shoes, or suggestive apparel at work
Do shower and make sure you are always clean	*Don't* overdo the cologne (or any body sprays)
Do make eye contact and offer a gentle but firm handshake	*Don't* grasp just the fingers when shaking hands
Do follow formal dining etiquette at work-related functions	*Don't* reach, grab, or overload your plate at the hors d'oeuvres table
Do say "please" and "thank-you" when appropriate	*Don't* assume that the other person knows you are thankful for his or her act of kindness

Concept Review and Application

Summary of Key Concepts

- Projecting an executive presence is important in demonstrating knowledge of basic workplace behavior
- The majority of first impressions are made through visual appearances
- Both your maturity and the importance you place on your job are reflected in the way you behave and dress at work
- Begin to create a work wardrobe today
- Visual body art/piercing and body rings/jewelry are offensive to some individuals and are not appropriate in a professional work environment. Consider the long-term consequences of getting a tattoo or piercing
- Follow business etiquette protocol and consistently utilize it in all areas of your life
- Make a habit of thanking individuals either verbally or in writing
- Appropriate etiquette at social functions and while dining is as important as professional behavior at work

Key Terms

appearance	casual workdays	courtesy
dress code	etiquette	executive presence
respect	work wardrobe	

If You Were the Boss

1. As the manager of a bank, one of your employees comes in on a Monday morning with a pierced tongue and purple hair. What should you do?
2. You have just hired a new employee who clearly has no concept of business etiquette. What specific steps would you take to teach your new employee how to behave professionally?

Learn More

To learn more about subjects addressed in this chapter attend a workshop on Business Etiquette.

Video Case Study: Dress for Success

This video presents expert advice on how to dress professionally at work. Refer to the CD that accompanies your text, watch this video, and answer the following questions.

1. What specifically are Franchesca and Brad wearing that makes their appearance professional?
2. What four items make Patricia's and Brian's appearance unprofessional?
3. What specific advice does the expert provide for looking professional regarding make-up, tattoos, jewelry, jeans, hair, and shoes?

Video Case Study: Business Lunch Etiquette

This video addresses a common business lunch sales meeting. Refer to the CD that accompanies your text, watch this video, and answer the following questions:

1. Name three things Brian did right or wrong?
2. What advice would you give Brian?
3. Midway through this lunch, how should Karen have handled this situation?

Web Links

http://www.ravenwerks.com/practices/etiquette.htm
http://www.youngmoney.com/careers//onthejob/149
http://www.letstalk.com/promo/unclecell//unclecell2.htm

Reference

Post, Peggy, and Peter Post. *The Etiquette Advantage in Business: Personal Skills for Professional Success.* New York: HarperCollins Publishers, 1999.

Activity 6-1

Assume you are starting a new job as an accounting clerk next week. You need a work wardrobe and are limited to a $50 budget. Make a list of what you need and could buy to get you through your first week of work. Include the cost.

What You Need to Buy	Cost
	$
Total Cost	$50

Prior to being faced with this scenario, what items can you purchase today to begin building your professional wardrobe?

Activity 6-2

Pretend you are at a business reception and you do not know anyone else in the room. Role-play formal introductions with a classmate, and then evaluate your partner's performance by identifying strengths and weaknesses.

STUDENT NAME

Strengths	Weaknesses

STUDENT NAME

Strengths	Weaknesses

Activity 6-3

Visit a (non-fast-food) restaurant to practice proper dining etiquette. While you are doing so, identify five acts of inappropriate behavior others are exhibiting.

Inappropriate Behavior	Why Behavior Is Inappropriate
1.	
2.	
3.	
4.	
5.	

Sample Exam Questions

1. The majority of first impressions are made by _____.

2. One of the first steps to determining appropriate attire for work is to identify _____

3. Give five tips for women for dressing professionally from head to toe. _____
   _____,
   _____,
   _____,
   _____,
   _____.

4. Give five tips for men for dressing professionally from head to toe. _____
   _____,
   _____,
   _____,
   _____.

5. A standard of social behavior is called _____.

6. When someone does something nice for you, you should _____
   _____.

7. A good handshake conveys _____.

8. Give five rules of thumb regarding dining etiquette. _____
   _____,
   _____,
   _____,
   _____.

Customer Service/Quality

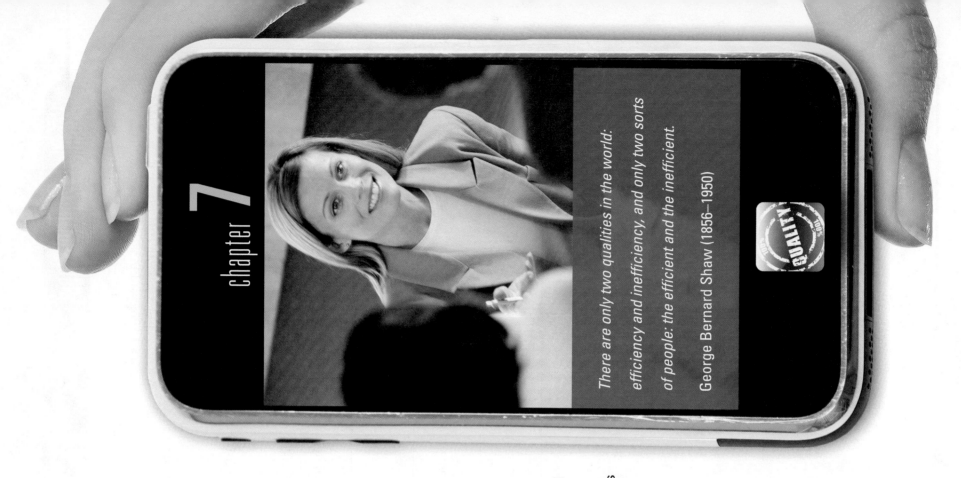

> There are only two qualities in the world: efficiency and inefficiency, and only two sorts of people: the efficient and the inefficient.
>
> George Bernard Shaw (1856–1950)

Objectives

- Define *productivity* and its impact on organizational success

- Identify and define *directional statements*

- Know the various types of plans used in an organization

- Define the primary business functions and their purpose in an organization

- Define *quality* and its importance in business

- State the difference between a *product*, a *good*, and a *service*

- Define *creativity* and *innovation*

- Identify and describe the importance of *customers* and *customer service*

- Describe how to handle a difficult customer

Productivity in the Workplace

Part of your workplace success will be based upon your understanding of the business, the way it is organized, and its overall purpose. Without an understanding of the business as a whole, it is difficult for you to be a good employee. This chapter addresses these issues.

The purpose of a business is to make a profit. The business has hired you to be productive. Workplace **productivity** means to perform a function that adds value to the company. Whatever you produce (called *output*) should always assist the company in achieving its mission. It is your responsibility to help the company be successful. There are several ways of doing this. First and foremost, behave ethically. Make ethical choices that serve the best interest of the company. It is your responsibility to take care of company resources that have been entrusted to you. This includes eliminating waste and producing quality products. As you learned in chapter 1, your attitude assists the company with becoming successful. Maintain a positive attitude. Be an active team member and work to create positive workplace relationships. Be open to learning new skills.

A company's **mission statement** is its statement of purpose. It identifies why everyone comes to work. An example of a college's mission statement is to contribute to student success. This means not only providing a solid education but also preparing students to succeed on the job or with their continuing education. If all college employees know their ultimate purpose is to contribute to student success, every activity they perform on the job should contribute to student success. Either prior to starting your job or within your first week at work, secure a copy of your company's mission statement. If possible, memorize it. A company's mission statement is typically included in the employee handbook and/or provided to you during the employee orientation. If this information is not provided, ask your supervisor or the human resource department for a copy.

A company will not survive without being profitable; even nonprofit organizations need to make a profit to accomplish their mission. However, a company is not successful just because it turns a profit. There are several important elements that contribute to a company's success. This includes satisfying customers who have purchased a quality product produced by motivated employees. Successful companies are accountable to various stakeholders including their investors, the community at large, the environment, and their employees. Factors within the business environment change, so it is important that companies constantly monitor changes and be proactive in meeting the needs of various stakeholders.

Once a company has identified why it exists, it must identify where it wants to be in the future. This is called a **vision statement**. A company's vision statement is its viable view of the future. For example, a college may want to be the top-ranked college in the nation. It will take work, but it is achievable. In addition to the company's mission and vision statements, each company should have a values statement. The **values statement** defines what is important to (or what the priorities are for) the company. This could include providing a healthy return to investors, taking care of the environment, taking care of its employees, and keeping customers satisfied. Included in the company values statement will typically be the company's code of conduct or ethics statement. As discussed in chapter 5, these statements discuss the importance of behaving ethically in all areas of business.

Together, the company's mission, vision, and values statements comprise the organization's **directional statements**. These statements create the foundation of why the company exists and how it will operate.

For example, Cory's company was updating its strategic plan and was asking for volunteers to sit on various committees. Cory wondered if new employees were able to sit on these committees. Cory decided to ask a coworker. The coworker encouraged Cory to participate and said it would be a great way for Cory to learn more about the company, get to know people throughout the organization, and help make positive changes for the company's overall success. Cory's coworker then showed Cory the back side of Cory's name badge. On it was printed the company's mission statement. "This," Cory's coworker proudly said, "is why we come to work everyday." Cory signed up for a committee that afternoon.

Each company should have a strategy. The company's **strategy** outlines major goals and objectives and is its road map for success. Typically, a **strategic plan** is a formal document that is developed by senior management. The strategic plan identifies how the company will secure, organize, utilize, and monitor its resources. **Company resources** include financial (fiscal), human (employees), and capital (long-term investments) resources. The formal strategic plan is generally not available to all employees. However, many companies provide brief summaries or overviews to all employees to keep everyone focused on priorities and goals. Just as you created a personal plan earlier in this text, all areas of the company will have smaller plans with stated **goals** and **objectives** that identify how their respective areas will assist in achieving the company's strategy. As defined in chapter 2, a goal is a broad statement while an objective supports a goal. Objectives are also referred to as *short-term goals*. Remember that an objective must be short-term and measurable. Each area of the company will utilize its respective resources and have its performance monitored based upon the company strategy and goals.

Exercise 7-1   Create Job Goals

Assume you started your new job today as a receptionist for a law firm. Write one goal and two objectives for your new job.

Goal

Objective 1

Objective 2

Lines of Authority

Company functions and resources within the business are organized according to the company's mission and strategy. The way a company is organized is called its **organizational structure**. The graphic visual display of this structure is called the company **organizational chart**. This chart not only identifies key functions within the company but also shows the formal lines of authority for employees. These formal lines of authority are also referred to as the *chain of command*. The formal lines of authority will identify who reports to whom within the company. Respect and follow the formal lines of authority within your company. For example, using the organizational chart in Figure 7-1, it is inappropriate for the accounts payable supervisor to directly approach the marketing vice president for a request without prior approval from the accounting director.

This story is a good example of why you should know your organizational structure and identify your superiors. One day Cory was left alone in the department while everyone was away at an important meeting. A tall man walked through the doors and asked to see Cory's boss. Cory explained that the boss was currently out. The gentleman began asking how Cory felt about the company, including how long Cory had worked for the company and if Cory were able to change one thing in the company what it would be. Cory found the questions strange but interesting. Cory was honest in the answers provided, always keeping the conversation polite and positive but constructive. The gentleman thanked Cory for the input and left. Two weeks later, Cory's boss returned from a meeting and told Cory that the CEO of the company had shared Cory's comments with key executives in identifying ways to improve employee morale. It was then that Cory realized that the earlier conversation was with the CEO of the company. Cory was relieved to have been polite and positive in the CEO conversation but regretted not recognizing the CEO when he first walked into the office.

Each company has a leader (see Figure 7-2). The leader is typically called the **president or chief executive officer (CEO)**. The president or CEO reports to the company **board of directors**. This group of individuals is responsible for developing the company's overall strategy and major policies. The people who become the company's board of directors are elected by shareholders or investors. Smaller companies may not have such a formal structure and/or titles, but each business has an investor(s), (owner(s)), and a leader (president). It is important to become familiar with your leaders' names and titles and the formal lines of authority. This will allow you to determine who you can go to if there is a question or problem. If possible, try to view updated photos of these individuals so that,

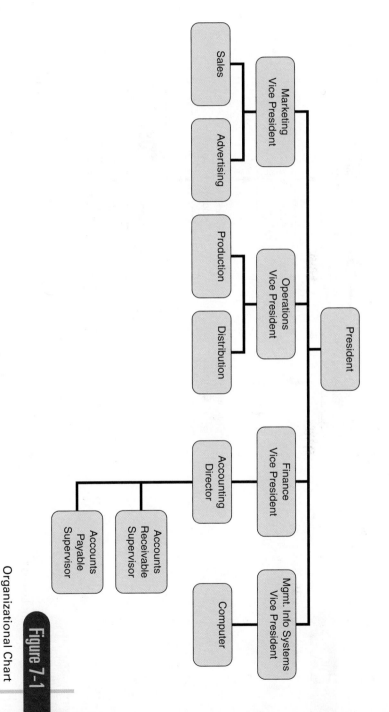

Figure 7-1

Organizational Chart

Figure 7-2

Formal Corporate Structure

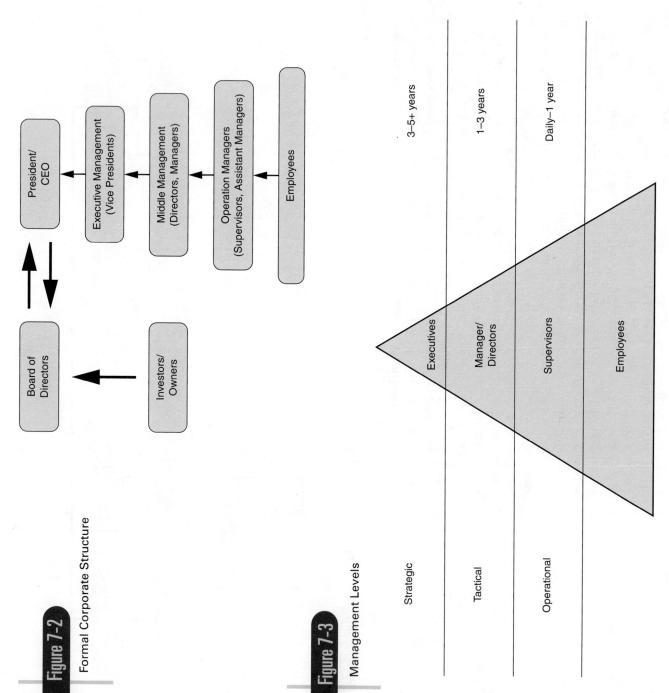

Figure 7-3

Management Levels

if the appropriate opportunity arises, as with Cory's experience, you can introduce yourself to them.

Within a typical company structure are three different levels of management (see Figure 7-3). These levels include senior management, middle management, and operations management. **Senior managers or executives** typically have the title of *vice president*. These individuals work with the president in identifying and implementing the company strategy. The time line for **strategic issues** typically ranges from three to five years or more. **Middle managers** typically have the title of *director* or *manager*. These individuals work on tactical issues. **Tactical issues** identify how to link the strategy into the reality of day-to-day operations. The time line for tactical issues is one to three years. **Operations managers**, typically *supervisors* and *assistant managers*, work on **operational issues**. These are issues within the company that occur on a daily basis and/or no longer than one year. As you begin to develop your career, you will have the opportunity to advance into a position of leadership. Your first step into a management position will be that of a **supervisor**. And, although supervisors only concern themselves with operational issues, successful employees and supervisors understand the bigger picture of the company's overall tactics and strategy.

As displayed in a typical organizational chart, companies are typically arranged by major functions. These major functions are frequently referred to as **divisions**. Within these divisions are **departments**. The departments carry out specific functions respective of their division. A number of major functions (divisions) are necessary in business. These include finance and accounting, human resources, operations, information systems, marketing, and legal counsel.

The **finance and accounting department** is responsible for the securing, distribution, and growth of the company's financial assets. Any invoices (company bills), incoming cash or checks must be recorded through the accounting department. The accounting department will work with the human resource department on payroll issues regarding your paycheck. Because the primary purpose of every company is to make a profit, you, as an employee, are accountable for how you utilize the company's financial resources. Just as you have a personal budget (refer to chapter 2), companies utilize **budgets**. A budget is a plan used to allocate money. There are several types of budgets including a **capital budget** and an **operational budget**. The capital budget is used for long-term investments including land and large pieces of equipment. An operational budget is used for short-term items including payroll and the day-to-day costs associated with running a business.

One of Cory's coworkers went on vacation. Before leaving, Cory's coworker showed Cory how to order office supplies online and asked Cory to order more supplies if the department fell short. Cory noticed that the department was running low on a few items and decided to place an order. As Cory clicked through the online catalog, Cory saw a lot of items that would be nice to have around the office, including a new hole punch, a label maker, and multicolored vinyl file folders. Cory also thought it would be nice to have a pair of new scissors, a tape dispenser, and other personal desk items. As Cory was about to place the order, Cory was shocked to see that the total was over $1,000. Cory realized that the coworker never gave Cory a budget, but knew that one existed. Cory decided to order only the necessities and wait to ask the coworker about the other items.

As illustrated in the Cory example, too frequently, employees do not think before they spend the company's money. Before you spend the company's money, ask yourself a simple question: "If I owned this company, would I spend my money on this item?" Answering that simple question makes you more accountable for your actions and makes you think like a business owner. You most likely will not spend your money on frivolous, unnecessary items and will pay more attention to not only adhering to a budget but also identifying ways to save money.

The **human resource department** deals with recruiting, hiring, training, evaluating, compensating, promoting, and terminating employees. This department deals with the employee (people) side of business. Your first contact with this function will be when you apply and interview for a job. You will also interact with the human resource department for any issue regarding company policy, complaints and grievances, and your terms of employment. The human resource function is discussed in greater detail in chapter 8.

The **operations** function deals with the production and distribution of the company's product. It is the core of the business. Even if your position does not directly contribute to the primary purpose of the company, it is your job to support individuals whose job it is to produce and distribute the product.

The **information systems (IS) department** deals with the electronic management of information within the organization. This division is responsible for ensuring that the company appropriately utilizes its computer/technology resources. As an employee, you assist and support the information systems department by only utilizing company technology for work-related business. Responsible employees know and practice computer basics such as routinely backing up files, emptying the electronic trash bin, and conducting routine virus checks. If your computer is not functioning normally, reboot the computer. Report any computer virus and system problems immediately.

Marketing is responsible for creating, pricing, selling, distributing, and promoting the company's product. As is discussed later in this chapter, there are internal and external customers and it is every employee's responsibility to assist in satisfying the customer's needs. Therefore, regardless of your position, it is your job to contribute to producing a high-quality, high-value product. You are a walking billboard for your company. Your behavior both at and away from work represents the company. Do not speak poorly of your company, coworkers, or the company's product.

Finally, the company's **legal counsel** handles all legal matters relating to the business. Check with the company's legal department prior to engaging in a contract on behalf of the company.

Large companies may have separate divisions for each of these functions, while smaller companies combine several functions into a single division, department, or position. Not all companies have all the formal departments, titles, or organizational charts described in this chapter. Most small businesses will not have such formal structures. However, to be successful, they will have someone who performs these important functions for the business.

Quality and the Company

If someone asked you to describe a company, you would most likely describe a building, its employees, and the product produced. These are major elements that define a company, but a company needs customers to succeed. Excellent service, quality, and innovation are what will persuade customers to purchase a company's product. More important, a successful company's employees and products must make customers want to make a repeat purchase.

As an employee, you are an important part of the company. Each job in the company has a purpose; therefore, each employee is important to a company. Although administration may lead what is being done in the company, your job is necessary to help run the company. This is what makes you an important part of the company. Therefore, perform your best at all times. **Quality** is a predetermined standard that defines how a good is to be produced or a service is to be provided. Customers demand quality not just in the product they purchase but also from the company employees. If customers do not perceive that they have received a quality product or service, they will not make a repeat purchase.

Customer loyalty is another important element that contributes to the success of a company. If a customer perceives he or she has received value and a quality product, he or she will display loyalty to your company by making a repeat purchase. Companies want to build brand loyalty with customers. This means that the customer will not substitute your product for that of a competing product. Customers will be loyal to a company and its products when quality products are consistently provided.

Employee loyalty is an employee's obligation to consistently support a company and its mission. Displaying loyalty contributes to a company's success. Employees show their loyalty in several ways. The most obvious is for you to do your job and do it well. Another way to show loyalty to the company is to show respect for company policies, your coworkers, and the company's customers. Make every effort to promote the company and its products. To do this, you must understand your company including its mission, strategy, and business structure.

The success of a company depends on profit. **Profit** is revenue (money coming in from sales) minus expenses (the costs involved in running the business). Help create profit for your company by monitoring and decreasing expenses and identifying ways to increase sales. Be aware of expenses you incur at work and make every effort to eliminate waste. Find ways to be involved with and take responsibility toward knowing your customers and the community. As profits increase, the company can grow. This means a company can expand into a larger space, add more sites, offer more services and/or goods, increase your pay and benefits, and/or hire additional employees. As an employee, this could result in raises or promotions.

Each company sells a **product**. A product is what is produced by a company. Products come in the form of goods and services. Some companies sell only goods, some sell only services and some sell both. A **good** is a tangible item, something that you can physically see or touch. Appliances, toys, or equipment are examples of tangible products. A **service** is an intangible product. In other words, you cannot always touch or see the product. Examples of services include haircuts, banking, golf courses, and medical services. The next section explains the difference between a company's service and customer service.

Who Is the Customer?

All functions of a company are important. However, a company cannot survive without customers. This makes it extremely important to know who your customers are and how to treat them. A **customer** is an individual or business that buys the company's product.

A company has internal and external customers. Internal customers are fellow employees and departments that exist within a company. External customers are individuals outside of the company. These include customers, vendors, and investors. You may have a job where you do not interact with the company's external customers, but you must serve and treat your internal customers as well as the company expects employees to treat its external customers. Doing so makes it easier for employees who interact with external customers to do so successfully.

Talk It Out

Identify common money wasters in the workplace.

Exercise 7-2   Identify Professional Treatment in the Workplace

As a customer, how do you expect to be treated?

_____

_____

How do you expect your coworkers to treat you?

_____

_____

A satisfied customer will make a repeat purchase. Maintaining satisfied customers is one of the best ways to sell your product or service because they will encourage others to buy your product. In contrast, unsatisfied customers will spread the word about their dissatisfaction even faster than satisfied customers spread the word about their satisfaction. Think about how many times you have been satisfied or unsatisfied with a good or service. When others ask you if you know about a particular product, you will tell them whether your experience was good or bad. The reason satisfaction is important is that most people will tell about the problems and bad experiences without anyone asking. You do not want people bad-mouthing your company or product.

To create a satisfied customer, a high-quality product or service and excellent customer service is necessary. This can only occur with quality employees producing their product with quality materials (inputs). This concept is illustrated in the quality equation found in Figure 7-4.

Quality

When it comes to quality, the expectation of customers is high. With increased technology and competition, customers demand high-quality products and services. Customers expect that a product will last. Customers also expect **value**,

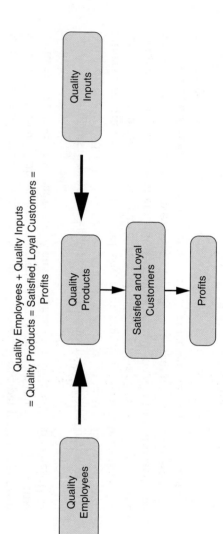

Quality Employees + Quality Inputs
= Quality Products = Satisfied, Loyal Customers =
Profits

Figure 7-4

The Quality Equation

which means customers believe they are getting a good deal for the price they have paid for a product. Companies that cannot compete on this issue cannot experience long-term success.

If your job is to help create a product, keep in mind that if you do your job well and the product is of high quality, customers will be happy and keep buying the product. High-quality products can only be produced if you, as an employee, are doing your job well.

Exercise 7-3   Taking Responsibility for Quality

As an employee, list three ways you can take personal responsibility for quality at work.

1. _____

2. _____

3. _____

Customers measure product quality by comparing your company's product to similar products. They also measure quality by how satisfied they are after consuming or using a product. Successful companies include performance monitors in their strategies. Performance monitors identify how success will be measured. Monitors, or standards, may include defect rates, expenses, or sales quotas. Another example would be employee evaluations. The evaluation can identify how an employee's performance contributes to customer quality. Performance monitors assess areas of quality and service that are done well and those that need improvement. Quality-focused evaluation criteria address areas such as response time, attitude toward customers, and the proper use of resources.

As mentioned earlier in this chapter, the marketing department is responsible for the price and unique, development, distribution, and promotion of a product. Although these functions are the primary responsibility of the marketing department, projecting a positive image and selling the company's product are the jobs of every employee within the organization. The premise that marketing is each employee's job is commonly referred to as the marketing concept.

Creativity and Innovation

As our economy becomes increasingly competitive, it is important for individuals to enhance their creativity. **Creativity** is the ability to produce something new and unique, such as a good, service, or system. Creativity is achieved when an individual looks at an object or situation differently than its intended use then identifies a new use or application to that object or situation. Creativity can only occur when an individual is not restrained by traditional thinking. A creative person will always ask, "what if?" instead of being constrained by the barrier of the item or services' original use.

Consider America's greatest inventor, Thomas Edison. He developed the phonograph when he was trying to improve the efficiency of the telegraph. Through the creativity of others, the phonograph evolved into a record player,

Web Quiz

Test your customer service skills.

http://www
.donnaearltraining.com/
Articles/CustomerService
Quiz.html

which ultimately evolved into today's portable music devices. If Edison had not developed the phonograph, imagine how life would be without easy access to music.

Employees need to enhance their workplace creativity. Doing so opens doors for new products and increased efficiencies. While creativity is important in the workplace, it is not useful if the new ideas are not acted upon. **Innovation** is the introduction of a new product. Think of innovation as putting your creative ideas into action. An important element of contributing to the success of any workplace is to continually identify new uses and applications for items and/or situations and then act upon those new ideas. Work on improving your creative and innovative skills in an effort to improve and/or contribute to your company's success.

Excellent Customer Service Defined

An important business concept relating to workplace quality is customer service. **Customer service** is the treatment an employee provides the customer.

Customers expect excellent customer service. They want to be treated with respect and kindness. They not only want but expect employees to be competent, dependable, and responsive. They expect the business environment to be clean, safe, and organized.

A **competent** employee is an employee who knows the product(s) his or her company offers. Competent employees are able to answer questions when a customer asks. Customers expect employees to be able to help them decide on a purchase by giving them correct information about the product. If you cannot answer a question, direct the customer to another employee who can assist the customer.

Dependable means that you are reliable and taking responsibility to assist a customer. Do not pretend to know something when you do not know the answer to a customer's question. Customers expect you to help them solve their problems. Admit when you do not know the answer. You will gain respect in admitting that you do not know all the answers but are willing to find someone who can assist the customer. If there is a situation in which you seek assistance from another employee when helping a customer, do not just hand the customer over to the other employee without explaining the situation. Whenever possible, stay with the customer and learn from your coworker so that, in the future, you will know the answer the next time someone asks.

A **responsive** employee provides a customer personal attention. Being responsive means that you are aware of the customer's need, often before the customer even realizes that need. Some customers like to be left alone to shop for a product but want you near if questions arise. Other customers would like you to guide them step by step when purchasing a product. When a customer approaches your area, make every effort to acknowledge the customer as soon as possible. Greet him or her and ask the customer if he or she needs assistance. Watch the customer's body language. The customer will let you know if he or she wants to be left alone or wants you to stay nearby. Use the customer's name if you know it. Using the customer's name creates a more personal and friendly atmosphere. Customers are different and need to be treated differently according to their needs. Learn how to satisfy these needs.

A customer also expects a welcoming, convenient, and safe environment. This includes the appearance of the building, as well as the appearance of the employees. As soon as a customer comes in contact with a business, an opinion is formed about that business. There is only one first impression, so it must be positive. The appearance of the building and/or employees can be the reason a customer visits your company in the first place. Keep your workplace clean, and immediately address any potential safety hazards. If there is trash on the floor or a spill of water, clean it up. Take responsibility for keeping your workplace clean and safe. Although addressed in greater detail in chapter 6, make every effort to maintain a professional appearance from head to toe. Your attitude, language, and attire are a total package that creates an image for your customers.

The Impact of Customer Service

Know your customers. Good customers will keep coming back to purchase your product if you have a high quality product and you make your customers feel valued. These customers will tell others about your business. Excellent customer service is the biggest reason customers return. With so many choices and increased competition, the same product can be purchased at many different places. Often times, the only thing that keeps customers coming back to your business may be the personal service that you have provided them. Your goal is to build a long-term relationship with customers that will make them loyal to you and your business. This is why so many businesses now keep records of their customers. The more information businesses maintain on their customers, the more they are able to provide personal service. With the increased use of technology, many companies maintain databases with such information as past purchases, birthdays, special interests, and return/exchange practices. This allows the company to establish a more personal relationship with the customer and to follow up on sales. It is common to notify customers of upcoming sales of frequently purchased products, send notification of upcoming events, or mail discounts and coupons. Customer information and records should be kept confidential and should only be used for business purposes.

For example, when Cory moved to a new neighborhood and wanted to order pizza, Cory found there were many different pizza parlors. The way to determine which one to try was to ask others for a recommendation or randomly try each one. Because Cory was new to the area and did not know many people, Cory called one of the pizza shops. When Cory called, the employee was friendly and sounded happy to assist with the order. Cory automatically formed a good impression about the pizza shop. When Cory went to pick up the pizza, the inside of the shop was clean, as were the employees. The pizza also tasted good. So the next time Cory wanted a pizza, Cory called the same place. Cory was really impressed when an employee at the pizza shop remembered what was previously ordered and called Cory by name. Cory experienced excellent service.

The success and profitability of a company depends on how you treat your customers. The happier the customers are, the more likely they are to come

Talk It Out

What customer body language would indicate a customer needs help and what body language would indicate a customer wants to be left alone?

back. A business needs satisfied customers to not only make repeat purchases but also to tell others about their favorable experience. Unhappy customers will tell others to avoid your business.

The Difficult Customer

Customers can sometimes be difficult to deal with. Historically, companies have had the motto "The customer is always right." But, in many instances, the customer may not be right. Although the customer may be wrong, adopt the attitude that the customer is unhappy and do all you can to help the customer solve his or her problem. Have patience, and sympathize with the customer.

Many times, a difficult customer will be unfriendly and may even begin yelling at you. If this occurs stay calm and do not take the customer's inappropriate behavior personally. By remaining calm, you are better able to identify the real problem and logically get the problem solved as quickly as possible in a manner that is fair to both the customer and your company.

In order to successfully resolve a difficult customer's complaint, do the following:

1. *Stay calm, let the customer talk, and listen for facts.* This may mean letting the customer vent for a few minutes. This is not easy when someone is yelling at you. However, do not interrupt or say "please calm down." This will only increase the anger. Pay attention, nod your head, and take notes if it helps you keep focused. Even though the person may be yelling at you, do not take the harsh words personally.

2. *Watch body language.* This may include the tone of voice, eye contact, and arm movement. If a customer avoids eye contact, he or she may be lying to you or not fully conveying his or her side of the story. Do not allow a customer to touch you, especially in a threatening manner. If you feel a difficult customer has the potential to become violent or physically abusive, immediately seek assistance.

3. *Acknowledge the customer's frustration.* Say, "I can understand why you are upset." Let the person know you have been listening to his or her concern by paraphrasing what you have understood the problem to be. Do not repeat everything, just a summary of the concern.

4. *Make sure the problem gets solved.* Whenever possible, take care of the problem yourself; do not send the customer to someone else. While it is tempting to call your supervisor or a coworker, whenever possible, take care of the customer by staying with him or her until you know the problem is resolved.

5. *Know company policy.* Some difficult customers are dishonest customers and attempt to frazzle employees by intimidation and rude behavior. Know company policies and do not be ashamed to enforce them consistently. If a customer challenges a policy, calmly and politely explain the purpose of the policy.

6. *Expect conflict, but do not accept abuse.* Difficult customers are a fact of life. Although customers may occasionally yell, you do not have to take the abuse. If a customer shows aggressiveness or is cursing, politely tell him or her that you cannot help him or her until he or she is able to treat you in a respectable manner. If the customer continues the inappropriate behavior, immediately call a supervisor.

Talk It Out

If a customer is angry with a raised voice, what would you say to that customer?

Workplace Dos and Don'ts

Do	Don't
Do read the company mission statement so you remember why the company pays you to come to work each day	*Don't* ignore the company's directional statements and their application to your job
Do know your internal and external customers. Also know what role you play in ensuring quality and how you contribute to your company's success	*Don't* assume that your only customer is outside of the company and that you have no influence on the company's overall success
Do take responsibility for producing and/or providing quality. Be a role model for other employees by eliminating waste and showing constant concern for quality	*Don't* ignore quality by allowing wasted materials and *don't* allow bad attitudes to affect your performance
Do display competence by knowing your company products and policies	*Don't* lie to customers and make up information you don't know regarding company products and policies
Do make every effort to build a professional relationship with your customers by learning their likes and dislikes	*Don't* become overbearing or intrusive when gathering or recording customer data
Do remain calm when dealing with a difficult customer, and seek assistance immediately if a customer becomes abusive	*Don't* tolerate foul language or violence

Concept Review and Application

Summary of Key Concepts

- Directional statements include the company's mission, vision, and values statements
- The company's strategic plan identifies how a company will secure, utilize, and monitor resources for success
- A company's organizational chart is a graphic display of the major functions and formal lines of authority within an organization
- Major functions (divisions) that are necessary within a business include finance and accounting, human resource management, operations, information systems, marketing, and legal counsel

- Excellent service, quality, and innovation are what will persuade customers to purchase a company's product or service
- Employees should work on improving their creative and innovative skills in an effort to contribute to a company's success
- Customers can be internal customers (other employees) or external customers (individuals outside of your company). A successful company has concern for both internal and external customers
- Employees that provide excellent customer service are competent, dependable, and responsive
- The customer is not always right, but you need to adopt the attitude that the customer is unhappy and do all you can to help the customer solve his or her problem

Key Terms

board of directors	budget	capital budget
company resources	competent	creativity
customer	customer service	departments
dependable	directional statements	divisions
employee loyalty	finance and accounting	goals
good	department	information systems
innovation	human resource	department
middle managers	department	marketing
operational budget	legal counsel	objectives
operations managers	mission statement	operations
president or chief	operational issues	organizational
executive officer (CEO)	organizational chart	structure
profit	product	productivity
senior managers or executives	quality	responsive
strategic plan	service	supervisor
tactical issues	strategic issues	value
vision statement	strategy	values statement

If You Were the Boss

1. How can you get your employees to better relate their workplace productivity to the department's budget?

2. You are the supervisor for a team of employees who have a high number of product defects. They also waste materials. You recognize that product defects and wasted materials impact your department's budget. You have told your team to decrease the amount of wasted materials, but your employees do not seem to care. How can you get them to increase their quality and decrease waste?

3. One of your best customers verbally abuses two of your employees every time she visits your store. Your employees have complained to you several times about this customer. What should you do?

Learn More

To learn more about subjects addressed in this chapter take a course in Introduction to Business and/or Introduction to Marketing.

Video Case Study: Customer Service Dialog

This video addresses an employee taking a service call from an unhappy customer. Refer to the CD that accompanies your text, watch this video, and answer the following questions:

1. If you were Frank Hallady, what would you have done differently? Explain your answer.

2. If you were the manager, what specific employee training would you implement based upon Mr. Rollins' experience?

Web Links

http://www.inc.com/resources/startup/articles/20050201/missionstatement.html
http://www.smartdraw.com/tutorials/orgcharts/tutorial11.htm
http://www.personnelinsights.com/customer_service_profile.htm

Reference

Deming, W. E. *Quality, Productivity and Competitive Position*, Cambridge, MA: MIT Press, 1982.

Activities

Activity 7-1

Review the following organizational chart and answer these questions.

1. Whom should Linda go to if there is a question about employee benefits?

_____

2. Who is Joyce's immediate supervisor?

_____

3. If Joyce's immediate supervisor is not available, whom should she seek assistance from?

_____

4. Who is ultimately responsible for creating, pricing, selling, distributing, and promoting the company's product?

_____

5. What is Brandon's title?

_____

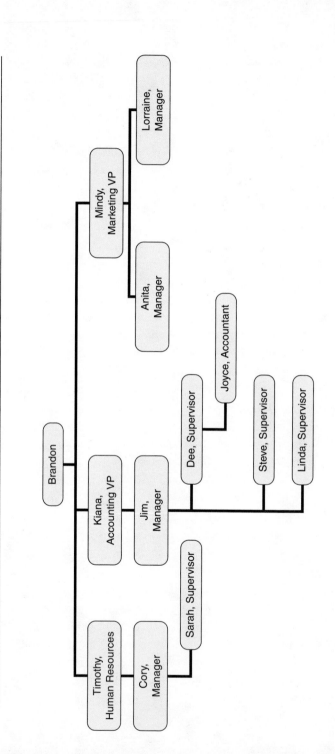

Activity 7-2

How would you measure performance in the following jobs?

Job	Performance Measures
Receptionist	
Customer service clerk	
Forklift driver	
Janitor	
Manager trainee	

Activity 7-3

What could you specifically do to communicate to your coworkers the importance customer service has on performance and profits?

Activity 7-4

When is it appropriate to ask your boss to assist you with a difficult customer?

Activity 7-5

Describe two different times when you received exemplary customer service. Be specific in identifying how employees behaved toward you.

Exemplary Service Act	Behavior Toward You
1.	
2.	

Sample Exam Questions

1. A company's _____ is its statement of purpose and identifies why everyone comes to work.

2. The _____ identifies how the company will secure, organize, utilize, and monitor its resources.

3. The _____ department is responsible for the securing, distribution, and growth of the company's financial assets.

4. _____ is a predetermined standard that defines how a product is to be produced or a service is to be provided. Customers demand _____ not just in the product they purchase but also from company employees.

5. Profit is _____ (money coming in from sales) minus _____ (the costs involved in running the business).

6. A/An _____ is one who buys a service or product.

7. Quality employees + quality inputs = _____ = satisfied, loyal _____.

   = _____.

8. _____ is when customers believe they received a good deal for the price they paid.

9. _____ is the treatment an employee provides the customer.

10. When dealing with a difficult customer, the first step is to _____, let the _____, and _____ for facts.

Human Resource Management

chapter 8

Eighty percent of success is showing up.

Woody Allen (b. 1935)

Objectives

- Identify the primary functions performed by the *human resource department*

- State the primary components of an *employee orientation program*

- Describe the purpose and use of an *employee handbook*

- Explain the concept of *employment-at-will* and *right-to-revise* clauses

- Identify the various types of employment status

- Name the primary types and appropriate use of employee benefits

- Explain the importance and appropriate use of an *open-door policy*

109

Human Resource Department

One of the first departments you will interact with at a new job is the **human resource department.** This department is responsible for hiring, training, compensation, benefits, performance evaluations, complaints, promotions, and changes in your work status. This important department exists to assist employees with work-related matters.

Employee Orientation

Typically, within the first few days of employment, you will experience an **employee orientation.** This is the time when the company's purpose, structure, major policies, procedures, benefits, and other important matters will be explained. You may also be issued company property at this time, including a name badge and keys. Begin meeting coworkers and identifying potential mentors. As you learned in chapter 2, mentors are individuals who will work with you in developing your skills and abilities.

Understanding your new company includes knowing the major products the company provides as well as the key people in charge. These questions are explained in the company's mission and the company's organization chart. As you learn about the company, pay attention to the names of key executives and their titles such as the company president, CEO, and/or vice presidents. If possible, view current photos of these individuals; if you ever have the opportunity to meet them in person, you will know who they are.

Employee Handbook

After a general overview of the company, you will be given a copy of the **employee handbook.** The employee handbook outlines an employee's agreement with the employer regarding work conditions, policies, and benefits. Some of these policies are legally required, while others address rules of conduct and/or benefits from the company. Keep this handbook and use it as a reference for major workplace issues. A representative of the company should review important sections of the handbook with you. Ask questions on topics that you do not fully understand. After the handbook is reviewed, you will usually be asked to sign a statement affirming that you have received the handbook, have read the handbook, and have agreed to its contents. This is a legal agreement. Therefore, do not sign the statement until you have completely read the handbook and fully understand its contents. Most employers will provide the employee a day or two to return the agreement.

During Cory's employee orientation, Cory received an employee handbook. With all new employees present, a representative from the human resource department went through the handbook. Unfortunately, Cory was so overwhelmed with new terms, policies, and signing forms that Cory was not confident that any information was truly understood. Cory kept the handbook along with all the other employment paperwork on the dining room table and thought about throwing it away. Cory figured the human resource department had copies of everything that was important but decided to keep all the information in case it was needed About three weeks later, Cory's friends wanted to take a minivacation on an upcoming holiday and invited Cory. Cory was not sure the company gave that day as a holiday but remembered that holidays were mentioned in the orientation meeting. Unsure of whom to ask without appearing foolish, Cory suddenly remembered the employee handbook. Using the handbook, Cory immediately identified company holidays and was thankful not to have thrown the policy book away.

Dress Code

Employees should be aware of the company **dress code.** A dress code is an organizational policy regarding appropriate workplace attire. Dress codes vary by company depending on the industry, the specific work area, and health/safety issues. If your company has a mandatory uniform, the company dress code is typically spelled out in detail. If a uniform is not required, identify what is and is not acceptable attire. Some codes include vague terms such as professional attire, while others are specific. Even if your company does not provide specific information regarding suitable workplace attire, dress appropriately. Work attire should pose no safety hazards. Unstable shoes and footwear that do not provide protection are not appropriate. Dangling jewelry that could be caught in equipment is also inappropriate for work. As discussed in chapter 6, undergarments, including bras, boxers, underwear, or thongs, should not be visible. You are expected to come to work clean (shower and brush your teeth). Cleanliness includes neatly maintained head and facial hair and hands, as well as control of body odor. Be conservative in the use of perfume, cologne, hair color and style, and jewelry. Clothes should be clean and well maintained. Finally, clothing should not carry offensive words or comments. If you have questions regarding the company dress code or appropriate attire, check with your boss or the human resource department.

Employment-at-Will and Right to Revise

Legally required in many states, a major policy statement that is usually placed at the very beginning of an employee handbook is called **employment-at-will.** This policy applies to any employee that is not hired as a contract employee for a stated period of time. Contract employees literally have contracts outlining the terms, start dates, and end dates of employment. Employment-at-will employees are not contractually obligated to work for the company for a specified period. You may quit anytime you want. On that same token, your employer may terminate your employment at any time.

An employer also has the **right to revise** or change employment policies. You may be asked to sign separate statements affirming that you understand both the employment-at-will and right-to-revise policies if they are applicable.

There should also be statements in the employee handbook regarding equal employment opportunity and discrimination. These policies state that the company does not discriminate nor allow unlawful harassment of any kind including sexual harassment, hostile workplace, or hate crimes.

Web Quiz

Find answers to questions on various labor topics by exploring the U.S. Department of Labor site.

http://www.dol.gov/dolfaq/dolfaq.asp

Employment Status

Another important section of most employee handbooks include employment status definitions, including introductory employees, part-time employees, full-time employees, and temporary employees. These classifications are typically determined by the number of hours worked per week and/or the length of employment with a company.

Part-time employees work less than forty hours a week. Depending on your employer, part-time work hours can vary based upon workload. **Full-time employees** work forty or more hours per week. Depending on the position, most entry-level employees who work more than forty hours per week are entitled to overtime pay. **Temporary employees** are hired only for a specified period of time, typically to assist with heavy work periods or to temporarily replace an employee on leave.

For most companies, new employees who are hired for full-time positions are first considered **introductory employees.** Historically, this was called a probationary period. There will be a period (typically one to three months) in which the employer will evaluate your performance and decide if you should continue as a regular employee. On that same note, you have that period to determine if you want to work for the employer. Near the end of this period, you may be given a performance evaluation. If the employer is satisfied with your performance, you become a regular employee and begin receiving benefits and/or other entitlements due to full-time employees. If the employer is not satisfied with your performance, he or she can terminate you without cause. No excuses need to be given. If your performance is not yet acceptable but the employer thinks you demonstrate potential, the introductory period may be extended for one to three additional months.

As a new employee, it is important that you identify

- Whether your company has an introductory period
- The length of your introductory period
- If and when you become eligible for benefits
- Factors that will be used to evaluate job performance

After determining the length of your introductory period, secure a copy of your job description and performance evaluation. A **job description** outlines job duties and responsibilities (i.e., why a company is paying you to come to work). A **performance evaluation** identifies how work performance will be measured. Performance evaluations contain various criteria that measure an employee's daily productivity, efficiency, and behavior. Common factors used to evaluate performance reflect the duties and responsibilities included in a job description. Additionally, your involvement in work-related activities, ongoing education, and ability to assume new responsibilities may be reflected in the evaluation. Both your job description and your performance evaluation will assist you in becoming a better employee and in moving past the introductory period and into that of a full-time, permanent employee.

How to Behave at Performance Evaluations

As previously mentioned, most employers typically provide performance evaluations immediately after completing an introductory period and once a year thereafter. Although the prospect of someone providing feedback on your

---

Talk It Out

What performance criteria would you use to evaluate a customer service employee?

performance can be a bit intimidating; this is a time for you to obtain information on how you can be a better employee. Performance evaluations provide a time not only for your supervisor to give you feedback on performance but also for you to share your desire for additional training and responsibilities. Each employee should receive advance notice of an impending evaluation and performance criteria. Based upon the preestablished criteria, keep a historical record of your past performance. This may include notes and letters from customers, coworkers, and vendors. It may also include personal documentation of events detailing when you displayed excellent judgment and/or behavior. On occasion, a supervisor provides the employee a blank copy of the upcoming evaluation form and asks the employee to complete a self-assessment. Use this opportunity to provide an honest review of your performance. Do not be overly favorable or overly critical in your self-assessment. Be honest. Refer to the evidence and documentation you collected to support your assessment. After you have completed your self-assessment, make a photocopy of your document and return the original to your supervisor.

During your formal evaluation, sit quietly and listen to your supervisor's assessment of your performance. If there is anything regarding your performance that is included in the evaluation that you do not agree with, take notes; but do not interrupt your supervisor. Share your concerns only when your supervisor is finished talking or asks for feedback. Support your comments with facts. Even if you do not agree with your supervisor's response after you have presented your evidence, do not argue or challenge your supervisor during the assessment. At the end of each appraisal form is an area for the employee's signature. Immediately under the signature area should be a sentence that states the employee's signature does not constitute agreement with everything contained in the assessment but only that the employee received an evaluation. If you do not agree with any statement included in your evaluation and the appraisal form *does not* contain the preceding statement, do not sign the evaluation. If you do not agree with any comments included in your evaluation and the appraisal form *does* include the statement, sign the evaluation; but attach a written response regarding what areas you specifically do not agree with and state why. Provide supporting documentation and evidence to your attached statement. Do not write an emotional response. Make your statements factual and professional, and do not attack your supervisor or anyone else. Employers usually allow a day to provide a written response. Both your original evaluation and your written response will be forwarded to the human resource department and will become a permanent part of your personnel file. Keep photocopies of your evaluations. They serve as legal documentation of your performance. If your evaluations are favorable they serve as excellent reference material for future employers.

Benefits

Most employees relate employee benefits with health care. Fortunately, employee benefits extend well beyond health benefits and vacations. During your orientation, someone will explain what benefits you will receive as a regular employee. These benefits may be **direct benefits** (monetary) and **indirect benefits** (nonmonetary) such as health care and paid vacations. Note that in most states employers do not have to offer health benefits. They do so as an incentive to attract a qualified workforce. Typically, only full-time, permanent employees are entitled to major benefits. During your employee orientation, you will learn when and if you qualify for benefits. Some employers allow employees to select which benefits best meet their lifestyle needs. Providing employees their choice of which benefits to choose is called a cafeteria plan. Most benefits become effective immediately, while others may become effective after employees have successfully passed the introductory period. If you are not clear as to when your benefits become effective, check with your human resource department.

If you qualify for benefits you will be given paperwork to complete. Provide accurate information. Your employer does not expect you to complete all the forms in one day and will most likely have you return them within a short time period. Keep copies of these forms in a secure place for easy reference. Personal medical information is confidential. Not even your boss should have access to this information. The only people within your company that will know your medical information will be those that are administering your health benefits.

Employers offer health benefits as an incentive to attract and keep good employees. Common health-related benefits include medical, vision, and dental insurance. **Medical benefits** include coverage for physician and hospital visits. Physician coverage sometimes includes psychological (therapy), chiropractic (bone alignment/massage), and physical therapy (rehabilitation) services. If you or someone in your family utilizes these services, make sure you understand the coverage and stipulations. Check for emergency room access and coverage, as well as coverage for pharmaceuticals (prescription drugs). **Vision benefits** include care for your eyes. Some plans pay for eyeglasses only, while others pay for contact lenses and/or corrective surgery. Once again, be familiar with your plan and its coverage. **Dental benefits** provide care for your teeth. Check to see how frequently you are allowed to see your dentist for routine checkups. Typically, this is twice a year. Identify if your plan pays for cosmetic dental care such as teeth whitening or braces.

Exercise 8-1 Choosing Benefits

Assume you are in a cafeteria plan and only qualify for four benefits from the following list. Which four would you choose and why?

Chiropractic
Vision
Well child care
Paid vacation
Paid holiday
Paid training
Family medical

Medical
Emergency
Day care
Life insurance
Free parking
In-house promotions
Bonuses

Dental
Company car
Prescriptions
Retail discounts
Personal days
Free meals
Flexible scheduling

Benefit	Why This Benefit Is Important to You
1.	
2.	
3.	
4.	

Most people utilize health benefits only when faced with an obvious health issue. While it is easy to put off routine checkups, it is in your best interest to practice preventive care. As soon as you become eligible for benefits, schedule an appointment with a physician for a routine physical. Get your vision checked, and see your dentist. This is important not only for preventive purposes but also to establish relationships with medical professionals. Because both you and your employer are paying for these benefits, it is important that you take advantage of these benefits when you become eligible. Finally, this may be a good time for you to evaluate your health habits. If you need to shed a few pounds or eliminate a poor habit such as smoking or drinking, now is a good time to change your behavior.

Employers may provide you several choices for health policies. While few if any policies pay 100 percent of your health expenses, employees typically need to pay a copayment, or small percentage of the total fee. Many health insurance programs provide a list of medical professionals and health facilities that accept their insurance. Any time you do not use one of these preferred providers, the health insurance will not pay for your care or it will only pay a percentage of the total. You are responsible for the rest of your bill. When selecting a health program, carefully review the list of providers and facilities for familiarity and convenience. Check emergency access, well child care, preventive care, or any other medical care you may need now or in the future.

Exercise 8-2   Health-Care Considerations

In selecting health-care providers for you and your dependents, what issues are important considerations?

Provider	Major Considerations
Physician	
Hospital	
Dentist	
Vision	
Pharmaceuticals	

As your benefits are being explained to you in detail, find out who else is entitled to these benefits. Frequently, benefits are available to an employee's spouse and children. You may have to pay a bit more if you add people to your coverage, but it may be worth the extra cost. As health-care costs continue to increase, it is important that you and your family have the security and needed access to quality health care.

Ask if your company offers a **retirement plan.** This is a savings plan for when you retire. Now is the time to begin thinking about saving for retirement. If your company has a retirement plan, join it and start saving. If you have retirement funds automatically deducted from your earnings prior to receiving your paycheck, you will most likely not miss the money but you will appreciate the funds as they increase. Many company-sponsored retirement savings plans are tax deferred,

Talk It Out

Identify health concerns and how they would affect the workplace.

which means you do not pay taxes on these funds until you retire. This provides an added incentive to begin planning for your future.

Payroll, paydays, accrued vacation, and sick days or sick leave are terms used to discuss monetary benefits. Your employee handbook identifies when you are paid. Typically, payday is every two weeks or on the fifteenth and thirtieth of each month. Your paycheck is in two parts. One part is the actual check (or a statement if your check is directly deposited into your bank account). The second part of your paycheck is called a pay stub. This stub contains very important information including hours worked, total pay, taxes paid, and any other deductions that were taken from your paycheck. Everyone pays taxes. Any money taken from your original earnings is documented on your pay stub. Keep payroll stubs in a file for tax purposes and later reference. The Internal Revenue Service (IRS) recommends you keep these records on file for three years.

Find out what vacations and holidays your new employer provides and if you get paid overtime for working on a holiday. Identify how many days of vacation you will receive and when it will become available to you. Some companies also provide a personal day. This is one day that an employee can take off without explanation. However, provide your employer ample notice prior to taking this day. Information regarding vacations and holidays should be clearly communicated in your employee handbook. If it is not, be sure to obtain this information from either your supervisor or the human resource department.

Cory's best friend has a family cabin and invited Cory to spend a long weekend at the lake. Unfortunately, Cory had only been on the job for two months and had not accumulated any vacation time. Cory really wanted to go to the cabin. Cory remembered that the company provides sick leave and one personal day a year. Being on the job for such a short period of time, Cory wondered if it would be okay to either call in sick or take a personal day. After some thought, Cory realized that it would be unethical to lie by calling in sick. Cory also thought it would not be responsible to take a personal day so early on the job. As a result, Cory called the friend and suggested that perhaps they could meet up at the cabin later in the year. As difficult as Cory's decision was, Cory valued the new job and did not want to do anything to risk losing credibility or responsibility at work.

If you have a family or are planning a family, identify company policies regarding pregnancy and family leave. There are laws to protect you from pregnancy discrimination and provide relief in these situations. Some employers even provide additional benefits beyond those required by law. Regardless of whether you currently have or are planning a family, emergencies happen with parents and other loved ones and you may need to take a leave of absence in the future.

Open-Door Policy/Grievance Procedures

An **open-door policy** is when management is available to listen to employees' ideas or concerns. Think of this policy as more of a "we're here to listen and help" policy. The purpose of an open-door policy is to communicate to employees that management and the human resource department is available to listen should the employee need to discuss a workplace concern. As discussed in chapter 12, the easiest way to deal with conflict is immediately, openly, and honestly. Doing so keeps a small problem from becoming and keeps problems from reoccurring. Do not be afraid to speak with your supervisor or the human resource department on any workplace issue that causes you concern.

Unions

Depending on the size and nature of your company's business, you may have the opportunity to join a union. A **union** is an organization whose purpose is to protect the rights of employees. This organization is a third party that represents you and your colleagues' interests to your employer. Theoretically, if managers are doing their jobs, there is no need for unions. Unfortunately, this is not always the case. Unions negotiate on behalf of employees and typically negotiate higher salaries, better benefits, and improved working conditions. This comes with a cost. Employees pay a fee to a union for this representation. As a union member, you are trusting that the union will act in your best interest. Employees have the right to unionize (become members of a union), and they also have the right to choose not to join a union. Union membership is only for non-management employees.

If your company's employees are represented by a union, the union will contact you and invite you to become a member when you begin employment. Additional employment issues, including the handling of grievances, holidays, vacations, and other issues are outlined in your **union contract.** The union contract is a document which states the rights of employees. The union contract and the employee handbook are equally important documents. The union contract addresses specific work-related issues that your employer and the union agree upon. These issues include work schedules, benefits, pay, performance measures, and a grievance procedure. Take time to carefully read the contract and keep it in a place where you can easily use it for later reference. Know the names of and how to contact union officials who can assist you with work-related issues.

Your primary union contact will be the shop steward or union representative. This individual is an employee of your company but has agreed to serve as a primary contact between company employees and the union. The shop steward or union representative knows the union contract in great detail and will make every effort to assist you with a work-related issue. Do not hesitate to contact the shop steward or union representative.

Once a new contract is presented, union members vote on approving the contract. It is imperative that you exercise your right to vote on a new contract. The union contract dictates work rules, benefits, and other issues important to your work environment. Not voting means that you do not care about these issues. At other times, the union will provide opportunities for employees to become union representatives. If you are interested in becoming more involved in the union, explore these opportunities. Union members will be given the opportunity to vote for their representatives. Exercise your right to vote on any union-related issue.

Take an active role in knowing what services are available to you through the union, the names of union officials who can assist you, and what value and services the union provides through its representation.

Workplace Dos and Don'ts

Do	Don't
Do read and keep your employee handbook for future reference	*Don't* ask your boss questions if you have not already referred to your employee handbook
Do utilize the employee handbook to identify paydays and company holidays	*Don't* demonstrate poor planning and be unaware of important days at work
Do maintain documentation for your performance evaluations	*Don't* interrupt during a performance evaluation
Do ask for clarification if you have questions regarding appropriate dress in the workplace	*Don't* dress in a manner that brings attention to you or does not professionally represent your company
Do immediately speak with your boss if there is a conflict regarding your work	*Don't* wait until a workplace issue gets out of control to share your concerns with your boss

Concept Review and Application

Summary of Key Concepts

- The human resource department is responsible for hiring, training, compensation, benefits, performance evaluations, complaints, promotions, and changes in your work status
- An employee orientation is the time to learn all about a company, its major policies, and employee services
- The employee handbook is an important document that outlines an employee's agreement with his or her employer regarding work conditions, policies, and benefits

- Employee benefits may include direct (monetary) benefits and indirect (nonmonetary) benefits such as health care and paid vacations
- Be aware of and take advantage of benefits that are available to you
- Be aware of paydays, paid holidays, and sick leave policies
- Unions are designed to protect the rights of employees

Key Terms

dental benefits	direct benefits	dress code
employee handbook	employee orientation	employment-at-will
full-time employee	human resource	indirect benefits
introductory	department	job description
employee	medical benefits	open-door policy
part-time employee	performance	retirement plan
right to revise	evaluation	temporary
union	union contract	employee
vision benefits		

If You Were the Boss

1. How should you handle an employee who keeps coming to you asking for information regarding major policies, vacations, and benefits?

2. How can a boss consistently communicate an open-door policy?

Learn More

To learn more about subjects addressed in this chapter take an introductory course in Human Resource Management

Video Case Study: Performance Evaluations

This video addresses how to behave during performance evaluations. Go to *MyProfessionalismKit* or your course website, watch this video, and answer the following questions:

1. What advice would you give Patricia regarding her behavior and conversation with Karen?

2. What can Patricia do in the future to improve her performance?

3. Did Karen handle the situation appropriately? Why or why not?

4. Was Regina's response appropriate? Why or why not?

Web Links

http://www.dol.gov/ebsa/publications/10working4you.html
http://www.busreslab.com/policies/goodpol2.htm

Reference

United States Equal Employment Opportunity Commission. Washington, DC. www.EEOC.gov

Activities

Activity 8-1

At the end of your orientation period, you may be given a formal performance evaluation. Identify and discuss three typical areas that employers look at in performance evaluations.

1. _____

2. _____

3. _____

Activity 8-2

Using the information from Exercise 8–2, Health-Care Considerations, assume you are now eligible for health benefits and must choose specific health-care providers. Identify a local physician, eye doctor, dentist, and hospital that you would utilize. Why did you select these providers? How did you go about selecting them?

	Name	Why Selected	How Selected
Physician			
Eye doctor			
Dentist			
Hospital			

Sample Exam Questions

1. During a/an _____, the company purpose, its structure, major policies, procedures, benefits, and other important matters are explained.

2. A/an _____ is a benefit that provides free and confidential psychological, financial, and legal advice.

3. Many companies offer _____ savings plans that are tax deferred for use at a later date.

4. A paycheck has two parts: the _____ and the _____.

5. What you wear to work should never pose a _____.

6. A/an _____ communicates to employees that management and the human resource department are always available to listen should the employee have a concern or complaint.

7. _____ exist to protect the rights of employees when management is not doing its job.

Communication

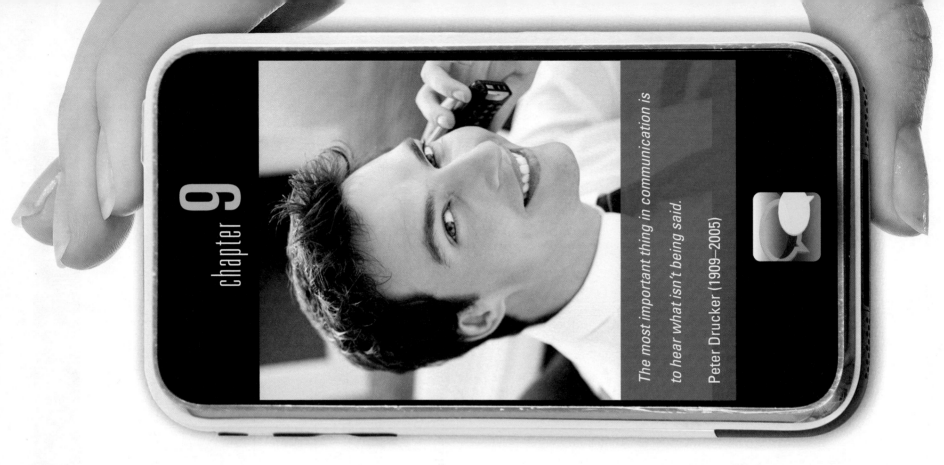

chapter 9

The most important thing in communication is to hear what isn't being said.

Peter Drucker (1909–2005)

Workplace Communication and Its Channels

Imagine going to work; sitting at your desk; and, for one day, sending and receiving no communication. If there were no face-to-face contact, no phones or text messages, no meetings, and no memos to receive or write, business would come to a complete standstill. No matter how talented you are at your job, if you cannot communicate with others, you will not succeed, much less keep a job. This chapter discusses the process and importance of effective communication in the workplace and provides information on how to improve your workplace communication skills.

At work, you have an obligation to share appropriate, timely, and accurate information with your boss, your coworkers, and your customers. Improving your communication skills is an ongoing process. As explained in chapter 5, information is power. In regard to workplace communication, your goal is to be known as an overcommunicator.

While eating lunch with employees from other departments, Cory listened to employees complain about how their bosses did such a poor job communicating with them. The employees complained that they never knew what was going on within the company. Cory had no reason to complain because Cory has a manager who makes every effort to share whatever information he knows with Cory's department. After each managers' meeting, Cory receives an e-mail outlining major topics that were discussed at the managers' meeting. During Cory's department meeting, Cory's manager reviews the information a second time and asks his employees if there are any additional questions. Cory appreciates the fact that the manager enjoys and values communicating important information with his employees.

In the workplace, there are two primary communication channels: formal and informal. Whether it is formal or informal communication, you have a professional obligation to share timely and relevant information with the appropriate people. **Formal communication** occurs through the formal lines of authority. This includes communication within your immediate department, your division, or throughout your company. Formal communication occurs either vertically or horizontally within an organization. Formal vertical communication comes down the organization chart (via written correspondence, policies and procedures, and directives and announcements from management), or goes up the organization chart (reports, budgets, and requests). Formal horizontal communication occurs among individuals or departments at the same or close organizational levels.

The second type of communication channel is informal. **Informal communication** occurs among individuals without regard to the formal lines of authority. For example, while eating lunch with friends, you may learn of a new policy. A major element of the informal communication network is called the **grapevine**. The grapevine is an informal network where employees talk about workplace issues of importance. Although the grapevine is an informal source of communication, it usually is not 100 percent accurate. While it is important to know about current events of the workplace, do not contribute negative information to the grapevine. If inaccurate information is being shared and you are aware of the facts, clarify the information. If someone shares information that is harmful to the company or is particularly disturbing to you, you have a responsibility to approach your boss and ask him or her to clarify the rumor.

When the grapevine is targeting individuals and their personal lives, it is called **gossip**. Gossip is personal information about individuals which is hurtful and inappropriate. Anytime you contribute to negative conversation you lose credibility with others. Spreading gossip reflects immaturity and unprofessional behavior. Should someone begin sharing gossip with you, politely interrupt and clarify the misinformation when necessary. Tell the individual that you do not want to hear gossip and/or transition the conversation to a more positive subject. You have a right to defend your coworkers from slander (individuals bad-mouthing others), just as you would expect coworkers to defend you. After a while, your colleagues will learn that you do not tolerate gossip at work and they will reconsider approaching you with gossip.

Refrain from speaking poorly of your coworkers and boss. As a result of human nature, you may not enjoy working with all of your colleagues and bosses. You do not have to like everyone at work, but everyone needs to be treated with respect. No matter how much someone annoys you at work, do not speak poorly of him or her. It only displays immaturity on your part and communicates distrust to your colleagues. Even if someone speaks poorly of you, do not reciprocate the bad behavior.

The Communication Process

Communication is the process of a sender sending a message to a receiver with the purpose of creating mutual understanding. As simple as this definition is, a lot of barriers hinder the process of creating mutual understanding and successful communication. Communication is important for maintaining good human relations. Without basic communication skills, processes break down and an organization may collapse. This is why you need to know and understand the communication process (see figure 9-1).

Communication starts with a **sender** wanting to convey a message. The sender must identify what message needs to be sent and how best to send this message. The sender has several options for sending the message. The message can be sent verbally, written, or nonverbally. Identifying the message and how it will be sent is called **encoding**.

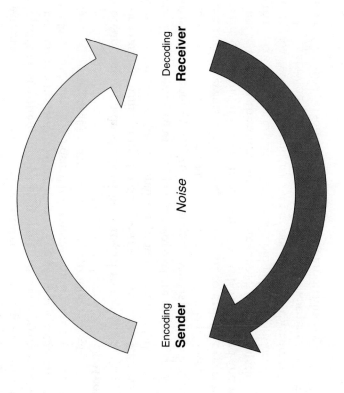

Figure 9-1

Communication Process

Once the sender encodes the message, the message is sent to a receiver. **Decoding** is when the receiver interprets the message. The receiver then sends **feedback** on the sender's message based upon the receiver's interpretation of the original message.

Due to barriers, the communication process can break down. First, the sender must clearly identify the message that needs to be sent. Once the message is identified, the sender needs to figure out how best to send (encode) the message in a manner that will be properly interpreted (decoded) by the receiver. If the sender is not a strong communicator, his or her verbal, written, or non-verbal communication may be misinterpreted by the receiver because the message was doomed before it is even sent. The receiver contributes to the communication breakdown if he or she incorrectly interprets the message.

Another barrier to effective communication is **noise**. Noise is anything that interrupts or interferes with the communication process. The noise can be audible (you can actually hear it with your ears), or the noise can occur through other senses such as visual, mental, and scent. This may also include emotions such as hurt, anger, joy, sadness, or surprise.

A supervisor in another department really irritates Cory. Cory has never shared this irritation with anyone. One day, Cory was asked to attend a meeting led by the irritating supervisor. As Cory sat in the meeting, Cory had a hard time focusing on the message. Cory's mind was wandering with both audible and mental noise. At the end of the meeting, Cory was embarrassed that there were no notes to share. Cory's dislike for the irritating supervisor affected Cory's ability to listen and be a good receiver. Cory learned a hard lesson that day and made a commitment to be open to every communication, regardless of Cory's like or dislike of the sender.

Communication can only be complete if all of the components of the communication process work together to effectively send the message as it is meant to be sent. In order for this to happen, the sender must choose the right medium and overcome noise. The receiver must then be willing to accept the message and provide feedback to acknowledge that the message has been received correctly.

As previously stated, a key element to effective communication is the communication medium (how the message will be sent). Communication media include verbal, nonverbal, and written communication. Let us further explore these three types of communication media.

Verbal Communication

Verbal communication is the process of using words to send a message. The words you select are extremely important. If you use only basic words in your communications, you may appear uneducated or inexperienced. In contrast, if you use a highly developed vocabulary, you may appear intimidating or arrogant. If others do not know the definitions of the words you are using, they will most likely not ask for clarification for fear of appearing ignorant. Therefore, your intended message will fail. When selecting words for your message, identify whether these words can be misinterpreted. Many times, we assume our receiver is thinking our same thoughts.

Learn to stop and listen. Too frequently, a person will have so much to say that he or she does not stop to give the receiver time to respond. The receiver's response is the only way a sender can verify that your message has been properly received. When improving verbal communication, identify when it is appropriate to not speak. Keys to effective listening include making eye contact with the sender and taking notes.

Nonverbal Communication

Nonverbal communication is what you communicate through your body language. You do not have to utter a word and you can still send a very strong message. Body language includes eye contact, facial expressions, tone of voice, and the positioning of your body. Nonverbal communication also includes the use of silence and space.

When people are nervous or excited, they frequently speak fast. When you increase the speed of your speech, you increase the probability that your message will be misinterpreted. Your tone of voice also conveys or creates images. It adds to others' perception of you, which either enforces your message or detracts from the message.

The most obvious form of body language is eye contact. When you look someone in the eye, you are generally communicating honesty and sincerity. At other times, looking someone in the eye and coupling that look with a harsh tone of voice and an unfriendly facial expression may imply intimidation. Those who fail to look someone in the eye risk conveying to their receiver that they are not confident or, worse, are being dishonest. Make eye contact with your audience (individual or group), but do not stare. Staring is considered rude and intimidating. Actively work at making appropriate eye contact with your receiver. If your direct eye contact is making the receiver uncomfortable, he or she will look away. Be aware of his or her response and adapt your behavior appropriately.

Eye contact is part of the larger communication package of a facial expression. A receiver will find it difficult to interpret your eye contact as sincere and friendly when your message is accompanied by a frown. A smile has immense power and value. On the other hand, make sure you don't smile when listening to someone who is angry or upset. He or she may interpret a smile as laughing at their distress. A nod implies that you are listening or agreeing with a sender's message. Even the positioning of your head can convey disagreement, confusion, or attentiveness.

Exercise 9-1   Body Language

With a partner, take turns communicating the following emotions through body language. Note how the sender signals to communicate the emotion.

Emotion	Signal
1. Concern	
2. Distrust	
3. Eagerness	
4. Boredom	
5. Self-importance	
6. Interest	

Another element of body language is the use and positioning of your body. Having your arms crossed in front of your body may be interpreted in several ways: as being physically cold, angry, or uninterested. When you are not physically cold, having your arms crossed implies that you are creating a barrier between yourself and the other person. To eliminate any miscommunication, it is best to have your arms at your side. Do not hide your hands in your pockets. In speaking with others, be aware of the positioning of your arms and those of your audience. Also, be aware of the positioning of your entire body. Turn your body toward those to whom you are speaking. It is considered rude to turn your back to or ignore someone when he or she is speaking. In this case, you are using your entire body to create a barrier. Avoid this type of rude behavior. This only communicates immaturity on your part.

The use of your hands is extremely important in effective communication. Through varied positioning, you can use your hands to nonverbally ask someone to stop a behavior, be quiet, or reprimand another. Be aware of the positioning of your hands. It is considered rude to point at someone with one finger. If you have nervous gestures such as popping your knuckles, biting your nails, or continually tapping your fingers, take steps to eliminate these habits.

Apart from a handshake, touching another person at work is not acceptable. People in our society frequently place a hand on another's shoulder as a show of support. However, others could interpret that hand on the shoulder as a threat or sexual advance. Therefore, keep your hands to yourself.

Be aware of the space you allow between you and your receiver. Standing too close may be interpreted as intimidation or may imply intimacy. Neither is appropriate for the workplace. Distancing yourself too far from someone may imply your unwillingness to communicate.

Another element that affects nonverbal communication is emotion. Make every attempt to not become emotional at work. However, reality may cause you to express emotions that oftentimes cannot be controlled. Make every effort to control your emotions in public. If you feel you are beginning to cry or have an outburst of anger, excuse yourself. Find a private area and deal with your emotion. If you are crying or distraught, splash water on your face and regain control of your emotions. If you are getting angry, assess why you are angry, control your anger, and then create a strategy to regain control of how best to handle the situation. Any overt display of anger in the workplace is inappropriate, can damage workplace relationships, and could potentially jeopardize your job. When you become emotional at work, you lose your ability to logically deal with situations. Practice effective stress management and think before you respond.

Finally, understand the appropriate use of silence. Silence is perhaps one of the most important communication tools you have. Silence communicates to your audience that you are listening and are allowing the other party consideration. Not immediately responding to a message gives the sender time to clarify or rephrase a message.

There are a lot of variables involved in effective nonverbal communication. Interpret body language within its entire context. For example, if you are communicating with a colleague with whom you have a positive working relationship and your coworker crosses his or her arms, your coworker is most likely cold. Consider the entire package: environment, relationship, and situation.

Written Communication

Writing is an important element of effective workplace communication. **Written communication** is a form of business communication that is either printed, handwritten, or sent electronically. Because the receiver of your message will not have verbal and nonverbal assistance in interpreting your message, take great care to ensure that the correct message is being communicated. Since you are not present when the message is received, the receiver will be drawing additional conclusions about you based upon the grammar, vocabulary, and presentation/formatting you use in your written communication.

As you advance in responsibility within an organization, you will be required to conduct an increasing amount of written business communications including writing memos, e-mail messages, and business letters. Written business correspondence represents not only your professionalism and intelligence but also that of your organization. Consistently present written correspondence in a professional manner. Make all written communication error free by proofreading the message prior to sending. The key to written communication is to choose words that clearly and concisely communicate your message. The three most common forms of written communication in the workplace are letters, memos, and electronic messages. Written communication should be typed. An exception to this rule is when you are sending a handwritten thank-you note.

The first step in any professional correspondence is to state an objective. Determine exactly what it is that you want to communicate. Write a draft message and make it free of anger or negative emotions. If the purpose of your correspondence is to address a negative situation (e.g., complaint), address the situation and do not negatively attack an individual. With all written forms of communication, do not send or write any message conveying anger. A good rule of thumb is to always put good news in writing and be cautious when sending negative information in writing. Put bad news in writing only when necessary.

After you have drafted your message and eliminated negative emotions, review your correspondence and delete unnecessary words. Keep written correspondence short and simple. Do not be wordy, and minimize personalization words (*I, my*) as much as possible. Written correspondence not only communicates your core message but also clearly communicates how you want the reader to respond to your communication. Include contact information and a deadline in your written communication if relevant.

Although it is important to keep your correspondence simple, you want to project a professional image, not that of an elementary student. Utilize a thesaurus to identify and substitute words that project a more mature image. Know the definitions of the words you are using and use these words appropriately. Utilizing a thesaurus is an excellent way to expand your vocabulary. Do not overdo it, and use words in the correct context.

After you have completed writing your message, identify who should receive the message. Share your correspondence only with individuals who need to know the information. However, make sure you have shared the information with individuals whom the correspondence affects. When writing business correspondence, you have several options. These include a business letter, business memo, an e-mail message, text message, and a thank-you note.

The Business Letter

A **business letter** is a formal written form of communication used when your message is being sent to an individual outside of your organization. External audiences may include customers, vendors, suppliers, or members of the community. With reliance on electronic communication, many businesses send formal business letters as attachments. Letters are to be written in proper business format and sent on company letterhead. Letters sent should be error free. Proofread, sign, and date the letter before mailing. Make sure your message and expected follow-up activity to the receiver is clear. The message needs to be conveyed to the receiver in a professional and concise manner.

Business letters are written on company letterhead. Company **letterhead** is paper that has the company logo and contact information imprinted on quality paper. Figure 9-2 shows the correct business letter format. Figure 9-3 provides an example of a business letter.

(Do not type QS and DS, these are shown for correct spacing.)	
	August 1, 2012
	QS (4 enters or returns)
Since most business letters will be on letterhead (preprinted business address), you need about a two-inch top margin before entering the current *date*.	
	Ms. Suzie Student
The *inside address* should include the title, first and, last name of receiver.	Word Processing Fun
	42 Learn Avenue
	Fresno, CA 93225
	DS (2 enters or returns)
	Dear Ms. Student:
The *salutation* should have title and last name only.	DS
	The first paragraph of a letter should state the reason for the letter. If you had any previous contact with the receiver, mention it in this paragraph.
	DS
For the *body*, all lines begin at the left margin. Use a colon after the salutation and a comma after the complementary closing.	The second (and possibly a third) paragraph should contain details. All information needing to be communicated should be included here.
	DS
	The last paragraph is used to close the letter. Add information that is needed to clarify anything you said in the letter. Also, add any follow-up or contact information.
	DS
Keep the *closing* simple.	Sincerely,
	QS
The writer's first and last name should be four enters or returns after the closing to give the *writer* room to sign (remember to have the writer sign).	*Sarah S. Quirrel*
	Sarah S. Quirrel
	Instructor
	DS
Typist's initials *Enclosure* is used only if you add something in the envelope with the letter.	sbb
	Enclosure

Figure 9-2

Letter Format

August 1, 2012

Ms. Suzie Student
Word Processing Fun
42 Learn Avenue
Fresno, CA 93225

Dear Ms. Student:

It was a pleasure speaking with you over the telephone earlier today. I am delighted that you have agreed to serve as a guest speaker in my Communications class. The purpose of this letter is to confirm the details of the upcoming speaking engagement.

As I mentioned in our conversation, the date for your scheduled lecture is Wednesday, October 14, 2012. The class meets from 6:00 p.m.–8:30 p.m. You may take as much time as you need, but if possible please allow a student question and answer period. There are approximately sixty students, and the classroom contains state-of-the-art technology. If you have specific technology requests, do not hesitate to contact me. Enclosed is a parking permit and map of the campus directing you to the appropriate classroom.

Once again, thank you for continued support of our students. I and my students are looking forward to you sharing your communications insight and expertise with us on October 14. If you have any additional information, please do not hesitate to contact me via e-mail at S.Quirrel@teaching.com or call me at 123-456-7890.

Sincerely,

Sarah S. Quirrel

Sarah S. Quirrel
Instructor

sbb
Enclosure

Figure 9-3

Letter Example

Another element of a business letter is the mailing envelope. The envelope helps create a first impression. Address the envelope with the same information that is in the inside address. The letter should be folded properly. This is done by folding in thirds; starting at the bottom and folding up one-third of the way. Then fold the top over the bottom and place it in the envelope with the opening on top. Number 10 envelopes are normally used for business letters.

The Business Memo

Business memos (sometimes called *interoffice memorandums*) are used internally, that is, when the written communication is being sent to a receiver within an organization. A memo includes the receiver's name, sender's name, date, and subject. As with a business letter, include all facts needed to properly communicate the message, but be brief and to the point. In general, memos are no longer than one page. Figures 9-4 and 9-5 illustrate the proper way to format and write a business memo.

(Do not type DS, these are shown for correct spacing.)

Start the memo two inches from the top of the page.

MEMO TO: Loretta Howerton, Office Manager

DS

FROM: Lawrence Schmidt, OA/CIS Trainer

DS

DATE: January 6, 2012

DS

SUBJECT: Memo Format for Internal Correspondence

DS

Double-space after each *heading.* Bold and capitalize only headings, not the information.

Use initial caps in the *subject line.*

A memorandum is an internal communication that is sent within the organization. It is often the means by which managers correspond with employees, and vice versa. Memos provide written records of announcements, requests for action, and policies and procedures. Use first and last names and include the job title.

DS

Body—single-space, no tabs, left align. Double-space between paragraphs.

Templates, or preformatted forms, often are used for creating memos. Templates provide a uniform look for company correspondence and save the employee the time of having to design a memo. Word processing software has memo templates that can be customized. Customize the template so it has the company name and your department name at the top. Make sure you change the date format (month, day, year). It should be as it is seen at the beginning of this memo.

DS

Reference *initials* (typist's initials)
Attachment notation, only if needed (if you attach something)

sbb
Attachment

Figure 9-4

Memo Format

MEMO TO: Loretta Howerton, Office Manager

FROM: Lawrence Schmidt, OA/CIS Trainer

DATE: January 6, 2012

SUBJECT: Accounting Department Computer Training

This memo is to confirm that the computer training for the accounting department will occur on February 1, 2012 in the large conference room. Although the training is scheduled from 9:00 a.m.–11:30 a.m., I have reserved the room for the entire morning, beginning at 7:00 a.m.

As we discussed last week, this may be a good opportunity to offer breakfast to the department prior to the training. If this is something you would like to pursue, please let me know by next Tuesday, and I will make the proper arrangements. Thank you again for the opportunity to provide computer training to your team.

sbb

Figure 9-5

Memo Example

The Business E-Mail

Electronic mail (e-mail) is the most common form of internal and external communications. With e-mail messages, you can directly type a message or attach a business memo or letter to your e-mail. E-mail creates more efficient communication within an organization and with individuals outside of the organization.

When sending an e-mail, include a descriptive subject in the subject line. The subject line should clearly state the purpose of the e-mail. Do not use *HI* or *HELLO* as the subject line. Because of the spread of common computer viruses, it is also inappropriate to use the words *URGENT, IMPORTANT, TEST* as a subject line.

As with the use of all workplace equipment, e-mail should only be used for business purposes. E-mail messages are an important element of professional workplace communication. Do not use emoticons (happy faces, winks) in your messages. Doing so at work takes away from your professional image. Refrain from forwarding messages that are not work related. Maintain an organized and updated electronic address book and make every attempt to preserve the confidentiality of your address book.

The Thank-You Note

As mentioned in the etiquette chapter, a thank-you note is a powerful tool for building relationships. When you express thanks, individuals are more likely to continue performing kind acts for you. A thank-you note is normally handwritten, in pen, and on a note card. However, for informal situations an electronic thank-you note is acceptable. Thank-you notes do not need to be lengthy; generally, just a few sentences are sufficient. Make it a habit to send a thank-you note when someone does something for you that takes more than five minutes or when someone gives you a gift. Deliver the note as soon as possible. Figure 9-6 shows the correct format and key elements of a handwritten thank-you note.

Documentation

One final element of effective communication is documentation. **Documentation** is an important paper trail that assists in remembering important events. Some industries require documentation to track a project's progress or employee's time for client billing. Documentation may be necessary for an employee evaluation, advancement, an instance in which a policy is not enforced, or an abnormal event has occurred that has the potential to evolve into conflict at a later date. These events may support performance issues, business relationships, and business operations. Employees should have some method of recording relevant business situations, such as a workplace injury, angry customer, or employee conflict, if needed for future reference to protect yourself and/or your employer. Although there are numerous methods of documenting and retaining important information and events, the basic elements to be recorded remain the same.

Depending on the purpose of your documentation, effective documentation records the *who, what, when, where,* and *why* of a situation. Basic elements in effective documentation include the date, time, and location the event occurred.

Note the event itself (e.g., who said what or did what). Also, note who was present when the event occurred and how witnesses to the event behaved or responded. Documentation can be kept electronically, in a journal, or through minimal notations on a calendar. If the documentation is for billing or client purposes your employer will provide the documentation format. Whatever system you choose, keep your documentation in a secure, private location. It is not necessary to record every event that occurs at work. If there are any supporting memos, keep copies in a secure location. If you are ever called upon to defend your actions, you will have the ability to easily gather pertinent information.

Presentations

Both formal and informal presentations are a normal workplace event and sometime in your career you will most likely be called upon to give a presentation. As with meeting etiquette, be prepared and professional. A successful presentation begins with a goal. Identify the purpose of your presentation and ensure that every word, visual aid, activity, and/or handout will support the overall goal of the presentation. After the purpose of the presentation has been identified, an outline of key points should be identified to reinforce the message you want individuals to respond to or remember.

Most formal presentations include three elements: the verbal content, the visual content, and support content. Verbal content includes all the detailed information you wish to share with the audience. Speak clearly and slowly, using professional and appropriate language. Face your audience. If you are using a screen, keep your back toward the screen. Beware of both verbal and nonverbal physical gestures. Nothing will distract an audience quicker than an overuse of "ums," "like," and "you know." Hands in pockets, crossed arms, or tapping feet are examples of distracting physical gestures. Dress professionally and do not wear anything that may distract from your message.

Visual content includes anything the audience will view or any activity the audience will perform during your presentation. Often times, this involves

---

Include the date.

Start your note with a salutation and the receiver's name.

Be brief but specific about why you are thanking the person. Include how you benefited from the person's kindness. Do not begin every sentence with *I*.

Use a complementary closing, and do not forget to sign your name.

June 3, 2012

Dear Ms. McCombs,

Thank-you for loaning me your book on business etiquette. I especially liked the chapter on social events and dining. Your constant encouragement and mentoring mean so much to me.

Sincerely,

Mason Yang

Figure 9-6
Thank-You Note

some type of technology including presentation software, videos, or music. When using presentation software, do not overdo the use of graphics, color, or animations. Test all equipment prior to the actual presentation. Preparation and practice ensures that your visual content and/or activities are the appropriate length. If you are including your audience in an activity (e.g., game), make directions simple and the activity brief. Keep your audience focused and do not allow the activity to serve as a distraction to your message.

Support content normally comes in the form of a handout. This is a good way to reinforce your verbal and visual message in writing. A popular format for a handout allows the audience to fill in the blanks as you present your message. Without becoming distracting, add professional and visual appeal to your handout. As you create your handout, follow the same order as the presentation outline. Check your visual presentation and support materials for spelling and grammatical errors. When you are certain your support content is error free and professional, make enough copies for each member of your audience.

Formal presentations are an excellent way to increase workplace credibility and individual confidence. In regard to workplace presentations, remember that success is in the planning and that practice makes perfect.

Telecommunication

With the increased use of technology in the workplace, the proper use of phones, voice mail, texting, and other communication devices becomes increasingly important. When using a communication device, keep in mind that there are proper times and places for its use. Just as it is impolite to verbally interrupt someone who is talking, it is also impolite to interrupt a conversation or meeting with incoming or outgoing electronic communications. There are two basic guidelines for using electronic communication devices. First, it is okay to use your communication device if you are alone and its use is permitted at your workplace. Secondly, when at a meeting or business activity, if the use of the device is not relevant to the discussion, turn your device off or put it on vibrate. If it vibrates, do not answer it. If you know it is an important call, politely excuse yourself from the room and take the message in private. Although these guidelines are for business purposes, they should pertain to personal use as well. Please review the information regarding telecommunication etiquette detailed in chapter 6.

Slang and Foul Language

Different generations, cultures, and technology use some form of slang. **Slang** is an informal language used among a particular group. Although slang is not always inappropriate, avoid using it in the workplace. Slang can be easily misinterpreted by others. Slang such as "cool" or "dude" when speaking in the business environment should be avoided. When sending e-mails and text messages to friends, it is common to use slang; however, slang should be avoided in both verbal and written workplace communications including e-mails and text messages. Become a more effective communicator in the workplace by eliminating the use of slang.

Your words reflect what is going on in your heart and mind. There is no appropriate time to use profane and offensive language at work. Even in times of stress or at social functions, you are representing your company and must do so in a professional manner. Practice self-control. Attempt to eliminate foul or offensive language from your personal and professional vocabulary. Doing so will rid your heart and mind of negativity. If you utilize inappropriate language at work, immediately apologize. Make a mental note of what situation caused you to behave poorly and learn from the experience. Ask yourself how you could have better handled the situation and mentally rehearse a proper, more acceptable method of verbally handling a challenging situation.

Potential Offensive Names

Names that could be considered sexist and offensive are inappropriate in a business setting. Using inappropriate names toward coworkers could expose you and your company to a potential sexual harassment lawsuit. These include names such as *honey*, *sweetie*, and *sexy*. Even if the individual being called these names acts as if he or she is not offended, the person may actually be offended or insulted but afraid to tell you. Eliminate potentially offensive names from your workplace vocabulary. In addition, do not use gender-specific titles when referring to certain jobs. For example:

Instead of	Use
Postman	Postal carrier
Policeman	Police officer
Waitress	Server
Stewardess	Flight attendant
Maid	Housekeeper

Not Always About You

Closing our discussion on communication, we address one word that often dominates written and verbal communication. This word frequently turns listeners off; unfortunately, too often, the sender is unaware of its overuse. The word is *I*. Be cautious with the use of this word. Self-centered people use it to draw attention, while others who lack self-confidence may subconsciously use the word to protect themselves. They may not know how to turn the conversation to others, so they choose to stay in a safety zone. When you are using verbal communication, think before you speak. If your initial sentence includes *I*, try to rephrase your message. Prior to sending written correspondence, review your message and reduce the number of sentences that begin with the word I.

Exercise 9-2   Checking for I

Take five minutes and interview a classmate about college and his or her career choice. While you are getting to know each other, keep track of how many times your new friend says the word *I*.

Workplace Dos and Don'ts

Do carefully think through your message and the appropriate medium	*Don't* be in such a hurry to send your message that an incorrect message is sent
Do demonstrate professionalism in the formatting, word choice, and grammar in your written communications	*Don't* write and send messages when you are angry
Do express kindness to others with both your words and body language	*Don't* utilize foul language at work or at home
Do leave professional voice-mail messages that include your name, a return number, and the purpose of your call	*Don't* have a cute or annoying message on your voice mail

Concept Review and Application

Summary of Key Concepts

- Effective communication is necessary for workplace success
- The goal of communication is to create a mutual understanding between the sender and the receiver
- There are appropriate times to utilize both the formal and informal communication channels
- The communication process involves a sender, a receiver, noise, and feedback
- Thoughtfully consider the right words to increase the chance of successful written and verbal communication
- Because the receiver of your message will not have verbal and nonverbal assistance in interpreting your message, take great care with all written messages
- Listening and silence are effective tools for effective communication

Key Terms

business letter	business memos	communication
decoding	documentation	encoding
feedback	formal communication	gossip
grapevine	informal communication	letterhead
noise	non-verbal communication	sender
slang	verbal communication	written communication

If You Were the Boss

1. One of your employees uses bad grammar that is reflecting poorly on your department's performance. How can you get a handle on this problem?

2. Employees keep saying they do not know what is going on at work. What steps would you take to increase workplace communication?

Learn More

To learn more about subjects addressed in this chapter take a course in Introductory Speech or Business Communication

Video Case Study: Language in the Office

This video addresses language in the office. Refer to the CD that accompanies your text, watch this video, and answer the following questions:

1. In the opening dialog between John and Regina, what specific advice would you give John? Why? What advice would you give Regina? Why?

2. Did Regina appropriately handle her telephone call? Please explain your answer.

3. Is the dialog between John and Brian appropriate? Provide specific examples.

4. Name two examples of how Brian could improve his language when speaking with Gerald.

Video Case Study: E-Mail Etiquette

This video presents expert advice on how to communicate professionally utilizing e-mail. Refer to the CD that accompanies your text, watch this video, and answer the following questions.

1. What should be included and what should be avoided in the subject line of an e-mail?

2. In what situations is it acceptable to utilize emoticons?

3. What is the appropriate e-mail use for non-work related matters?

Web Links

http://owl.english.purdue.edu/handouts/pw/p_memo.html

http://network.justjobs.com/profiles/blogs/using-foul-language-in-the

Reference

http://www.cedresources.ca/docs/modules/comm.do

Activities

Activity 9-1

Without infringing on someone's privacy, discreetly observe a stranger's body language for approximately five minutes. Stay far enough away to not hear him or her speak. Name at least two assumptions you can make by simply watching the person's gestures, movements, and expressions.

Gesture, Movement, or Expression	Assumption
1.	
2.	
3.	

Activity 9-2

Watch a television news show for a half hour. Document at least two facial expressions of an individual being interviewed. Did the individual's facial expressions match his or her statements?

Facial Expression	Match Statements: Yes or No
1.	
2.	

Activity 9-3

Review the following letter and identify five formatting errors. How should they be corrected?

April

Sandra Wong, Vice President
Human Resource Department
Robinson Enterprises
55123 W. Robinson Lane
Prosperity, CA 99923

Dear Sandra Wong

It was a pleasure speaking with you this afternoon regarding the average salary you pay your receptionists. This data will be useful as our company begins creating a new receptionist position for our California site.

I am most appreciative of your offer to mail me a copy of your most recent salary guide for all production positions. I look forward to receiving that guide in the mail. As a thank-you for your kindness, I am enclosing coupons for our company product.

If there is any information I can provide to assist you, please let me know. Thank-you again for your cooperation.

Sincerely,
Cory Kringle

What Are the Errors?	How to Correct
1.	
2.	
3.	
4.	
5.	

Activity 9-4

Review the following memo and identify five errors. How should they be corrected?

MEMORANDUM

Re: Budget Meeting

To: Mason Jared

From: Cory Kringle

Date: May 1

Hey Mason. I wanted to remind you that we have a meeting next week to talk about next year's budget. Bring some numbers and we'll work through them. Bye.

-Cory

What Are the Errors?	How to Correct
1.	
2.	
3.	
4.	
5.	

Activity 9-5

What would you say to someone who is inappropriately talking on his or her cell phone, such as someone interrupting your meeting.

Sample Exam Questions

1. The two types of workplace communication include _____ and _____ communication.

2. A major form of the informal communication network is called _____.

3. When the _____ is targeting individuals and their personal lives, it is called _____.

4. When _____ are displayed at work, it becomes difficult to think and behave in a logical manner.

5. Nonverbal communication is what we communicate through our _____.

6. _____ communicates to your audience that you are listening and are allowing the other party consideration.

7. Check that all _____ is error free by proofreading prior to sending.

Accountability and Workplace Relationships

> *You cannot escape the responsibility of tomorrow by evading it today.*
>
> Abraham Lincoln (1809–1865)

chapter **10**

Objectives

- Define and link the concepts of *empowerment, responsibility,* and *accountability*

- Describe how best to deal with your boss

- Describe how to respond when a workplace relationship turns negative

- Identify appropriate and inappropriate relationships with your boss, colleagues, executives, and customers

- Identify basic workplace expectations regarding social functions and gift giving

Empowerment

In politics, business, and education, individuals need to be held accountable for their actions. Unfortunately, too many people do not know what it means to be accountable. This chapter discusses the concepts of accountability and workplace relationships. The concepts of empowerment, responsibility, and accountability are all about personal choices. These personal choices not only impact how successfully you will perform at work but have a tremendous impact on workplace relationships.

In chapter 5 we discussed power bases and how workplace power affects politics and ethical behavior. Employees in the workplace have power. Unfortunately, many people in the workplace do not use their power appropriately or at all. As companies place an increased focus on quality and performance, correct decision making by employees becomes more and more important.

Empowerment is pushing power and decision making to the individuals who are closest to the customer in an effort to increase quality, customer satisfaction, and, ultimately, profits. The foundation of this basic management concept means that if employees feel they are making a direct contribution to a company's activities, they will perform better. This will then increase quality and customer satisfaction.

Consider the case of a manager for a retail customer service counter telling his employee to make the customer happy. The manager feels he has empowered his employee. However, the next day, the manager walks by the employee's counter and notices that the employee has given customers refunds for their returns, even when the return did not warrant a refund. The boss immediately disciplines the employee for poor performance. Didn't the employee do exactly what the manager asked the employee to do? Did the manager truly empower his employee? The answer is no. Telling someone to do something is different than showing someone the correct behavior. The employee interpreted the phrase "make the customer happy" differently from the manager's intention. The proper way for the manager to have empowered the employee would have been to discuss the company's return policies, role-play various customer scenarios, and then monitor the employee's performance. If or when the employee made errors through the training process, the wrong behavior should have been immediately corrected while good performance should have immediately received positive reinforcement.

When you, as an employee, demonstrate a willingness to learn, you have taken responsibility. **Responsibility** is accepting the power that is being given to you. If you are not being responsible, you are not fully utilizing power that has been entrusted to you. The concept of empowerment and responsibility is useless without accountability. **Accountability** means that you will report back to whoever gave you the power to carry out that responsibility. Employees at all levels of an organization are accountable to each other, their bosses, their customers, and the company's investors to perform their best.

One of the best ways to gain respect and credibility at work is to begin asking for and assuming new tasks. If you are interested in learning new skills, speak up and ask your boss to teach or provide you opportunities to increase your value to the company. Assume responsibility for these new tasks and report back (become accountable) on your performance. Worthwhile activities support the company's overall mission. Each project for which you assume responsibility must have a measurable goal. If it lacks a goal, it will be difficult to be accountable for your performance.

As you increase your workplace responsibilities, do not be afraid to seek assistance. Learning and success comes from others and past experiences. When you make mistakes, do not blame others. Determine what went wrong and why. Learn from mistakes, and view them as opportunities to do better in the future.

Cory is rapidly becoming more confident on the job. Cory wanted to be of more value to the company and began studying the concept of personal responsibility and accountability. Cory was excited about the new concepts that were learned and began requesting extra projects at work. Cory gladly kept the boss informed on the status of each project and reported when each project was successfully completed. The boss noticed how Cory took responsibility not only for personal growth but also for the success of the department. As a result, the boss informs Cory that he is impressed with Cory's willingness to improve and is considering Cory for a promotion.

Personal Accountability

In today's uncertain economy, it is even more important that employees show up to work with a positive attitude and give 100% effort when at work. All companies are continuously exploring methods to increase efficiencies and decrease waste. Each employee must take personal responsibility for his or her performance and be accountable for his or her actions and workplace choices. Good employees contribute to this effort by taking personal accountability for their actions while at work. Be on time and do what is expected of you. Do not miss work and do not call in sick unless you are ill. Reserve personal leave days for emergencies, funerals, or other such situations. During working hours, work. Do not surf the Internet or waste company time on personal activities. When an employee is constantly late, absent, or not completing his or her duties, other employees must take over the responsibilities of this employee. Not being accountable to your coworkers leads to poor workplace relationships.

Workplace Relationships

People who are mature and confident behave consistently around others, while those who are not as secure frequently behave differently around the boss or selected colleagues. Some could argue in favor of this behavior, but it is wrong and immature to behave inconsistently at work. Consistently behave professionally and respectfully, no matter who is around or watching. This section explains the dynamics of workplace relationships and its impact on performance.

Because many people spend more time at work than at home, workplace relationships have a profound impact on productivity. Treat everyone respectfully and professionally. It is easy to be respectful and professional to those we like; it is much more difficult doing so with those we dislike. Chapter 12, regarding the topic of conflict at work, addresses the sensitive issue of working productively with those whom we do not like. Unfortunately, strong friendships at work can be equally as damaging as workplace enemies if we fail to keep professional relationships separate from our personal lives. Socializing with our coworkers is both expected and acceptable to a degree, but do not make workplace relationships your only circle of friends. Doing so is dangerous because it becomes difficult to separate personal from work issues. It has the potential to create distrust among employees who are not included in your circle of workplace friends. Finally, it creates the potential for you to unknowingly or subconsciously show favoritism toward your friends. Even if you are not showing favoritism, those who are not within the circle of friends may perceive favoritism and may become distrustful of you.

As you become more comfortable with your job and company, you will be in various situations that provide opportunities to strengthen workplace relationships with coworkers, executives, investors, vendors, and customers. The following section discusses selected situations and how best to behave in these circumstances.

Executives/Senior Officials

It is often difficult for new employees to know how to behave in a room full of executives or board members. There may be occasions when you are in the presence of executives and board members. These may include meetings, corporate events, and social functions. While it is tempting to pull a senior official aside and tell him or her stories about your boss or how perfect you would be for an advanced position, be aware that some may view this behavior as both inappropriate and unacceptable. Do not draw attention to yourself. Project a positive, professional image. Highlight the successes of your department instead of personal accomplishments.

If you are in a meeting that you do not normally attend, do not dominate the discussion. If it is convenient, before or after the meeting, it is acceptable to introduce yourself to senior officials. Do not interrupt. Be confident, extend a hand, and state, "Hello, Mrs. Jones, my name is Tim Brandon. I work in the accounting department. It's nice to meet you." Keep your comments brief and positive. Your objective is to create a favorable and memorable impression with the executive. When introducing yourself make eye contact when talking so that the executive can connect a face, name, and department. Do not speak poorly of anyone or a situation. It is also inappropriate to discuss specific work-related issues, such as wanting to change positions, unless you are in a meeting specifically to discuss that issue. Allow the executive to guide the conversation and make sure to read the executive's body language. If the executive's body language includes a nodding head and his or her body is facing you, continue talking. If the executive is glancing away or his or her body is turning away from you, that body language is communicating the executive's desire to be elsewhere. Therefore, tell the executive it was nice meeting him or her, excuse yourself, and leave. Use encounters with executives as opportunities to create favorable impressions for you and your department.

Your Boss

Typically, there is no middle ground when it comes to workers and their feelings for their bosses. We either love them or hate them. There are three common types of bosses: the good boss, the incompetent boss, and the abusive boss.

Before we discuss how to handle each type, remember that bosses are human. Like us, they too are learning and developing their skills. Although they are not perfect, we should assume they are doing their best.

If you have a **good boss**, be thankful but cautious. A good boss is one who is respectful and fair and will groom you for a promotion. It frequently becomes tempting to develop a personal friendship with a good boss. Keep the relationship professional. While it is okay to share important activities occurring in your personal life with your boss (e.g., spouse and child issues, vacation plans), do not divulge too much personal information. Having a good boss may provide an opportunity to have him or her become a professional mentor. Identify what management qualities make your boss valued and begin imitating these qualities in your own workplace behavior.

An **incompetent boss** is one who does not know how to do his or her job. As with any work situation, no matter how bad the boss, remain professional and respectful. Make it your mission to make your boss look good. Doing so demonstrates your maturity and diminishes the tension between you and your boss. Do not worry about your boss receiving credit for your hard work. Incompetence rises to the top. If your boss is a poor performer, others in the company will discover your boss is not producing the good work being presented. If you are doing good work, it will get noticed by others in the company. If your boss really is not incompetent and you and your boss just have a personality conflict, do not allow your personal feelings to affect your performance. Focus on staying positive and being of value to your boss. Even when your coworkers want to bad-mouth the boss, do not give in to temptation. Remain professional and respectful. Use your bad boss experience as a time to learn what not to do when you become a boss.

Sometime in your career, you may experience an **abusive boss**. The abusive boss is one who is constantly belittling or intimidating his or her employees. Abusive bosses generally behave this way because they have low self-esteem. Therefore, they utilize their legitimate and coercive power to make themselves feel better by knocking someone else down. There are several ways to deal with an abusive boss. If the abuse is tolerable, do your best to work with the situation. Do not speak poorly of your boss in public. If the situation becomes intolerable and is negatively affecting your performance, seek confidential advice from someone in the human resource management department. This expert can begin observing, investigating, and documenting the situation and take corrective action or provide needed management training to your boss if necessary. Be factual in reporting inappropriate incidents. Human resource managers only want facts, not emotions. While tempting, do not go to your boss's boss. Doing so implies secrecy and distrust. If your boss's boss does not support you and/or your immediate boss finds out, your plan can backfire. Finally, if it looks as if nothing and no one can improve your boss's behavior, begin quietly searching for another job in a different department within the company or at a new company. As an employee, you have rights. If your boss ever acts discriminatory or harassing toward you, document and report the behavior immediately. Your boss should not make you perform functions that do not reasonably support those identified in your job description. Abusive bosses may have employees run personal errands or perform duties not appropriate for your job. If you are asked to perform unreasonable functions, politely decline. Regardless of what type of boss you have, give your personal best.

Web Quiz

Rate your relationship with your boss.

http://careerpath.com/
career-tests/?lr=cbmsn&
siteid=cbmsnchcpath

Colleagues

Having friends at work is nice. Unfortunately, when workplace friendships go awry, it affects your job. It is for this reason that you should be cautious about close friendships developed at work. A close friend is someone whom you trust and who knows your strengths and weaknesses. While you should be able to trust your coworkers, they should not know everything about you. It is important to be friendly to everyone at work. There will be some with whom you want to develop a friendship outside of work, but beware. If there is a misunderstanding either at work or away from work, the relationship can go sour and affect both areas. If one of you gets promoted and suddenly becomes the boss of the other, it also creates an awkward situation for both parties. Even if you can both get beyond this issue, others at work may feel like outsiders or feel you are playing favorites with your friend. If you only socialize with friends developed at work, you risk the danger of getting too absorbed in work issues. The one common thread that binds your friendship is work. Therefore, it is work that you will most likely discuss when you are together. This can be unhealthy and could potentially create a conflict of interest in work related decisions.

Others Within the Organization

The topic of friendships in the workplace extend to those throughout the organization. Increase your professional network by meeting others within your company. As discussed in chapter 5, as we build our connection power, we are gaining additional knowledge and contacts to assist us in performing our jobs and perhaps earning future promotions. When interacting with others in the organization, keep conversations positive and respectful. Even if another individual steers the conversation in a negative direction, respond with a positive comment. Defend coworkers when another employee is talking negatively about them.

For example, one day, Cory and a friend were sitting in the break room when Vicki, the department's unhappy coworker, walked in. "I just can't stand John!" declared Vicki. "That's too bad. John's a friend of mine," responded Cory's friend, Dee. Vicki stood there red-faced, turned around, and left the room. Cory told Dee that Cory never knew she and John were close. "Well," responded Dee, "we're not personal friends, but we all work together." Dee went on to explain that it is easy to eliminate negative conversation when you immediately communicate that you will not tolerate bad-mouthing others. Cory thought that was pretty good advice.

Each company has a **corporate culture (organizational culture).** Corporate culture is the company's personality being reflected through its employees' behavior. The company's culture is its shared values and beliefs. For example, if the company's management team openly communicates and promotes teamwork, the company will most likely have excellent communication and successful teams. In contrast, executives who are stressed and reacting to crisis situations will create a workplace atmosphere based on stress and crisis management. A company's corporate culture has an enormous impact on **employee morale.** Employee morale is the attitude employees have toward the company.

Exercise 10-1   Improving Morale

What can you do to help improve employee morale in your workplace?

_____

_____

_____

What workplace relationships contribute to poor employee morale?

_____

_____

_____

When Relationships Turn Negative

Unresolved conflict happens to the best of relationships. Due to a conflict or misunderstanding, a relationship may go bad. Unfortunately this happens at work. Sometimes you have no idea what you have done wrong. In other cases, you may be the one that wants to end the relationship. As stated earlier in the text, you do not have to like everyone at work, but no one should know who you dislike. Show everyone respect and behave professionally, even toward your adversaries.

If you are part of a bad workplace relationship, take the following steps in dealing with the situation:

- If you harmed the other person (intentionally or unintentionally), apologize immediately.
- If the other person accepts your apology, demonstrate your regret by changing your behavior.
- If the other person does not accept your apology and your apology was sincere, move on. Continue demonstrating your regret by changing your behavior.
- If you lose the relationship, do not hold a grudge. Continue being polite, respectful, and professional to the offended coworker.
- If the offended coworker acts rude or inappropriate, do not retaliate by returning the poor behavior. Respond in kindness.
- If the rude and inappropriate behavior negatively impacts your performance or is hostile or harassing, document the situation and inform your boss.

Erin had been one of Cory's favorite coworkers since Cory's first day at work. They took breaks together and at least once a week went out for lunch. One day Cory was working on a project with a short deadline. Erin invited Cory out to lunch and Cory politely declined, explaining why. The next day, Cory asked Erin to lunch and Erin just gave Cory a funny look and turned away. "Erin, what's wrong?" Cory asked. Erin just shook her head and left the room. Cory left Erin alone for a few days, hoping whatever was bothering her would blow over and things would be better. After a week of Erin ignoring Cory, things only got worse. Cory decided to try one last time to save the relationship. As Cory approached Erin, Cory said, "Erin, I'm sorry for whatever I've done to upset you and I'd like for us to talk about it." Unfortunately, Erin again gave Cory a hollow look and walked away.

The toughest step when addressing a broken relationship is when the other individual does not accept your apology. Most of us have grown up believing that we must like everyone and that everyone must like us. Because of human nature, this simply is not possible. We cannot be friends with everyone at work. People get their feelings hurt and some find it hard to forgive. Any behavior that is not respectful and professional interferes with performance. Your focus at work should be, first and foremost, getting the job done. The company is paying you to perform. Therefore, if a sour relationship begins to impact performance, you must respond. Ask yourself if your behavior is contributing to the unresolved conflict. If it is, change your behavior immediately. If your wronged coworker is upset or hurt, it is common for the coworker to begin bad-mouthing you. Do not retaliate by speaking negatively about your coworker. This only makes both of you look petty and immature. Document the facts of the incident and be mature. If the bad behavior continues for a reasonable period of time and negatively affects your performance, it is time to seek assistance. This is why documentation is important.

At this point, contact your immediate supervisor for an intervention. When you meet with your supervisor, explain the situation in a factual and unemotional manner making sure to communicate how the situation is negatively impacting the workplace and productivity. Provide specific examples of the offensive behavior and document any witnesses. Do not approach your supervisor to get the other individual in trouble. Your objective is to secure your boss's assistance in creating a mutually respectful and professional working relationship with your coworker. The boss may call you and the coworker into the boss's office to discuss the situation. Do not become emotional during this meeting. Your objective is to come to an agreement on behaving respectfully and professionally at work.

Dating at Work

A sticky but common workplace relationship issue is that of dating other employees, vendors, or customers of your place of employment. Because we spend so much time at work, it is natural for coworkers to look for companionship in the workplace. While a company cannot prevent you from dating coworkers who are in your immediate work area, many companies discourage the practice. Some companies go as far as having employees who are romantically involved sign statements releasing the company from any liability should the relationship turn sour. It is inappropriate for you to date coworkers and bosses, or if you are a supervisor for you to date your employees. Doing so exposes you, your romantic interest, and your company to potential sexual harassment charges. Your romantic actions will most likely negatively impact your entire department and make everyone uncomfortable.

If you date customers and vendors/suppliers of your company, use caution. In dating either customers or vendors, ask yourself how the changed relationship can potentially impact your job. You are representing your company 24/7.

Therefore, do not share confidential information or speak poorly of your colleagues or employer. Be careful to not put yourself in a situation in which you could be accused of a conflict of interest. It is best to keep your romantic life separate from that of the workplace.

Socializing

Work-related social activities such as company picnics, potlucks, and birthday celebrations are common. While some individuals enjoy attending these social functions, others do not. You do not have to attend a work-related social function outside of your required work hours. However, it is often considered rude if you do not attend social functions that occur at the workplace during work hours. If you are working on an important deadline and simply cannot attend, briefly stop by the function and apologize to whoever is hosting the event. If you are invited to attend a work-related social function, check to see if guests are being requested to bring items to the event. If you plan on attending, bring an item if one is requested. It is considered impolite to show up to a potluck empty-handed. It is also considered rude to take home a plate of leftovers unless offered. Alcohol should not be served on work premises.

Attendance at work-related social events occurring outside the work site is considered optional. As discussed in chapter 6, if the invitation requires an RSVP, send your reservation or regrets in a timely manner. If you choose not to attend an off-site activity, thank whoever invited you to maintain a positive work relationship. If you do attend an off-site social function check to see if guests are being requested to bring something. If the function is at someone's home, a host or hostess gift is also appropriate. Thank the host for the invitation when arriving and when leaving. If alcohol is being served at an off-site work-related function, use caution when consuming alcohol. It is best to not consume at all; but, if you consume, limit yourself to one drink.

Shared Work Areas

In an effort to facilitate teamwork and fully utilize workspace, many worksites utilize cubicles. While cubicles open up a work area, it is important to respect the privacy of each workspace as if it were an individual office. When working or conducting business in a shared work area, avoid making loud noises, smells, or distractions that may interrupt or annoy others. Speak quietly. Imagine that each cubicle has a door. Just as you would not walk into someone's office unannounced or without knocking, avoid walking into someone's cubicle space without permission. Stand at the entrance of the cubicle and quietly knock or say "excuse me." Wait for the individual to invite you into his or her work area. If you are conducting business and the discussion is lengthy, utilize a nearby conference/meeting room so as to not disrupt others. Respect the privacy of others' workspace. Do not take or use items from someone's

---

Talk It Out

What are common distractions that employees should avoid doing in a common work area?

desk without permission.

Breaks and the Break Room

It is a common practice for offices to make coffee available to everyone in the office. In most cases, the company does not pay for this benefit. The coffee, snacks, and other supplies are typically provided by the boss or someone else in the office. It is common for people to informally contribute to the coffee fund. If you routinely drink coffee or eat the office snacks, contribute funds to help pay for this luxury. The same goes for office treats such as doughnuts, cookies, or birthday cakes. If you partake, offer to share the cost or take your turn bringing treats one day. Many offices have a refrigerator available for employees to store their meals. Do not help yourself to food stored in the community refrigerator. If you store your food in this area, remember to throw out unused or spoiled food at the end of each workweek. Finally, clean up after yourself. If you use a coffee cup, wash it and put it away when you are finished. Throw away your trash, and leave the break room clean for the next person.

Miscellaneous Workplace Issues

While it is tempting to sell fund-raising items at work, the practice is questionable. Some companies have policies prohibiting this practice. If the practice is acceptable, do not pester people nor make them feel guilty if they decline to make a purchase.

It is common and acceptable to give a gift to a friend commemorating special days such as birthdays and holidays. However, you do not have to give gifts to anyone at work. If you are a gift giver, do so discreetly so as to not offend others who do not receive gifts from you. When you advance into a management position, do not give a gift to just one employee. Managers who choose to give gifts must give gifts to all employees and treat everyone equally.

It is also common for employees to pitch in and purchase a group gift for special days such as Boss's Day and Administrative Assistant's Day. While it is not mandatory to contribute to these gifts, it is generally expected that you contribute. If you strongly object or cannot afford to participate, politely decline without attaching a negative comment. If price is the issue, contribute whatever amount you deem reasonable and explain that you are on a budget. If you are the receiver of a gift, verbally thank the gift giver immediately and follow up with a handwritten thank-you note.

Good employees take ownership of common work areas and practice common courtesy with such issues as refilling a coffee pot when it is empty and/or filling the copy machine when it is low on paper. If a piece of office machinery is broken or a copy machine is jammed, do not leave the problem for someone else to solve. Take responsibility and solve the problem yourself. If you are unable to solve the problem alert someone who knows how to fix the problem.

Workplace Dos and Don'ts

Do take responsibility for your performance and success at work	*Don't* wait for someone to tell you what to do
Do display consistent, professional behavior	*Don't* behave appropriately only when the boss is around
Do make your boss look good	*Don't* speak poorly of your boss
Do create positive relationships with co-workers	*Don't* make your workplace friendships your primary friendships away from work
Do practice business etiquette at work-related social functions	*Don't* ignore the importance of behaving professionally at work-related social functions

Concept Review and Application

Summary of Key Concepts

- Take responsibility for the job you perform by being accountable for your actions
- Keep workplace friendships positive, but be cautious that these relationships are not your only friendships away from the workplace
- If a workplace relationship turns negative, remain professional and respectful
- It is best to refrain from dating anyone at work
- Practice good etiquette at social functions that occur within the office

Key Terms

abusive boss
corporate culture (organizational culture)
empowerment
incompetent boss
accountability
employee morale
good boss
responsibility

If You Were the Boss

1. How can you get employees excited about assuming additional responsibilities?
2. If you noticed employee morale dropping in your department, how would you respond?
3. How would you handle two employees whose friendship had turned negative?
4. You never give your employees gifts, but one of your employees always gives you gifts for holidays, birthdays, and boss's day. Is it wrong for you to accept these gifts?

Learn More

To learn more about subjects addressed in this chapter take a course in organizational behavior.

Video Case Study: Workplace Etiquette

This video addresses business etiquette in a shared workspace. Refer to the CD that accompanies your text, watch this video, and answer the following questions:

1. Were Brian, John, and Joe acting appropriate at the start of the video? Why or why not?
2. When is it appropriate to borrow another person's desk items?
3. Is Brian dressed appropriately, why or why not?

Web Links

http://www.librarysupportstaff.com/coworkers.html#principles
www.themeetingmagazines.com/index/Default.aspx?tabid=439

Reference

Deming, W. E. *Quality, Productivity and Competitive Position*, Cambridge, MA: MIT Press, 1982.

Activities

Activity 10-1

You are supposed to attend a meeting the next day. Overnight, you have a family emergency. What should you do? Explain your answer.

_____

_____

_____

Activity 10-2

Your boss bad-mouths or belittles coworkers. You do not like it and you wonder what he or she says about you when you are not around. What should you do?

_____

_____

_____

Activity 10-3

The company that services your office equipment has hired a new salesperson. This person does not wear a wedding ring and flirts with you. If you go out on a date with this person, what are three potential problems that could occur (work related)?

1. _____

2. _____

3. _____

Activity 10-4

Is it appropriate to discuss the following company information with individuals outside of the company? Why or why not?

Information	Yes or No	Why or Why Not?
1. Key clients/customers		
2. Financial information		
3. Boss's work style		
4. Company mission statement		
5. Names of members of the company board of directors		

Sample Exam Questions

1. _____ is the attitude employees have toward the company.

2. If you ever harm another, immediately _____ _____.

3. Any behavior that is not _____ or professional interferes with _____.

4. Be cautious in engaging in _____ with coworkers, customers, vendors, or your boss.

5. You _____ have to attend any work-related social function outside of your normal work hours.

6. If _____ is being served at a work-related function off of the work site, use caution when consuming, or better yet, do not _____.

7. If you partake of office treats, it is good manners to _____ in the break room.

8. Just like at home, _____ in the break room.

9. It is best to not sell _____ items at work.

Teamwork, Motivation, and Leadership

chapter 11

Objectives

- Define a *team* and its function

- Identify the characteristics of a team player

- Describe the elements of successful presentations and meetings

- Describe what motivates team players

- Identify the characteristics of effective *leadership*

- Identify leadership styles

- Describe ways to develop leadership skills

The price of greatness is responsibility.

Sir Winston Churchill (1874–1965)

Teams and Performance

Good human relations are all about attitude and getting along with others. Most individuals have experienced being part of a successful team. Perhaps it was a sports team, or maybe it was in school when a group of students successfully completed a big project. Whatever the task, these individuals were part of a team that comprised individuals who shared a goal and respected each other. These important factors resulted in success. Learning to get along with others is a skill that is necessary in the workplace. You will most likely be working with others in a group or as part of a team. Each team should strive toward creating synergy. **Synergy** is that extra excitement that occurs when people are truly working together as a team. This chapter discusses teamwork, factors vital for team success, and the impact teams have on an organization's overall performance.

In the workplace, working in a **group** means you and one or more people share a common goal. Every group has one leader that defines what happens in the group in order to reach a goal. The most common group in a workplace is a department. As a department, your boss will be the one assigned to lead your group in accomplishing the department's goal.

Companies use **teams** to accomplish goals. You and one or more other people will make up a team. The team will be assigned the task of reaching a goal. As opposed to a group that has one leader, in a team setting every member takes a leadership role and decides how and when to reach a goal. Each team member needs to have a sense of ownership for the team's performance. This occurs when team members are active participants and are accountable to fellow team members.

Several types of teams exist at work. Teams that occur within the organizational structure are formal teams. **Formal teams** are developed within the formal organizational structure and include functional teams (e.g., individuals from the same department) or cross-functional teams (individuals from different departments). **Informal teams** are comprised of individuals who get together outside of the formal organizational structure to accomplish a goal. Examples of informal teams include a company softball team and a group of coworkers collecting food for a local charity. In each team situation you are involved with, you need to get along with your team members and act professionally. Your performance for getting the job done depends on this team effort. A team comprised of individuals who behave professionally performs better.

Teams go through five stages of team development: forming, storming, norming, performing, and adjournment. In the **forming stage,** you are getting to know and forming initial opinions about your team members. Assumptions are based on first impressions. Sometimes these impressions are right; other times, they are wrong. In stage two, the **storming stage,** some team members begin to have conflict with each other. When team members accept other members for who they are (i.e., overcome the conflict), the team has moved into the **norming stage.** It is only then that the team is able to enter the **performing stage** where they begin working on the task. Once the team has completed its task, it is in the **adjourning stage,** which brings closure to the project. Note that it is normal for a team to go through these phases. Some teams successfully and rapidly move through the forming, storming, and norming phases and get right to work (performing), while other teams cannot get beyond the initial phases of forming or storming. Make every effort to move your team along to the performing stage, and recognize that minor conflicts are a part of team development. Successful teams move beyond the conflict and accept each member for his or her unique talents and skills.

You may work with team members you know and see every day in the workplace. However, you may have to work with a team of people you have never met before. Some team members may be from your immediate department (functional teams), some may be outside of your department (cross-functional teams), and some may be from outside of the company. Good people skills and a willingness to lead are what make employees valuable to a team.

In a team situation, you will usually have your own job to do but you are also accountable to your fellow team members. The success of others within the company depends on how you do your job. Although you may be working independently from your team members, it is still important that you get your job done on time and correctly. An effective team member is able to work with everyone on the team. You may have to work with a person with whom you do not care to work. No matter what disagreements you may have, you need to get along with this person and be professional at all times. This is a skill needed for any job.

Characteristics of a Team Member

A good team member is one who does his or her job in a manner that is contributing to the end project. This means being trustworthy, being efficient, and communicating at all times. Common team projects include improving product quality, providing excellent customer service, and creating and/or maintaining company records.

As a team member, know the objectives and goal of the team. The activity performed for your team should support the team's objectives and goal. In chapter 2, you learned how to create personal goals. Organizations do the same thing. When there is a team working on a specific project, there is a goal; so the first step is to set objectives to reach that goal. Do not just jump into a project without a clear understanding of the expected outcome. Do not reinvent the wheel or waste time and money. The best way to avoid these common mistakes is to solicit ideas and input from all team members.

Once the team has identified its goal and objectives, the team can identify various alternatives or solutions on how best to successfully achieve the goal. One popular way of doing this is through brainstorming. **Brainstorming** is a problem-solving method that involves identifying alternatives that allow members to freely add ideas while other members withhold comments on the alternatives. Brainstorming is successful because it is fast and provides members the opportunity to contribute different and creative ideas. Brainstorming starts with the presentation of a problem, for example, how to improve office communication. Members then have a set time to make any suggestion for improving office communication. The suggestions can be obvious (e.g., a newsletter) or fun and creative (have a daily off-site office party). No matter the suggestion, members are to withhold comment and judgment on the idea until the brainstorming session is over. Recommendations are recorded on a board for the team to view. In effective brainstorming sessions, even an off-the-wall comment such as the suggestion to have a daily off-site office party may spark a more practical idea that contributes to solving the problem (e.g., have a companywide gathering).

Although conflict is a natural part of team development, occasionally, there are teams that are filled with hard-to-resolve conflict. As you will learn in chapter 12, there are various ways to overcome conflict. Do not let one member ruin the

Exercise 11-1   Brainstorm for Saving

Working in a small group, brainstorm as many ideas as possible to help you and/or your classmates save money while going to college. List the top three ideas.

1. _____

2. _____

3. _____

synergy of the team. If possible, confidentially pull the member aside and ask that person what it is about the team or project that he or she finds objectionable. Also, ask that team member how he or she feels the issue can best be resolved. Calmly and logically help the individual work through the issues. Accept the fact that he or she may not (1) recognize there is a problem, (2) share, or (3) want to come to a solution. If you or others on the team attempt to solve the problem with the difficult team member and he or she rejects the effort, your team needs to move forward without that person. Do not give one member so much power that he or she negatively affects the efforts of the entire team. Although team conflict is a natural stage of team development, it should not cripple a team. When the problem team member is not around, do not allow other team members to talk negatively about the individual. Your job is to be a productive, positive team member who assists in successfully accomplishing the team's goal.

In addition to knowing the goals of the project and what your roles and responsibilities are in the team effort, you also need to know the responsibilities of all the other team members. Whenever possible, identify ways to support other team members and assist them in accomplishing the team's objectives. Take responsibility to attend all team meetings and be on time. Participation, sharing, support, understanding, and concern are all part of being on a team. During team meetings, make every effort to be involved in discussions and determine what work is needed for accomplishing the goal. Do not be afraid to speak up during team meetings. The key is to successfully complete the team goal. Some of your ideas may not be considered, but that does not mean they are not important. Be responsible and finish assignments in a timely manner. As a group, review all aspects of the project together before completing the project. To make the project successful, team members must be accountable to each other.

Cory's department was having problems meeting its production goal. The manager asked the department to form a team and create a plan for increasing production. Cory volunteered to be on this team. It was the first team project Cory had been involved in, and Cory did not know what to expect. Fortunately, Cory had a good team leader. The team leader sat down with the team and helped identify its goal and objectives so that team members knew exactly what needed to be done. At the next meeting, the team leader led a brainstorming session. Some good ideas were mentioned. Cory had an idea but was not sure it should be mentioned. Remembering that members need to freely add ideas during brainstorming, Cory decided to share an idea. It turned out the team liked the idea, and it became an important part of the project plan.

Communication is a key element of effective teamwork. Do not make assumptions about others or a team project. If you have questions regarding any aspect of a project, respectfully speak up. As mentioned earlier in this chapter, it is normal for teams to experience conflict. If others do not agree with your ideas, keep a positive attitude. If your team takes a wrong turn, do not waste time on blame; take corrective action and learn from any mistakes that are made. Each team member should be able to state his or her position and ideas; it should then be a team effort to decide which ideas to use. Do not assume that any team member's idea will not be worth hearing. The whole point of a team project is to get as many ideas as possible in order to come up with the best solution for reaching the goal. If the team makes a decision with which you did not agree and you have expressed and explained your objection and the team still decides to continue, support the team's decision, and continue assisting the team in achieving its goal. Conflict is a normal part of teamwork, learn to work through conflict. This is where open, honest, and timely communication with all team members is important.

Your team members need to trust you to do your part in getting the work done. Do not allow team members to do your work because you know they will do it for you. Many times, in a team situation, one member contributes nothing because that member knows he or she can. If you have a lazy team member, continue to do your best and try to work around that person. Eventually, that person will lose respect from other team members and they will not work with that person on projects. Try talking to the poorly performing team member and identify why he or she is not doing his or her share. If the team member provides a good reason, suggest that he or she excuse himself or herself from the team. If the team member just simply refuses to perform, you may need to talk to your supervisor and get him or her replaced.

Exercise 11-2   Good Team Member Characteristics

Name the two most important characteristics you would want to see in your team members. Be specific and explain why these characteristics aid in a team's success.

Characteristic	How Does this Help the Team Achieve Success?
1.	
2.	
3.	

Meetings

A common form of team interaction and workplace communication is a meeting. Meetings are either informational, discussion driven, decisional, or some combination of the three. Meetings can be formal or informal. The most common form of meetings in the workplace is a department meeting where a boss meets with his or her employees.

Prior to meetings, a **meeting agenda** is normally distributed to all attendees. A meeting agenda is an outline of major topics and activities that are scheduled to be addressed during the meeting. Some agendas have time limits attached to each item. If you receive an agenda prior to a meeting, take time to read the agenda and become familiar with the topics of discussion. If there is an item you would like placed on the agenda, notify the person in charge of the meeting. If you are responsible for an agenda item, plan what you are going to share and/or request prior to the meeting. Prepare handouts for each attendee if necessary.

The most common type of meeting is a face-to-face meeting where all parties are physically present in one location. When you arrive at a face-to-face meeting, arrive early. Depending on the size of the meeting, there can be one table or many tables filled with meeting attendees. If there is a head table, do not sit at the head table unless you are invited to do so. If there are no assigned seats and you are speaking, sit toward the front of the room. The **meeting chair** is the individual who is in charge of the meeting and has prepared the agenda. This person normally sits at the head of the table. If the chair has an assistant, the assistant will usually sit at the right side of the meeting chair. Other individuals in authority may sit toward the front of the table or they will sit at the opposite end of the table. If you are unsure of where to sit at a conference table, wait to see where others sit and then fill in an empty seat.

It is important for employees to show up on time and be prepared for meetings. Most formal business meetings will follow some form of **Robert's Rules of Order,** a guide to running meetings. Robert's Rules of Order is oftentimes referred to as parliamentary procedure. At the start of a meeting, the meeting chair will call a meeting to order and, if appropriate, review the minutes from the last meeting. After the review of minutes, the meeting chair will ask that the minutes be approved. Once the minutes are approved, the agenda issues will be addressed in the agenda order. At the close of the meeting, the meeting chair will adjourn the meeting.

As a meeting participant, take your turn speaking by contributing thoughtful and relevant information when appropriate. Keep your discussion to the topic at hand and assist the meeting chair by keeping the discussion moving, with all contributions being professional, respectful, and focused on the goals of the company.

When distance separates meeting participants, virtual meetings take place. These meetings occur through the use of technology such as videoconferencing, telephone, or the Internet. In some situations, such as teleconferencing, you may not have the ability to see other participants. In situations such as these, state your name each time you speak. For example, prior to contributing, say, "Hi, this is Ted. I would like to provide a status report on the Bear project." Because virtual meetings require a special emphasis on listening, be quiet when others are speaking and do not do anything distracting. As with face-to-face meetings, be prepared and actively contribute.

Team Presentations

Some work situations require employees to create and provide a presentation as a team. The presentation material presented in chapter 9 applies to team presentations. First, agree upon the presentation goal. Then, as a team, create the presentation outline. Using the outline as a foundation, discuss and agree upon the verbal, visual, and support content. Just as with other team situations each member needs to take responsibility and be accountable to each other. Do not just split up sections and piece a presentation together at the last minute. Team presentations must be complete and reviewed by the entire team before presenting. Demonstrating positive human relation skills is a key to the success of a team. Each member must communicate, share duties, and behave in a respectful and professional manner.

Motivation

Motivation is an internal drive that causes people to behave a certain way to meet a need. The way individuals behave at work is a result of trying to fill a need. If needs are not met, your behavior changes. Team members need to be motivated to achieve success. Several factors can contribute to motivating team members. The most obvious motivation factor is money. However, when working in teams, monetary payment often may not be the primary motivating factor.

Motivation comes from within. A team member's motivation may be a sense of accomplishment or the achievement of a goal. The motivating factor may be the social acceptance received from others for being part of a successful team. For some, the motivation factor may just be a matter of keeping their job. Abraham Maslow created a hierarchy of needs (see figure 11-1). This hierarchy of needs essentially states that throughout one's lifetime, as individuals' needs are met, they move up a pyramid (hierarchy) until they self-actualize and have realized their potential. Organizational behaviorists have adapted Maslow's hierarchy to a typical workplace. Maslow's lowest level, **physiological needs,** translates to basic wages. People work to receive a paycheck, which is used for food and shelter. The next step up the pyramid is **safety needs.** Individuals desire not only a safe working environment but also job security. It is only after individuals receive basic wages and experience job security that they invest in workplace relationships, thus reaching the **social needs** level. Employees

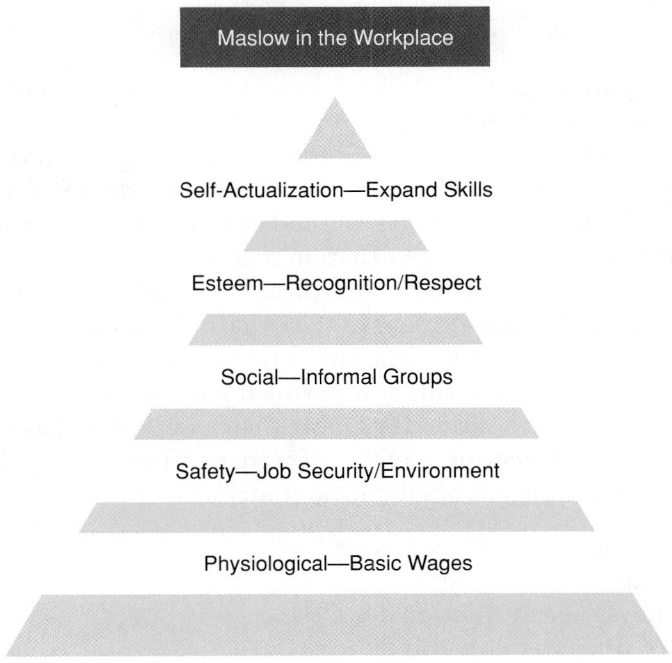

Maslow in the Workplace

Self-Actualization—Expand Skills

Esteem—Recognition/Respect

Social—Informal Groups

Safety—Job Security/Environment

Physiological—Basic Wages

Figure 11-1

Maslow's Hierarchy of Needs

cannot progress to the next level until positive workplace relationships are realized. The next level on the pyramid is **self-esteem needs.** This is when employees flaunt workplace titles, degrees, and awards. Their need is to inform others of their accomplishments. The final stage of the hierarchy is that of **self-actualization.** In a workplace, this is when employees have successfully had their basic needs met and now desire to assist others in meeting their needs. They do so by becoming mentors or coaches or by finding other means of helping others achieve their goals.

Maslow's theory is still used today to explain what motivates employees and how humans respond to motivational factors. Each level of the pyramid addresses different ways people need to be motivated. As a team member, recognize that not everyone is motivated by the same factors; nor do others have the same needs as you. Observe other members' behaviors and words, then try to determine where they are on the pyramid. Once you identify others' needs, you assist in creating an environment that helps meet these particular needs. Motivation is an internal drive, you are the only one that can motivate yourself. Others can only provide a motivating environment.

Talk It Out

Where is the majority of the class currently on Maslow's hierarchy?

Exercise 11-3   Identify the Need

Evaluating the following comments and determine what need on Maslow's hierarchy is being expressed. Refer to figure 11-1.

Comment	Need Expressed
I have done a similar project in the past; can I help you?	
I need a raise this year.	
Anyone want to join me for lunch?	
I received a sales award; would you like to see it?	

One final point regarding Maslow's theory is that individuals can quickly move from one level to another. It is common to have an off day in which you are not motivated to perform. If you find yourself having an off day, take time out and ask yourself what situation put you in a nonproductive frame of mind. Use positive self-talk to get back on track and be productive. In some situations, you may not be able to control the situation that affected your performance. An example may be work layoffs or a workplace safety issue. In one of these instances, try to identify what element of the situation you can control and work from there. You are the only one who can control your attitude.

If you find yourself in a situation in which you no longer have a desire to work and this lack of motivation lasts more than a week, you may be experiencing job burnout. **Job burnout** is a form of extreme stress that results in the desire to no longer work. Signs of job burnout include:

- Being frequently tardy or absent
- Continual complaining
- Poor physical and emotional health
- Lack of concern for quality

- Clock-watching and being easily distracted
- Gossiping
- Desire to cause harm to the company (theft or damage property)

If you have seriously tried to improve the current work situation and still find yourself at a dead end, you may need to consider a job change. Continuing in a job in which you have not been motivated in for a long period of time is destructive not only to you but also to your company and coworkers.

Leadership

When reference is made to *leaders*, people think of managers. But the reality is that each employee should display leadership. **Leadership** is a process of one person guiding one or more individuals toward a specific goal. At work we need to behave as leaders. A leader does not need to be a manager or a supervisor. Note that not all bosses behave as leaders. Leaders motivate others through relationships. At work, these relationships are based on trust, professionalism, and mutual respect. A leader is one who will help guide and motivate others. In other words, a boss who is not a leader will tell others what job to complete without guiding and motivating.

There are three primary leadership styles: autocratic, democratic, and laissez-faire leadership. **Autocratic leaders** are very authoritarian, meaning they make decisions on their own. **Democratic leaders** make decisions based upon input from others. **Laissez-faire leaders** allow team members to make their own decisions without input from the leader. There is no best leadership style and the appropriate leadership style is dependent on the situation.

You do not need a title or degree to be a leader. At work, make an effort to assume a leadership role. In a leadership role, know the project and its purpose. Know the team players' (or coworkers') strengths and weaknesses and be someone others can trust. Successfully working with others is a team process, not just your own process for completing a job. As a good leader, problem-solve and form and communicate a plan, then follow up on projects. In order to do this, know your job. A good leader will also know when to allow others to lead.

Effective leaders do not do all the work themselves. They learn to **delegate.** Delegating is when a manager or leader assigns part or all of a project to someone else. As a leader, you are ultimately responsible for a project's successful completion. Leaders empower others, teach others, and mentor others. In a team situation, contribute to the success of a project. Ultimately, leaders take responsibility. Take your responsibilities seriously and consistently perform in a quality manner.

Becoming a Leader

At work, you may be assigned a leadership position by your boss or your team or simply because no one else wants to lead. No matter how a leadership position is obtained, be willing and prepared to lead at all times. Volunteer to serve on a team and learn what skills are necessary to be a successful team leader. Begin preparing today by learning new skills, by joining committees, training, and attending workshops. Observe successful leaders and/or find a mentor to help

Talk It Out

Which leadership style is most appropriate for a football team? For a gaming designer? For rearranging office space? Explain your answers.

Web Quiz

What is your leadership style?

http://psychology.about .com/library/quiz/ bl-leadershipquiz.htm you develop good leadership skills. Learning new skills will enable you to think and act like a leader. You will also improve your communication skills, which is necessary for effective leadership.

Effective leaders display characteristics that make them stand out from others. These skills include excellent communication skills, the ability to work with and earn the trust of others, consistent ethical behavior, and focus and vision. Although these skills are not developed overnight you do have the ability to become a successful leader not only in your workplace but also in every other area of your life.

Exercise 11-4   Leadership Characteristics

List three people whom you consider leaders. Next to their names, list the characteristic that makes them a successful leader.

Leader	Leadership Characteristic
1.	
2.	
3.	

Workplace Dos and Don'ts

Do be an active participant by being accountable to fellow team members	*Don't* ignore team meetings and deadlines
Do be a good team member by being trustworthy and efficient and by communicating at all times	*Don't* allow negative team members to disrupt the team's performance
Do express yourself during team meetings	*Don't* think your ideas are not of value
Do recognize that people are motivated by different factors	*Don't* ignore initial signs of burnout
Do make every effort to increase your leadership skills	*Don't* leave the leadership process up to others

Concept Review and Application

Summary of Key Concepts

- Most companies use teams to accomplish goals
- An effective team comprises individuals who share a goal and respect for each other
- A good team member is one who does his or her job in a manner that is productive toward the end project
- Although team conflict is a natural stage of team development, do not allow conflict to cripple a team
- Communication is a key element of effective teamwork
- Motivation is an internal drive that causes you to behave a certain way to meet a need
- Everyone has the ability to become a successful leader

Key Terms

adjourning stage	autocratic leaders	brainstorming
delegate	democratic leaders	formal teams
forming stage	group	informal teams
job burnout	laissez-faire leaders	leadership
meeting agenda	meeting chair	motivation
norming stage	performing stage	physiological needs
Robert's Rules of Order	safety needs	self-actualization
self-esteem needs	social needs	storming stage
synergy	teams	

If You Were the Boss

1. You have assembled a group of employees into a team to reach the goal of improving customer service in your department, but all they do is argue when they meet. What should you do?
2. Your employees have successfully met their production goals this week. Based on Maslow's hierarchy of needs, how can you motivate them to meet next week's goals?

Learn More

To learn more about subjects addressed in this chapter take an Introduction to Management course.

Video Case Study: Meetings

This video addresses meeting behavior and etiquette. Refer to the CD that accompanies your text, watch this video, and answer the following questions:

1. Out of the four employees which one demonstrated appropriate meeting behavior? Provide specific examples.

2. How did technology assist the meeting and how did technology hinder the meeting?

3. What perception of the company may the client have from the conference call? Provide two examples.

4. Name four inappropriate actions of the employees.

Web Links

http://www.nwlink.com/~donclark/leader/leadhb.html

http://www.associatedcontent.com/article/317564/the importance_of_teamwork_in_the_workplace.html

http://www.accel-team.com/human_relations/hrels_02_maslow.html

http://www.deepermind.com/20maslow.htm

References

Lewin, K., Lippit, R., and White, R. K. (1939). "Patterns of aggressive behavior in experimentally created social climates." *Journal of Social Psychology, 10,* 271–301.

Maslow, Abraham. *Motivation and Personality,* 2nd ed. New York: Harper & Row, 1970.

Maxwell, J. C. *The 21 Irrefutable Laws of Leadership.* Nashville: Nelson Business, 1998.

Tuckman, B. W., and Jenson, M. A. C. "Stages of Small Group Development Revisited." In *Group and Organizational Studies,* 2nd ed., 419–27. 1977.

Zemke, Ron. "Maslow for the New Millennium." *Training* (December 1998): 54–58.

Activity 11-1

Write about a time when you belonged to a successful team. Identify at least three specific factors that made the team successful.

Team Situation

1.

2.

3.

Activity 11-2

Research President Abraham Lincoln and answer the following questions.

What key leadership qualities made him unique?

_____

_____

What challenges did he face?

_____

_____

How can you apply lessons learned from your President Lincoln research to your leadership development?

_____

_____

Activity 11-3

If you were teaching this class, what specific topics or activities could you include in the course to help students better meet each level of Maslow's hierarchy?

Level	Motivation Factor
Self-Actualization	
Esteem	
Social	
Safety	
Physiological	

Sample Exam Questions

1. _____ hierarchy of needs is used to explain _____.

2. Every team goes through _____: forming, _____, norming, _____, and _____.

3. _____ is a way for teams to identify various alternatives or solutions on how best to successfully achieve the goal.

4. A/An _____ is one who will work with others to help guide and motivate.

5. Communication with all team members must be _____, _____, and _____.

6. _____ is an internal drive; therefore, no one can motivate you. Others can only provide a _____ environment.

7. _____ is the desire to no longer work. It is most commonly caused by _____.

8. At work, _____ are based on trust, professionalism, and mutual respect.

Conflict and Negotiation

chapter 12

Whenever you're in conflict with someone, there is one factor that can make the difference between damaging your relationship and deepening it. The factor is attitude.

William James (1842–1910)

Objectives

- Define *conflict* and its impact on performance

- Name and describe the various conflict management styles and the appropriate time to utilize each one

- Describe the process and purpose of *negotiation*

- Define the various forms of workplace *harassment*

- Identify resources available to employees who are confronted with workplace harassment

- Describe how to deal with a hostile work environment or *workplace bully*

- Name warning signs of workplace violence

Conflict

Unfortunately, a common element of working with individuals is conflict. Although most individuals regard conflict as a negative experience, it does not have to be negative. Conflict can result in a positive experience if you approach it with the right attitude. This chapter addresses the issue of conflict and its impact on performance. Various methods of dealing with conflict in addition to tips on how to deal with difficult people is also presented. Finally, the issues of harassment, workplace violence, and negotiation are discussed.

Conflict occurs when there is a disagreement or tension between two or more parties (individuals or groups). Although conflict at work cannot be avoided, you can control your reaction to the conflict. Conflict means that individuals are looking at a situation from different perspectives, which is not always a bad thing. Different perspectives mean diversity of thought. If you disagree with a coworker and no one else is involved, it is courteous to discuss the matter in private.

If you view conflict as a breakdown in communication, work on overcoming the problem instead of finding fault or blame. How an individual deals with conflict reflects his or her attitude, maturity level, and self-confidence. When someone disagrees with you or hurts you, a natural tendency is to become angry. A common reaction to anger is to retaliate or get even. Unfortunately, this behavior does not reflect that of an individual who is striving to become a logical, mature professional. Follow these basic rules when dealing with conflict:

- Remain calm and unemotional
- Be silent and listen
- Try to see the disagreement from the other person's perspective
- Explain your position and offer a solution
- Come to a solution

Rarely, if ever, does anyone win when people respond in anger. An individual who becomes emotional has difficulty managing his or her logic in resolving the issue. When confronted with conflict, remain calm and unemotional. Acknowledge your hurt feelings or anger, but do not let it dominate your response. With a clear mind, it is easier to view the disagreement from your opponent's side. Try to identify why your opponent behaved the way he or she did. Before responding, identify what message was being sent. Look for facts and feelings. This will help you identify if the message was misinterpreted because of a miscommunication of facts or an emotional response. It could just be a difference of opinion.

After thinking about the disagreement from the other person's perspective, calmly and rationally explain your position along with a solution. This is the step that could easily lead to an argument if you become emotional. While explaining your position, your opponent may interrupt and state his or her position. Do not argue. Allow your opponent to talk while you remain quiet and listen. This is tough because we want to defend our opinions. Respond in a mature, professional manner. When the opponent is done speaking, take your turn. If your opponent again interrupts, ask him or her if you can take your turn responding. In your conversation, look for common ground. Identify what the disagreement is about. Try to give several alternatives to solving the problem, and then agree on a solution. In the workplace there may be situations where both parties may need to agree to disagree.

The following list offers several basic concepts to deal with conflict in the workplace:

- Only you can control how you respond to a situation.
- Do not let feelings dictate actions. Remain calm and unemotional.
- Attempt to resolve a conflict immediately; work with the offender.
- Accept responsibility for your actions and apologize if necessary.
- Retaliation (getting even) is not the answer.
- Keep your conflict issues confidential.

If the conflict is negatively affecting your job performance:

- Document the offensive or inappropriate behavior regarding the conflict.
- Seek assistance within the company to resolve the conflict. If possible begin with the supervisor.
- If an internal remedy cannot be reached, seek outside assistance.

Exercise 12-1   Handling Interruptions

Role-play a conversation with a classmate about the best way to take notes in class. Have the other classmate interrupt you several times. Practice handling the interruption in an adult, mature manner. What did you say to that person?

_____

_____

_____

Conflict Management Styles

Depending on the offense and workplace situation, there are several conflict management styles. These include forcing, avoiding, accommodating, compromising, or collaborating.

If a behavior is offensive or unacceptable, use the **forcing conflict management style.** This style deals with the issue directly. Remain calm and unemotional. Do not turn the discussion into an argument. Your goal is to communicate that the inappropriate behavior is unacceptable and provide your solution to the problem. Forcing behavior means you are trying to make someone do things your way. The other party has no say whatsoever.

The **avoiding conflict management style** is used when you do not want to deal with the conflict so you ignore the offense. Sometimes we avoid a conflict because the offense is not a big enough deal to upset others. Other times, we avoid the conflict because we are not strong or confident enough to stand up for our rights.

If preserving a relationship is a priority, you may use the **accommodating conflict management style.** Allow the other party to have his or her way without knowing there was a conflict.

A **compromising conflict management style** occurs when both parties give up something of importance to arrive at a mutually agreeable solution to the conflict. This differs from the **collaborating conflict management style** in which both parties work together to arrive at a solution without having to give up something of value.

When faced with conflict, your goal is to create a solution that is fair to all involved parties. This is called **negotiation.** Both sides can come to an agreement if both parties:

- Want to resolve an issue
- Agree on an objective
- Honestly communicate their case/situation
- Listen to the other side
- Work toward a common solution that is mutually beneficial

In working toward a successful negotiation, practice good communication skills. As stated in the preceding list, listen. Do not interrupt or pass judgment until the other side has stated its case. Watch the other party's body language through hand and arm gestures and body positioning. Attempt to identify whether the other party is willing to resolve the issue. Also evaluate the party's ability to make eye contact. Put aside your personal feelings and focus on coming to a mutually agreeable solution.

If two parties are not able to resolve an issue themselves or if the issue affects workplace performance, it is common for a neutral third party to serve as a **mediator.** The mediator's primary objective is to assist the two feuding parties in coming to a mutually agreeable solution.

If you consistently allow others to have their way, you are displaying passive behavior. While it is acceptable to use **passive behavior** at times, there are appropriate times to use **assertive behavior.** Assertive behavior is when you stand up for your rights without violating the rights of others. Professionals should behave in an assertive manner. This is done by displaying confidence and not being ashamed to defend your position by sharing your concerns in an inoffensive manner. Individuals exhibiting **aggressive behavior** stand up for their rights in a way that violates others' rights, in an offensive manner. Others do not have to be harmed or put down for you to be heard or for you to have your way. Someone loses when aggressive behavior is exhibited. Treat others in a respectful, professional manner. If you are offended or see that someone else's rights are being violated, speak up. You can stand up for your rights (or those of another) without harming others. Do not demean others as a form of retaliation when someone displays aggressive behavior toward you.

Talk It Out

How can you become more assertive?

Harassment

As discussed in chapter 8, the human resource department is your advocate for unlawful harassment. The Equal Employment Opportunity Commission (EEOC) defines **sexual harassment** as unwanted advances of a sexual nature. The two types of sexual harassment are quid pro quo and hostile behavior. **Quid pro quo harassment** is behavior that is construed as reciprocity or payback for a sexual favor (e.g., you sleep with your boss and he or she gives you a raise). The EEOC states that quid pro quo harassment can include "verbal, visual or physical conduct of a sexual nature." **Hostile behavior harassment** includes any behavior of a sexual nature by another employee that you find offensive. The EEOC states this behavior can include "verbal slurs, physical contact, offensive photos, jokes, or any other offensive behavior of a sexual nature." Sexual harassment can occur between a man and a woman, a man and another man, or a woman and another woman. It does not limit itself to a boss and employee relationship.

In addition to a sexual harassment policy, companies should also have a policy regarding professional behavior. Each employee is entitled to be treated in a respectful and professional manner by coworkers. A policy regarding workplace behavior prevents workplace incivility and communicates to all employees that unprofessional behavior will not be tolerated. In the workplace, there will be individuals whom you may not care to befriend. You do not have to be friends with all of your coworkers, but you are required to respect your colleagues and treat them in a professional manner. There is no place for rudeness in the workplace. Choose to be courteous. You also do not have to like your coworkers, but they should not be aware of your negative feelings toward them. Mature adults treat coworkers with courtesy and respect.

Exercise 12-2   Identify Harassment

What kind of behavior have you exhibited that could be construed as harassing?

_____

_____

How can you change your behavior or attitude to ensure that no one is offended by or could misinterpret your behavior as inappropriate?

_____

_____

1. If the behavior is offensive but relatively minor, tell the individual that his or her behavior is offensive and ask him or her to stop. Document the conversation in your personal notes. Include the date, time, and any witnesses to the incident.

2. If the behavior continues or if the behavior is extremely inappropriate and/or outrageously offensive, immediately contact your supervisor or human resource department. Tell the person you contact what happened, that you are offended by the harassing behavior, and that you want to file harassment charges. Provide facts and names of anyone who witnessed the offensive behavior.

All companies should have an antiharassment policy. Employers need to provide antiharassment training and a protocol for filing and investigating a complaint. If you are a victim of harassment, take the following steps:

Once you have filed a complaint with your employer, he or she has a legal obligation to conduct a confidential investigation. Everyone is innocent until proven guilty. Do not feed the rumor mill with information regarding your complaint. Remain professional and reserve comments for the investigative interview. Document the dates and times of whom you speak with regarding the complaint, interviews, and comments made. When the investigation is complete, the supervisor or human resource department will render a decision. If you are not satisfied with the outcome, you have the right to file a complaint with the Department of Fair Employment and Housing or the Equal Employment Opportunity Commission. It is unlawful for an employer to retaliate against or punish anyone who files a sexual harassment claim, even if the claim is found to be without merit. No one should be punished for filing a claim.

Harassment policies are extremely important policies. Behave appropriately and do not exhibit behavior that could be offensive to others. This includes off-color jokes, inappropriate touching, inappropriate conversations, and suggestive attire. Many times, individuals think they are joking when in fact their behavior is offensive to others.

Katie, the mailroom clerk who works in Cory's office, returned from a vacation at the beach. When Cory asked Katie about her new tattoo, she told Cory and Cory's officemates all about her new tattoo. One of Cory's coworkers, John, asked where on her body she got her tattoo. Katie grinned at John and patted her chest. The next day, when Katie delivered the mail, John again asked Katie when he would get to see her tattoo. Katie grinned and went on her way. For the next few days, John kept asking about the tattoo and Katie kept grinning and walking away. The following week, John was called into the boss's office. Cory later found out that Katie filed sexual harassment charges against John based on John's curiosity regarding Katie's new tattoo.

Web Quiz

Take the quiz to find out if you understand appropriate workplace behavior.

http://www.workrelationships .com/site/quiz/

Exercise 12-3   Identify Violations

Whose rights were violated in the previous story regarding Katie, John, and the tattoo? Justify your answer.

_____

_____

If you were Katie, how should you have handled the situation differently?

_____

_____

If you were John, what would you have done differently?

_____

_____

Workplace Bullies

Even if you are treating everyone with respect, you may have a coworker who is not reciprocating with the same respectful and professional behavior. Many times in a workplace, there is an employee who is rude and unprofessional. This type of employee is called a **workplace bully.** Workplace bullies seek ways to intimidate or belittle coworkers. Sometimes bullies publicly harass coworkers.

Other times, they are discreet in their harassing tactics. Employees who are consistently rude and who bad-mouth other employees or demonstrate intimidating behavior are displaying workplace incivility. Both bullying and incivility can result in a hostile work environment, which contributes to both an increase in stress-related performance issues and, worse yet, workplace violence. Workplace bullying and incivility are not only immature behavior; they are unacceptable at work. If you experience workplace bullying:

- Do not retaliate with the same bad behavior. Remain calm and unemotional. Remember that the bully enjoys seeing that he or she has upset you. While it is tempting to seek sympathy from coworkers, keep the issue confidential.
- Document dates, words, and witnesses of inappropriate behavior.
- Share your factual and documented information with your boss or human resource department, and file a formal complaint.
- If you think your company has not appropriately resolved the issue in a reasonable time and manner, seek outside assistance. This assistance can come from a union, a counselor or mental health professional, state or federal agency, or private attorney.

Know Your Rights

Each employee has a right to work in an environment free from harassment, discrimination, and hostility. Your boss and human resource department cannot assist you in resolving conflict if they are not aware of the issue. Share your concerns regarding harassment, discrimination, and workplace incivility immediately with your superiors. Prior to seeking outside assistance, exhaust all internal remedies (company resources that exist to take care of these issues). If you think you need outside assistance to preserve your rights, several state and federal resources are available to assist you. These include your state's Department of Fair Employment and Housing, the Federal Equal Employment Opportunity Commission, your State Personnel Board, the Department of Labor/Labor Commission, and the Department of Justice. These resources are available to act on your behalf and ensure you are being treated in a fair and nondiscriminatory manner.

Resolving Conflict at Work

Several steps should be taken when attempting to resolve a conflict at work. They are presented in figure 12-1. Whenever you are faced with a conflict, attempt to resolve the issue as quickly as possible. Too often, individuals ignore a problem and hope it will go away. Unfortunately, these unresolved molehills frequently grow into giant, unresolved mountains. If you choose to utilize an accommodating or avoiding conflict resolution style, accept your decision to not bring the conflict to the attention of the offender and move on without holding a grudge.

If the conflict is negatively affecting either yours or someone else's performance, inform your immediate supervisor. During this step, think like a boss and ask yourself if the matter is appropriate to be brought to the attention of a superior. You do not want to appear as a complainer. Document relevant information and conversations. If the problem continues and you are not satisfied

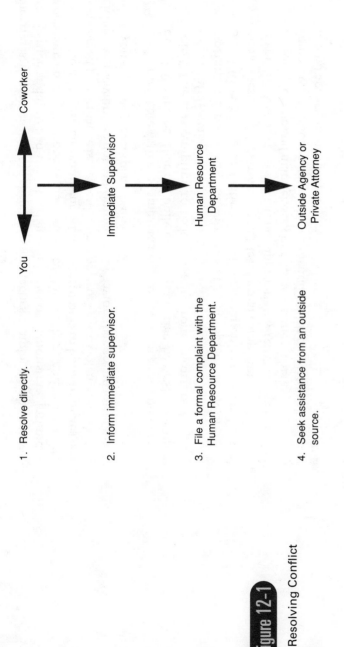

1. Resolve directly.

    You ⟷ Coworker

2. Inform immediate supervisor.

    Immediate Supervisor

3. File a formal complaint with the Human Resource Department.

    Human Resource Department

4. Seek assistance from an outside source.

    Outside Agency or Private Attorney

Figure 12-1

Resolving Conflict

with the way your immediate supervisor is handling the situation, contact the human resource management department. Members of this department will review existing policies and, if the situation warrants, they will conduct an investigation. If you are not fully satisfied with their decision or handling of the situation, you have the right to seek assistance from a private attorney or an outside government agency identified earlier in this chapter. Prior to seeking assistance from any outside agency, attempt to resolve the problem within your organization's structure. If you have representation from a union, involve the union as early in the process as possible.

Resolving a Conflict Under a Union Agreement

If you belong to a union and you have a conflict with your supervisor or any other member of management, refer to your union contract to identify what steps and rights are afforded you by being a union member. Each workplace represented by a union has a shop steward. The **shop steward** is a coworker who is very familiar with the union contract and procedures available to assist you in resolving a workplace conflict. A problem or conflict that occurs in a union setting is called a grievance. Go to your shop steward and share your concern, along with any documentation or evidence you may have. The shop steward will meet with you and your supervisor to attempt to resolve the issue. If the issue cannot be resolved at this level, a union representative will meet with the human resource management department. The issue will continue to work up the chain of command until it is resolved. This process is called a **grievance procedure.** If you are represented by a union, your union representatives will assist you in protecting your rights through the grievance process. However, the union's purpose is not to shield you from punishment if you are guilty of wrongdoing. The purpose of the union is to enforce the union contract.

Workplace Violence

Unresolved conflict has the potential to escalate into workplace violence. According to the U.S. Department of Labor, workplace violence is the third leading cause of workplace fatal injuries. Workplace violence includes any type of harassing or harming behavior (verbal or physical) that occurs in the workplace. This violence can come from coworkers, a boss, a customer, or a family member. It is vitally important that you recognize the warning signs and take appropriate precautions to decrease the probability that you become a victim.

If you are a victim of harassment, seek assistance and report unprofessional behavior to your boss or to the human resource department before the behavior escalates to violence. Personal issues can impact workplace performance as well. If you have a personal issue that you feel may negatively impact the workplace, share your concerns and seek confidential assistance from a coworker, your boss, or the human resource department as soon as possible. Some companies offer **employee assistance programs (EAP)**. This benefit typically provides free and confidential psychological, financial, and legal advice. An EAP benefit is generally extended to everyone who lives in your household. If you are experiencing a stressful situation at work or home, take advantage of this benefit. Even if your company does not offer an EAP, it may be able to help you identify an appropriate community resource.

Cory shares a cubicle with a woman who is newly married. She appeared to be happily married and had told Cory about the romantic dinners and gifts her new husband provided. One day, the woman showed up to work and kept to herself. Throughout the morning, Cory found it strange that she kept covering her face. Finally, as it neared lunch hour, Cory asked the woman if everything was okay. The woman looked up at Cory with a black eye and a bruised face and told Cory that she was leaving her husband. She went on to tell Cory that the husband had become increasingly jealous of any friendship the woman had with other men and had hit her the night before. Cory asked her if she felt safe. The woman responded, "No." Cory reminded the woman about the confidential and free EAP benefit their company offered. Cory then assisted her in getting an immediate appointment.

As exemplified in Cory's experience, stress at home can impact performance at work. Many times, victims of domestic violence fail to seek assistance out of embarrassment or fear. Your employer will want to assist you. If you feel your conflict (either at work or at home) does not warrant professional assistance, find a friend with whom you can confidentially and neutrally discuss the issue. Take responsibility at work to ensure a safe working environment. Do not be afraid to ask for an escort to and from your car if you are working nontraditional work hours or park your car in a remote location. Keep emergency phone numbers posted in a visible area next to your phone and know where all the emergency exits are located. Finally, report suspicious behavior or situations that have the potential to become violent. It is much better to be safe than sorry.

Agree to Disagree

As we learned in this chapter, conflict frequently cannot be avoided. In your efforts to work in harmony with coworkers, you will find that others may hurt you. As important as it is to apologize when we have harmed others, it is equally as important as it is to forgive. Too often, coworkers have apologized and the harmed individual has failed to forgive. Forgiving does not mean that you have forgotten the hurt. It does mean that you will give the individual another opportunity to prove his or her apology was sincere by a change in behavior.

A mature coworker is always willing to forgive and not hold grudges. Those who hold grudges never forgave in the first place and may be seeking a means of retaliation. Doing so demonstrates immaturity. You do not have to like all of your colleagues, but demonstrate professionalism and respect toward them. Conflict at work is inevitable. How you allow the conflict to affect your performance is your choice.

Exercise 12-4   Resolving Issues

Identify grudges you have held or people you need to forgive. Make a point of resolving one of those issues within the next week.

_____

_____

Workplace Dos and Don'ts

Do resolve a conflict as quickly as possible and at the lowest organizational level	*Don't* allow a small conflict to grow over time
Do utilize the appropriate conflict-management style	*Don't* demonstrate aggressive behavior when standing up for your rights
Do know your rights regarding sexual harassment and discrimination issues	*Don't* utilize offensive language or hostile behavior
Do document any activity that you feel may escalate into potential problems	*Don't* retaliate when a workplace bully behaves inappropriately
Do agree to disagree when a conflict cannot be resolved	*Don't* hold grudges or behave in an immature manner

Concept Review and Application

Summary of Key Concepts

- A natural element of working with others is conflict
- How you deal with conflict determines your maturity level and professionalism
- Depending on the offense and workplace situation, there are several methods of dealing with conflict
- Employees have a right to work in an environment free from harassment
- Immediately report any harassing behavior
- Attempt to resolve conflict at the lowest level, as soon as possible
- Recognize the warning signs and take appropriate precautions to decrease the probability that you become a victim of workplace violence
- It is considered immature to hold grudges. If you cannot resolve a conflict, sometimes it may be best to agree to disagree

Key Terms

accommodating conflict management style
assertive behavior
collaborating conflict management style
conflict
forcing conflict management style
hostile behavior harassment
negotiation
quid pro quo harassment
shop steward

aggressive behavior
avoiding conflict management style
compromising conflict management style
employee assistance program (EAP)
grievance procedure
mediator
passive behavior
sexual harassment
workplace bullies

If You Were the Boss

1. A fellow supervisor usually argues about an issue before arriving at a decision. Knowing this is typical of this person's behavior, how should you handle your next confrontation?
2. One of your employees tells you that another employee has been harassing him. What should you do?

Learn More

To learn more about subjects addressed in this chapter attend a workshop on workplace negotiation.

Video Case Study: Conflict

This video addresses workplace conflict during a brainstorming session. Refer to the CD that accompanies your text, watch this video, and answer the following questions:

1. If you were leading this meeting, how would you have handled Jane's behavior?

2. If you were a member of this team, would you have intervened in the conflict between Rachel and Jane? Why or why not?

3. What were the conflict management styles exhibited by each team member? What conflict style should have been exhibited by each team member?

Video Case Study: Sexual Harassment

This video addresses the topic of sexual harassment. Refer to the CD that accompanies your text, watch this video, and answer the following questions:

1. Was there anything inappropriate about Kenneth's comments to Rachel? If so, please be specific in which comments were inappropriate and explain why.

2. Did Rachel make any workplace-related mistakes to contribute to Kenneth's perception of her? If yes, please explain.

3. Did Rachel handle the conversation appropriately? Why or why not?

4. Based upon the conversation between Kenneth and Rachel, what should be Rachel's next steps? Be specific.

Web Links

http://www.cdc.gov/niosh/violcont.html
http://www.boston.com/jobs/galleries/workplaceconflict/
http://humanresources/about.com/cs/conflictresolves/a/conflictcourage.htm

References

Rahim, M. A., and Bonoma, T. V. "Managing Organizational Conflict: A Model for Diagnosis and Intervention." *Psychological Reports* 44 (1979): 1323–44.

State of California Department of Fair Employment and Housing. *The Facts about Sexual Harassment.* CADFEH-185 (04.04). Sacramento, CA, 2004.

U.S. Department of Labor Office of Labor-Management Standards within the Employment Standards Administration, Washington, DC www.dol.gov.

United States Equal Employment Opportunity Commission. Washington, DC www.eeoc.gov.

United States Occupational Safety and Health Administration. U.S. Department of Labor, Washington, DC. www.osha.gov.

Activity 12-1

Based on what you learned in this chapter, identify the proper way to deal with these poor boss behaviors.

Poor Management Quality	How to Deal With
1. Uses foul language	
2. Steals company property	
3. Tells you to lie	
4. Allows employees to harass other employees	
5. Takes all the credit for everyone else's work	

Activity 12-2

Name at least three specific steps you can take to decrease the probability of workplace violence occurring in your office.

1. _____

2. _____

3. _____

Activity 12-3

You need a new printer and have decided to approach your boss and negotiate for the new piece of equipment.

What key information should you prepare before your meeting?

_____

_____

What key points should you share during the meeting?

_____

Activity 12-4

Identify a time you felt you were harassed or had your rights violated.

Based on the information you learned in this chapter, what should you have done differently?

_____

_____

What outside resource could/should you have contacted?

_____

_____

Sample Exam Questions

1. _____ occurs when there is a disagreement or tension between two or more parties (individuals or groups).

2. Your goal when _____ is to create a win-win situation for all involved parties.

3. There are two types of sexual harassment: _____ and _____.

4. _____ harassment is when payback is expected for a sexual favor. It can also be construed as verbal, visual, or physical conduct of a sexual nature.

5. A/An _____ includes any behavior of a sexual nature by another employee that you find offensive. This may include verbal slurs, offensive photos, jokes, or any other offensive behavior of a sexual nature.

6. _____ seek ways to intimidate or belittle coworkers.

7. If you belong to a/an _____, refer to your _____ and you have a conflict with and rights are afforded you by being a union member.

8. _____ to identify what steps _____ when you have harmed others.

Job Search Skills

chapter **13**

Choose a job you love, and you will never have to work a day in your life.

Confucius

Objectives

- Utilize the *self-discovery* process to identify the right career

- Conduct a targeted job search and create a *job search portfolio*

- Ensure a professional *electronic image*

- Identify references to be used in your job search

- Identify sources for job leads

- Define *networking* and create a professional *networking list*

The Job Search

As with all business activities, success is in the planning, and any human resource professional will tell you that successful interviews start with solid preparation. This chapter is designed to help you create a job search strategy. A successful job search strategy identifies what type of job you will be looking for, what tools and resources you will need, and how these tools and resources are best used to secure an interview. The ultimate goal of a job search is to secure an interview which paves the way toward obtaining the job of your dreams.

Deciding on the Right Career

Deciding on the right career involves **self-discovery**. Self-discovery is the process of identifying key interests and skills built upon the career goals you set in chapter 2. Knowing your key selling points and linking these with your career goals will assist you in landing a job that you will enjoy. The process of a career self-discovery includes identifying key interests and accomplishments from your work, educational, and personal experiences. A method for identifying key interests is creating an accomplishments worksheet. This is done by inventorying skills you have acquired from either your work or nonwork experience. Education and nonwork experience such as volunteerism are career-building experiences. The following trigger words assist you in identifying accomplishments:

Trigger Words

Adapted	Developed	Motivated
Addressed	Earned	Organized
Analyzed	Established	Planned
Arranged	Financed	Projected
Assisted	Implemented	Recommended
Built	Increased	Risked
Calculated	Instructed	Saved
Chaired	Installed	Staffed
Cleaned	Introduced	Taught
Coached	Investigated	Typed
Communicated	Learned	Updated
Coordinated	Located	Won
Created	Managed	Wrote
Determined		

Your accomplishments will be used to identify the right career, and they will also provide an excellent foundation when you begin to build your resumé.

After you have completed your accomplishments worksheet, reread your responses. They will most likely reveal a targeted career of interest to you.

Talk It Out

Review your completed accomplishments worksheet. What career area do you believe suits your skills and previous experiences?

Exercise 13-1 Complete the Following Accomplishments Worksheet

Prior to answering each question, review the trigger words. Whenever possible, quantify your answers by documenting how many, how often, and how much. Do not worry if you cannot answer every question. The purpose of this exercise is to begin identifying accomplishments.

Question	Your Response Quantify Your Answers
1. What have you done in your career or career-building activities that you are most proud of?	
2. List something that you have achieved at work or school.	
3. What tasks have you performed at work and in career-building activities?	
4. What results have you produced from the tasks performed?	
5. List three things that demonstrate your ability to produce results.	
6. What have you done that shows an ability to successfully work with people?	
7. What else have you accomplished professionally or educationally that makes you proud?	
8. What extracurricular activities have you been involved with?	
9. List special skills or foreign languages you speak or write?	
10. What areas of interest do you have?	

Web Quiz

Take the following quiz "Career Planner Quiz" to get a snapshot of your target job.

http://careerpath.com/career-tests/?lr=cbmsn&siteid=cbmsnchcpath

A second means of identifying key skills and career areas of interest is by taking a career assessment. Common career assessment tools include the Myers-Briggs Type Indicator, the Golden Personality Type Indicator, and the Strong Interest Inventory. Many college career centers offer this assessment, as do various online sources.

Career Objective and Personal Profile

A foundation for both your job search strategy and building a winning resumé is to write a career objective or personal profile. A **career objective** is an introductory written statement for individuals with little or no work experience. A **personal profile** is an introductory written statement for individuals with professional experience related to their target career. These statements are used on a resumé to relate to the target career and/or employer; briefly introduce key skills, and express interest in a position. The responses from your completed accomplishments worksheet and career assessment provide a good summary of your current career goal based upon the knowledge, skills, and abilities you possess. Use this information as a foundation to create a statement that briefly and professionally describes you and your career goals. Depending on the layout of your resumé, this information will either have the heading Career Objective or Personal Profile. This statement will be the first item listed on your resumé.

As mentioned earlier, a career objective is an introductory written statement for individuals with little or no work experience. This is a brief statement which will include your interest in a specific position, a brief one-line description of your skills related to the position, and how you will utilize your skills. The career objective is the only place on a resumé where it is acceptable to use the words "I" and "my."

Examples of Career Objectives

Objective: Seeking a position with an established accounting firm where I can utilize and apply my current accounting and computerized skills toward the excellence of Bell Company.

Objective: To obtain an Account Clerk position at Bell Company where I can demonstrate and increase my general accounting skills to contribute to the success of the company.

Those with extensive work experience will utilize a personal profile. In creating a personal profile, review your key skills and accomplishments and group these items into general categories. Also identify key qualities that you possess that are required for your target job. Take this information and turn it into a two- to three-sentence statement that provides a snapshot of your professional qualifications in a manner that sells your knowledge, skills, and abilities.

An Example of a Personal Profile

Personal Profile: Highly professional and detail-oriented accounting professional with demonstrated leadership and success in the areas of payroll, collections, and project management. Excellent analytical, communication, computer, and organizational skills. Bilingual (English/Spanish).

Industry Research

A step toward a successful job search is research. When a job fits your personality and skills, you will more likely succeed. Success comes from working at a company and doing a job that you enjoy. In chapter 2 you created goals for your career and personal life. Conducting industry research will reinforce that you have made the right career decision. In order to determine what type of industry to research, identify industries that require your key skills. You may realize there is more potential for jobs that require your key skills than you thought.

Once you have identified the industries fitted to your skills, begin identifying specific jobs in these industries. Note the different job opportunities that exist. In addition, look at various job titles. Being aware of the different job titles you qualify for allows you more flexibility when job searching. After determining industries and job titles that fit your skills, identify the various environments available including where the jobs are located and specifically what type of environment you want to work in.

For example, if you finished college with a business degree, you begin by conducting industry research on the skills you have acquired. Many different industries need employees with a business background, such as health care, educational institutions, and marketing. Once you have determined which industry or industries you want to work for, you can then start looking at the job titles that fit the skills you have acquired in college, such as Financial Analyst, General Accountant, Marketing Assistant, or Human Resources Generalist. After identifying job titles, decide what type of environment you may want to work in. If you select health care, you may have the choice of working in a hospital, a surgery center, or a doctor's office.

By conducting this research you will provide yourself with the tools that will make your job search easier and more successful. Instead of sending out hundreds of resumés in hopes of getting any job, target the companies that are a good match with you, your skills, and your desired work environment.

The Targeted Job Search

After you have identified jobs that suit your personal and career goals and have a clearly defined career objective, it is time to begin a targeted job search. A targeted job search leads you through the process of discovering open positions for which you are qualified in addition to identifying companies for which you would like to work.

Part of a job search is to determine in what city you want to work. If your job search is limited to your local area, you will be restricted to employers in your community. If you are willing to commute outside of your area, determine how far you are willing to commute (both directions) on a daily basis. If you wish to move out of the area, identify what locations are most appealing.

Exercise 13-2   Identify Target Employers

Identify three companies/employers in your target location that may be of interest to you.

1.

2.

3.

Preparation

When you embark on a job search your personal life may be exposed in the job search process. Ensuring you have a favorable **electronic image** is important. An electronic image is the image formed when someone is communicating and/or researching you through electronic means. This includes conducting an Internet search on you through personal pages and search engines. Since the majority of information on the Internet is public information, an increasing number of employers are conducting web searches on potential employees to gain a better perspective of the applicant's values and lifestyle. With today's overabundance of electronic social networking and information sites, be aware that defamatory photos, writings, or other material not be a barrier in your job search. Conduct an Internet search on yourself and remove any information that portrays you in a negative light. If you are actively involved in social networking sites, carefully evaluate any personal information that is contained on the sites of your friends. If negative information is contained on sites of your friends, explain your job search plans and politely ask them to remove the potentially harmful information.

An additional move toward ensuring a clean electronic image is to maintain a professional e-mail address. Sending a potential employer an e-mail from the address "prty2nite" is not the image you want to project. If necessary, establish a new e-mail address that utilizes some form of your name or initials to maintain a clean and professional electronic image. Two final considerations in maintaining a professional electronic image are, as mentioned in the communication chapter, the maintenance of a professional voice mail message and the avoidance of text slang in all written communication. Your job search strategy will involve extensive communication with employers and other individuals who will assist you with your job search. Interaction with these individuals needs to be professional.

Job Search Portfolio

A **job search portfolio** is a collection of paperwork used for job searches and interviews. You will use the items you collect for your portfolio to keep organized and prepared while job searching.

It is best to have a binder with tabs to keep this paperwork organized and protected. Do not punch holes in original documents. Place original documents in plastic notebook protectors. When you begin collecting items for your portfolio, keep your original and at least two copies of each item available at all times. The copies are used for interviews.

Items in your job search portfolio assist you in your job search and interview process. You will not necessarily take all of the items from your job search portfolio with you to each job interview. You will create an **interview portfolio** to take with you to an interview. An interview portfolio and its purpose will be discussed in chapter 15.

A useful networking and introduction tool is the use of a personal business card. A personal business card is a small card that contains contact information including your name, mailing and e-mail addresses, and phone number. It is a good practice to share a personal business card with anyone you meet. Doing so makes it easier for your new acquaintance to remember and contact you in the future. Personal business cards are inexpensive and valuable networking tools and need not be professionally printed. Templates are available on the web and can easily be printed on cardstock paper or you can purchase special business card packages at an office supply store. When designing a personal business card, ensure it contains all relevant contact information and that it reflects a professional and clean image. Use an easy-to-read font style. Do not include fancy graphics and too many words. Simple is better.

The following is a list of items to keep in your job search portfolio. These items and their purpose will be discussed in this and the next two chapters.

Talk It Out

What type of photos, writings, or materials do you think are inappropriate for a potential employer to see?

Item	Description
Network list	A list of professional relationships used for job contacts
Personal business cards	Cards with personal contact information used to share for job leads
Resumé	A formal profile that is presented to potential employers
Cover letter	Introduces a resumé
Reference list	A list of individuals who will provide a professional reference
Letters of recommendation	A written professional reference to verify work experience and character
Transcripts	Documents that verify education. Have both official (sealed) and copies available. Sealed transcripts may be required
State licenses	Documents that verify the ability to practice certain professions
Awards, certificates, work samples	Documents that demonstrate proficiency in specific skills that are shared with an employer during an interview
Completed generic application	Generic job application that makes information readily available
Copy of ID and/or driver's license	A valid ID and proof of ability to drive (if driving is a job requirement)
Personal commercial	Statement that assists with interview
Small calendar, note pad, pen	To track important dates and make notes
Performance appraisals from previous jobs	Proof of positive work performance

Employment Applications

Have a completed generic application in your job search portfolio so that when you are asked to complete an application you will have the information readily available. Complete the application in its entirety, but do not list your Social Security number or birth date. This information is not given to a prospective employer until you are a finalist for the job.

An employment application is a legal document. When completing the application, read the fine print prior to signing the application. Commonly, at the end of the application, there will be a statement that grants the potential employer permission to conduct reference checks and various background checks including a credit check if a credit check is relevant to the job for which you are applying. You need to fully understand why this background information is necessary and how it will be used in the hiring process. If you do not fully understand the statements on the application, clarify these statements prior to signing the application.

It is common for employers to request that the applicant complete an employment application and submit this document along with the resumé package. If you only submitted a cover letter and resumé, you may be asked to complete an application after you have been interviewed. A typed employment application is best. Many employers provide downloadable applications online. If this is not possible, complete the application by printing neatly in black ink.

Personal References and Recommendations

Create a list of professional references that a potential employer can contact to verify your work experience and personal character. References are not to be included on your resumé. Create a separate page for references. Do not send your reference list with your resumé unless it is requested by the employer. However, have a copy available to share during your interview in case the employer requests references during the interview. Prior to including individuals on your reference list, ask each person if he or she is willing to serve as a reference. Be sure each person on this list will provide a positive reference. Have at least three names to submit as references. Include each reference's name, contact phone number, mailing address, relationship, and e-mail address. References can be past or present employers and supervisors, coworkers, instructors, or someone with whom you have volunteered. Do not use relatives, friends, or religious leaders unless you have worked or volunteered with or for them.

In addition to reputable references, it is wise to have at least three **letters of recommendation.** A letter of recommendation is a written testimony from another person that states that you are credible. Letters of recommendation need to reflect current job skills, accomplishments, and positive human relations skills and should be no older than one year. Letters of recommendation can be from past or present employers, coworkers, instructors, or someone you worked for as a volunteer. It is common and acceptable to have someone write a formal letter of recommendation and serve as a personal reference.

In addition to routinely updating your resumé, keep updating your reference list. Provide references who are relevant to your career. Occasionally check with your references and verify if they are still willing to serve as references. Keep these individuals current on your job search status and career goals.

Exercise 13-3   List Your References

List three people you can use as references. Then list three people you can ask to write you a letter of recommendation. Include their relationship to you.

References

	Relationship
1.	
2.	
3.	

Letter of Recommendation

	Relationship
1.	
2.	
3.	

Sources of Job Leads

There are many sources for job leads. The first and most obvious job lead is directly from your targeted company. Information regarding open positions within your targeted company can be obtained from the company web site or from visiting the company's human resource department. This is where you will find a list of open positions. If you do not have a targeted company but have an area where you would like to work, conduct an Internet search using the targeted city and target position as key search words. Check online message boards and popular job search sites such as monster.com, CareerBuilder.com, and hotjobs.com. Many larger cities and counties offer one-stop centers for job seekers. These government-funded agencies provide job seeker assistance and serve as a link between job seekers and local employers. Other job sources include job fairs, newspaper advertisements, industry journals, industry associations, and current employees who work in your targeted industry and/or company. Most individuals rely on posted job positions. However, many jobs are unsolicited (not made public). The way to become aware of these unsolicited jobs is to use your professional network. Inform network members of your desire for a job and ask for potential job leads.

In situations where you will be distributing your resumé, meeting a potential network contact, or visiting a company to identify open positions, treat the job search situation as if you are going to an interview. Dress professionally, have extra copies of your resumé, display confidence, and bring your interview portfolio. The interview portfolio will be discussed in detail in chapter 15. In networking situations where there are many job seekers, such as a job fair, be polite and professional in your interactions with everyone. Do not interrupt or be rude to other job seekers. Take the lead in introducing yourself to company representatives. Sell your skills and ask the company representative if he or she has an open position where your skills can assist the company. Your goal in such a situation is to stand out from the rest of the crowd, share your resumé, and arrange an interview. In situations where you are collecting and/or completing applications apply these same professional behaviors.

If you are unable to find a job lead, send an unsolicited cover letter and resumé to your target company. When sending an unsolicited resumé, send two copies: one to the human resource manager and the other to the manager of your target job. Prior to sending your resumé, call the company to secure the names of both individuals. Ensure you have identified the correct spelling and gender for the individuals to whom you will be sending your resumé. Sending two resumés to the same company increases the opportunity of securing an interview. The targeted department manager will most likely read and file your resumé for future reference. The human resource manager will also review your resumé and may identify other jobs for which you are qualified.

Networking

Throughout this text you have learned how to be successful in the workplace. The importance of maintaining a positive attitude throughout your career cannot be stressed enough. This holds true during your job search.

During the time you will be looking for a job or advanced position, establishing a professional network and maintaining this network throughout your career is important. **Networking** is the act of creating professional relationships. Think of networking as a connection device.

Professional networking is necessary throughout a job search. Developing a professional network is easy. You tell one person that you are looking for a job. That person tells others, then those people tell others, and soon you have many people who know that you are looking for a job. View figure 13–1 to see how a network grows.

Almost every person you know may be a part of your network, including the following individuals:

- Coworkers
- Supervisors
- Instructors
- Family
- Friends

Cory has been working as an account clerk for a year. Throughout the year, Cory has acquired new accounting skills, learned new software packages, and has graduated with an accounting degree. Now is the time to begin networking. Cory begins by telling supervisors and coworkers what skills and education have been acquired. In addition, Cory mentions the new skills and software packages learned over the last year and shares future goals. Cory then tells family members and friends the same information. This is the beginning of Cory's professional network. Cory creates a database of people on the network list and begins tracking and updating these people. Cory will continue to update the people on the network list about new skills acquired and job search progress.

Exchange personal business cards with your network contacts and use the information on their business card to update your network list. In addition to adding people you know to your network list, use other methods to expand your network such as volunteering for community organizations. Volunteering provides a chance to meet people in different organizations and learn about new positions throughout the community. Join clubs and professional organizations. Attend workshops, conferences, and seminars to meet people from corporations that are in your targeted career field. Another great method to grow your professional network is for you to

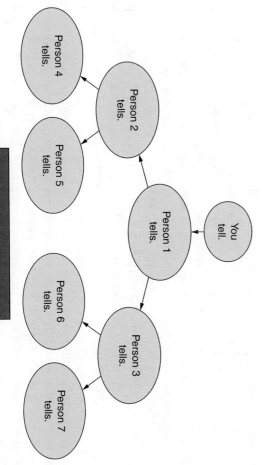

You tell.

Person 1 tells.

Person 2 tells.

Person 3 tells.

Person 4 tells.

Person 5 tells.

Person 6 tells.

Person 7 tells.

And this networking continues.

Figure 13-1

Networking

conduct **informational interviews.** An informational interview is when a job seeker meets with a business professional to learn about a specific career, company, or industry. You are not asking for a job during an informational interview. You are only expanding your professional network. During an informational interview, ask the business professional questions about targeted careers, hiring, and the culture of the company. By meeting and talking with business professionals, you have added to your professional network. When you network, ask those with whom you network for additional contacts who may be able to assist you.

Networking is done in many ways such as when you:

- Attend professional or trade association meetings
- Talk to other parents when attending a child's sporting or music event
- Volunteer for community service
- Visit with other members of social clubs or religious groups
- Talk with neighbors
- Strike up a conversation with a stranger while waiting in line in public places
- Post messages on online discussion boards, chat rooms, and/or social networking sites
- Talk to salespeople and/or vendors in the workplace

Exercise 13-4   Identify Your Current Network

Name at least three places where you have met people who could be on your professional network list.

1. _____

2. _____

3. _____

Once you have established a professional network, maintain that network. Stay in touch with the people on your network list by routinely updating them with your career growth and plans. Keep track of who is included in your network and note the last time you provided those on your network updated information on your job search. A **network list** is a written list of all network contact's names, mailing addresses, phone numbers, and e-mail addresses so you can easily contact each person for quick reference. Provide each contact who is actively assisting with your job search a copy of your most current resumé. Keep all contacts on your network list updated throughout your job search. When keeping in contact with members of your network, be sensitive to their time. Do not annoy or be inconsiderate in your interactions with individuals in your network.

Another element of professional networking is to know how to meet and greet others. This is done by initiating a conversation. Start the conversation with a simple introduction. For example, "Hello, my name is Diane Patty. I work in production. I don't believe we've ever met." When introducing yourself, extend your hand and practice the art of a good handshake. This important social skill was addressed in chapter 6. As the person is telling you his or her name, listen to the name and make a mental note to remember the name. An excellent way to remember someone's name is to repeat it immediately after it is shared. Try to relate that person's name to someone else who shares the same name. For example, "It's nice to meet you, Carol. When I was growing up, I had a neighbor named Carol." This will make it easier for you to remember the name in the future and will also increase your personal workplace power as explained in chapter 5.

Protecting Your Privacy

The job search process involves sharing personal information. Be cautious and only share personal information with reputable sources or you may become a target for identity theft. If you are applying for a job and have never heard of the employer, conduct research to verify that the employer is legitimate. Do not share your birth date or Social Security number with any employer until after you are a finalist for the job.

Cory's friend, Connor, was looking for a job. Connor found a job on an online classified job site that sounded legitimate. The employer asked that Connor submit a resumé online. Within a few days after sharing his resumé, Connor received an e-mail telling him that he was a finalist for the job. The only step left in the process was for Connor to forward a copy of his credit report. Although Connor was desperate for a job, he thought this was a little strange, so he asked Cory what Cory thought of the situation. Cory conducted an Internet search for Connor and could not find any evidence that the company Connor was applying to even existed. Cory asked Connor if he completed an application that gave the potential employer permission to view Connor's credit information and Connor said no. Cory and Connor agreed that sharing personal information with an unknown company was not a good idea.

Keeping the Right Attitude

The job search process is a lot of work and can sometimes be frustrating. Do not get discouraged if you do not get an interview or job offer on your first try. In tight job markets, it may take many interviews before receiving a job offer. To maintain a healthy attitude during this time of transition, follow these tips when looking for a job:

1. *Stay positive:* Start each day with a positive affirmation. Speaking aloud, tell yourself that you are a talented and great person who deserves a good job (and believe what you say). Your attitude is reflected in your actions. If you allow negative elements to influence your job search, you will be at a disadvantage.

2. *Stay active:* Create a daily and weekly "to do" list. Every day, check the web sites of your targeted industries and companies in addition to checking relevant job sites. Schedule time for industry and company research as well as time for networking. A job search is a job in itself. You do not want to be an unproductive employee in the workplace, so begin creating good work habits now by making the most of your time in a job search.

3. *Keep learning:* Use job search down time to learn or develop a skill. As with your routine industry and company research and daily review of targeted job postings, schedule learning time. Identify a skill that will assist you when you are offered a job. Finances do not have to be a barrier to learning new skills. There are many free tutorials available on the Internet. Topics to consider include computer skills, writing skills, or any skill specific to your chosen industry.

4. *Stay connected:* Although it is natural to not want to socialize with others when discouraged, the job search period is the time that you most need to be in the presence of others. In addition to keeping your current network updated on your job search, identify

additional methods of expanding your network. Attend association meetings and events, volunteer, and schedule informational interviews. Plan at least one meeting and/or activity each day. As opposed to sitting around the house waiting for the phone to ring, dressing professionally and networking every day will contribute to maintaining a positive outlook.

5. *Stay focused:* During a job search, manage your professional job search, your personal health, and your environment. Manage your professional job search by maintaining an up-to-date calendar with scheduled follow-up activities relating to your job search. Because a job search is a stressful experience, practice healthy stress management techniques including a proper diet, regular exercise, and positive self-talk. Invest a portion of your time in something of interest other than your job search. Consider volunteering for an organization of special interest to you. Doing so will provide a mental break, provide possible new network contacts, and provide you the satisfaction of helping others. Managing your personal environment includes the proper management of your finances. Be cautious and conservative with your money. Make thoughtful purchases and avoid stress spending. Finally, surround yourself with individuals who are positive and supportive of you and your efforts.

If you are currently working and you begin looking for a job, keep your job search confidential. If you are listing your supervisor as a reference, let him or her know you are looking for a new job and briefly explain why. Do not quit your current job before accepting a new job. Also, do not bad-mouth your company or anyone that works for your current or former employer(s).

Workplace Dos and Don'ts

Do keep your original job search documents in a portfolio	*Don't* give employers your original documents and expect them to be returned to you
Do keep a network list and keep the people on your list updated	*Don't* be annoying or inconsiderate of your network contacts' time
Do realize that a targeted job search takes time	*Don't* get discouraged if you do not get an interview or job offer on your first try
Do explore various sources of job leads including your personal network, the Internet, and industry journals	*Don't* limit your job leads to one source

Summary of Key Concepts

- The career objective or personal profile is a brief statement that sells your key skills and relates to your self-discovery
- A targeted job search leads you through the process of identifying open positions for which you are qualified in addition to identifying companies for which you would like to work
- Ensure you have a professional electronic image while job searching
- Professional networking is the act of creating professional relationships
- In addition to people you already know, develop additional network contacts through various sources of job leads
- Creating and maintaining a job search portfolio will keep you organized and prepared during the job search process
- Create a list of professional references for employers

Key Terms

career objective	electronic image
informational interviews	interview portfolio
job search portfolio	letters of recommendation
network list	networking
personal profile	self-discovery

If You Were the Boss

1. What information would you supply to a job seeker during an informational interview with you?

2. If you discovered that one of your top interview candidates had an un-professional web site, what would you do?

Video Case Study: Job Fair

This video addresses inappropriate and appropriate behavior when participating in a job fair. Refer to the CD that accompanies your text, watch this video, and answer the following questions:

1. What inappropriate behaviors did Kevin exhibit at the job fair?
   Be specific in your answer.

2. What inappropriate behaviors did Sean exhibit at the job fair?
   Be specific in your answer.

3. What appropriate behaviors did Rachel exhibit at the job fair?
   Be specific in your answer.

4. Did Rachel close her interview appropriately? Why or why not?

Video Case Study: Job Search Strategies

This video presents expert advice on how to conduct a professional job search. Refer to the CD that accompanies your text, watch this video, and answer the following questions.

1. What are important considerations and activities that should take place during the research phase of a job search?
2. What is a network and how do you create it?
3. What specific advice does the expert provide regarding cold call applications?

Web Links

http://www.rileyguide.com/network.html#netprep
http://jobsearch.about.com/od/networking
http://www.truecareers.com
http://www.weddles.com/associations/index.cfm
http://money.cnn.com/magazines/fortune/rankings/
http://www.glassdoor.com/index.htm

Reference

Keirsey, David. *Please Understand Me II: Temperament, Character, Intelligence.* Del Mar, CA: Prometheus Nemesis Book Company, (1998).

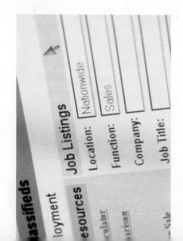

Activity 13-1

Create a reference list with at least three names; include the following information.

Reference 1

Name

Job title

Place of employment

Address

Telephone number

E-mail address

Relationship (why is he or she a reference?)

Reference 2

Name

Job title

Place of employment

Address

Telephone number

E-mail address

Relationship (why is he or she a reference?)

Reference 3

Name

Job title

Place of employment

Address

Telephone number

E-mail address

Relationship (why is he or she a reference?)

Activity 13-2

Using the following network table to create a networking list. At a minimum, include each contact's name, address, phone number, and e-mail address.

NETWORK TABLE

Network List				
Name	Address	Phone No.	E-Mail Address	Last Date of Contact

Activity 13-3

Using an Internet job site or other job sources, identify three specific industry job leads that match your career goals and current qualifications.

Industry	Job Titles	Environment
1.		
2.		
3.		

Activity 13-4

Design a personal business card.

┌─────────────────────────────┐
│   │
│   │
│   │
│   │
│   │
│   │
└─────────────────────────────┘

Activity 13-5

Secure a job application online or from a local employer. With the exception of your signature, complete the application. Include this document in your job search portfolio.

Sample Exam Questions

1. The act of creating professional relationships is referred to as _____.

2. The following people could be included in a professional network: _____, _____, and _____.

3. One of the most obvious job sources is utilizing your _____.

4. Keep your phone message _____.

5. The process of identifying your key interests and skills built upon career goals is known as _____.

6. The _____ or _____ is an introductory written statement at the beginning of a resumé.

7. A _____ is an image formed when someone is researching you through a computer search.

8. An employment application is a _____.

Resumé Package

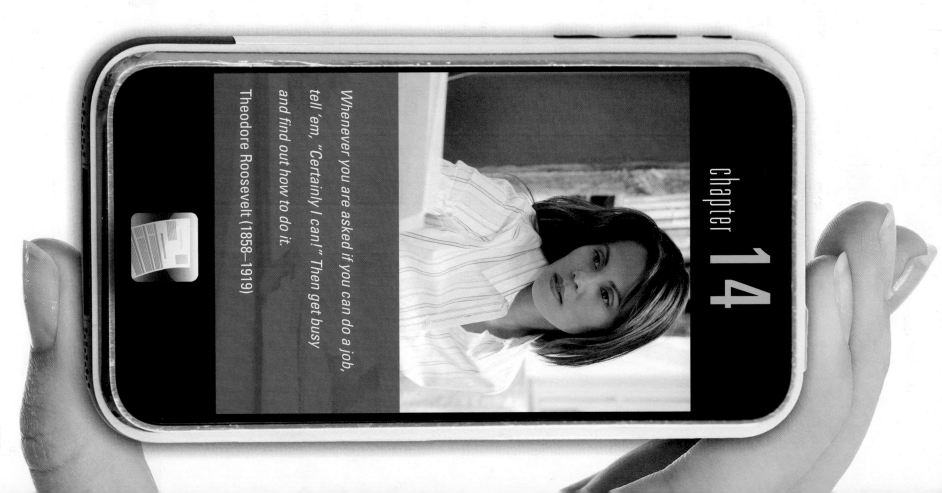

Whenever you are asked if you can do a job, tell 'em, "Certainly I can!" Then get busy and find out how to do it.

Theodore Roosevelt (1858–1919)

Objectives

- Identify the steps for building a resumé

- Write a career objective or personal profile

- Distinguish between a functional resumé and a chronological resumé

- Identify job-specific skills and transferable skills

- Create a winning resumé

- Create a cover letter

Building Your Resumé

An important tool in your job search is your resumé. A **resumé** is a formal written profile that presents a person's knowledge, skills, and abilities to potential employers. Throughout your career continually update your resumé. You may not be planning to find a new job or get promoted today, but a time will come when a current resumé is needed. Do not wait until that time to create or update your resumé. As you increase your job skills and accomplishments, add these new skills and experiences to your resumé.

When you begin to create your resumé, you will quickly discover that there are various types of resumés and resumé formats. You may also receive conflicting advice as to how the perfect resumé should look and what it should include. The appropriate type of resumé used will depend on your work experience. A well-written resumé makes it easy for potential employers to quickly and easily identify your skills and work experience. The following information walks you through five steps to building a winning resumé:

- *Step One:* Career Objective/Personal Profile
- *Step Two:* Gathering Information
- *Step Three:* Proper Layout
- *Step Four:* Skills, Accomplishments, and Experience
- *Step Five:* The Final Resumé

As you construct your resumé, make every word, visual presentation, and information sell your skills and career accomplishments.

Step One: Career Objective/Personal Profile

The first step in developing a winning resumé is to write a career objective or personal profile. As presented in the previous chapter, a career objective is a statement that presents your key skills in a brief statement for individuals with little or no work experience. A personal profile is used for individuals with more extensive career experience. Create a career objective or personal profile using the information from chapter 13. Use your career objective or personal profile as the foundation for your resumé. Make your career objective or personal profile specific to the job for which you are applying.

Exercise 14-1   Your Career Objective or Personal Profile

Write a career objective or personal profile.

_____

_____

_____

Step Two: Gathering Information

The second step in building a resumé is to create a draft document with key headings. This step involves collecting and merging all relevant information into one document. Begin identifying and listing the following information into an electronic document:

1. *Education.* List schools, dates, degrees, certificates, credentials, GPA, licenses, etc., including military experience.
2. *Skills.* List all skills you possess.
3. *Employment.* Starting with the most recent job, list the employer, dates of employment (month and year), job title, and responsibilities.
4. *Languages.* List all foreign languages, fluency levels, and if you can read, speak, and/or write the foreign language.
5. *Honors and Awards.* List any honors and awards you have received.
6. *Professional/Community Involvement.* Include volunteer work and community service projects. Include any leadership role you took in these activities.

Exercise 14-2   Gather Information

Complete the following table:

	Education (list most recent first)			
School Name	City, State	Dates	Degree, Certificate, Credential, Licenses,	GPA

Skills		

Exercise 14-2   Gather Information (Continued)

Employment (list most recent first)

Employer	Employment Dates	Job Title	Duties

Languages

Fluency (Read, Write, and/or Speak)

Honors and Awards

Dates	Place

Professional/Community Involvement

Step Three: Proper Layout

The third step in developing a successful resumé is to identify and arrange your information in the proper resumé layout. If you are at the start of your career and/or do not have extensive work experience, create a resumé using the **functional resumé layout**. This layout is used to emphasize relevant skills when you lack related work experience. A functional resumé focuses on skills and education. When writing a functional resumé list your career objective, relevant skills, and education before any work experience. Only include your high school in the education section if you are using a functional layout and have not graduated from college. Most functional resumés are only one page in length. Refer to figure 14-1 for the functional resumé layout and see figures 14-2 and 14-3 for examples of a functional resumé with and without career related work experience. Additional career specific examples are available on the author's website.

Those with extensive career experience should use a **chronological resumé layout**. In the chronological layout, note that the Career Objective is replaced with a Personal Profile. General skills emphasized in a personal profile are key skill sets. These skill sets will be used as subheadings in the Professional Experience section on a chronological resumé. The chronological layout presents related work experience, skills, and significant accomplishments under each respective skill set subheading. When writing a personal profile, include key general skills and key qualities desired by your target employer. Specific skills will be detailed under each respective Professional Experience subheading. Share major accomplishments and responsibilities from each position. Include important activities you have accomplished in your job. If necessary, add a second page to your resumé. A chronological layout best highlights, communicates, and sells specific job skills and work accomplishments. Refer to figure 14-4 for the chronological resumé layout and see figures 14-5 and 14-6 for examples of chronological resumés.

For both functional and chronological resumé layouts, present employment history and education in reverse time order (most recent job first). When listing work history, bold your job title, not the place of employment. When listing dates of employment, use only month and year. Be consistent in how dates are listed on the resumé.

When you have determined which resumé layout is best for your current situation, electronically arrange the information you have compiled into the correct resumé layout. Avoid resumé templates. Resumé templates can be difficult to update, modify and personalize.

Step Four: Skills, Accomplishments, and Experience

Once you have electronically arranged your information into the correct layout, it is time to move to the fourth step in developing your resumé. This involves detailing the information listed in your skills, work experience, and professional accomplishments. Work experience includes the learned skills, job duties, and accomplishments. Professional accomplishments communicate specific activities you achieved beyond your job duties. Whenever possible, quantify your skills, responsibilities, and professional accomplishments. Do not assume the reader will know what you have done. As you insert professional accomplishments into your electronic file, include both job-specific skills and transferable skills. **Job-specific skills** are those that are directly related to a specific job or industry. If you were to leave that job and change careers, job-specific skills would probably not be useful. For example, if you are a medical billing clerk who knows how to use a specific software program such as Medical Manager, you will not need to use this skill if you become a preschool teacher.

Transferable skills are skills that are transferred from one job to the next. If you change careers, you will still be able to use (transfer) these skills in any job. For example, if you are a medical billing clerk, you may have learned customer

Functional Resumé Layout
See Figure 14-1 on page 218.

Functional Resumé Example with Minimal Career Work Experience
See Figure 14-2 on page 219.

Function Resumé Example without Career Work Experience
See Figure 14-3 on page 220.

Talk It Out

Which resumé layout is best for your situation? Why?

Chronological Resumé Layout
See Figure 14-4 on page 221.

Chronological Resumé Example with Degree
See Figure 14-5 on pages 222–223.

Chronological Resumé Example with No Degree
See Figure 14-6 on pages 224–225.

service skills from consistent contact with patients and must practice being positive when dealing with customers. If you become a preschool teacher, the customer service skill of being positive is transferable to the children in your classroom. Employers need employees with job-specific skills and transferable skills. List both job-specific and transferable skills on your resumé. The term **soft skills** refer to the people skills necessary when working with others in the workplace. Employers want employees that are reliable, team players, good communicators, and able to get along well with others.

When listing workplace experiences on your resumé, include the job title, company name, city, and state where the company is located, and the duties of the position. When listing job duties, be specific with common workplace skills, such as computer skills. The term *computer skills* can be too general and typically includes many different areas: networking, programming, applications, data processing, and/or repair. An employer needs to know what specific computer skills you possess. For example, inform the employer of your computer skill level (e.g., basic, intermediate, or advanced) with a specific software. When listing your skills, list the skills relevant to your target job first. If you are bilingual (speak or write a second language), include this information in your resumé. Let the employer know if you read, write, or only speak that language.

Resumés do not normally contain complete sentences. They contain statements that sell your skills, qualifications, and work experience. Except for the career objective on a functional resumé the words *I* and *my* should not appear.

Exercise 14-3   Detail Your Skills

List as many as possible of your job-specific skills and your transferable skills. If you do not have any job-specific skills, list the job skills you will have after finishing your schooling.

Job-Specific Skills (Related to Your Career Job)	Transferable Skills (Can Be Used in Any Job)
1.	1.
2.	2.
3.	3.
4.	4.
5.	5.

When applying for a specific position, identify the key required knowledge, skills, and abilities the employer desires. General information will be listed in the job announcement. If possible, secure a copy of the job description. If this is not possible, conduct an occupational quick search on the O'Net database. This database of occupational information was developed for the U.S. Department of Labor and provides key information by job title. Identify key skills required by employers and emphasize these required skills on your resumé.

Organize your skills and work experience by first listing the key skills required for your target job. When communicating your skills, experience, and accomplishments, write with energy. Use action verbs, also referred to as **power words**. Power words are action verbs that describe your accomplishments in a lively and specific way. For example, instead of stating "started a new accounts receivable system," use "developed a new accounts receivable system that reduced turnaround time by 20 percent." Power words are listed in table 14-1 and table 14-2.

Exercise 14-4   Accomplishments

Refer back to the accomplishments worksheet you completed in exercise 13-1. Review these accomplishments and turn them into powerful action statements. Quantify whenever possible.

Choose Your Top Five Accomplishments from Exercise 13-1	Change to Powerful Action Statements
1.	
2.	
3.	
4.	
5.	

Table 14-1   Skills Power Words

Power Words for Skills Section

- Ideal oral and written communications skills
- Understanding of office practices and procedures; ability to operate fax machine, copy machine, and ten-key machine; ability to enter data; ability to effectively interpret policies and procedures; work well under the pressure of deadlines; establish and maintain a positive working relationship with others; ability to communicate
- Accurate typing skills at _____ wpm
- Experienced with Microsoft Office, including Word, Excel, Access, PowerPoint, and Outlook
- Excellent English grammar, spelling, and punctuation skills
- Accurately proofread and edit documents
- Strong attention to detail
- Accurately follow oral and written instructions
- Excellent attendance and punctual record
- Maintain confidentiality
- Positive attitude, motivated, and organized

Table 14-2   Experience Power Words

Power Words for Work Experience

- Prepared reports and other materials requiring independent achievement
- Enjoy working in a flexible team situation
- Established and maintained positive and effective working relationships
- Planned, scheduled, and performed a variety of clerical work
- Maintained office equipment and supplies
- Proofread forms and materials for completeness and accuracy according to regulations and procedures
- Processed and prepared materials for pamphlets, bulletins, brochures, announcements, handbooks, forms, and curriculum materials
- Provided training of temporary or new employees
- Maintained department files and records
- Demonstrated ability to receive incoming calls and route them efficiently
- Processed purchase requisitions, ordered and distributed supplies, and maintained inventory control
- Responsibly planned and conducted meetings

Step Five: The Final Resumé

Prior to finalizing your resumé, ensure that you have added all information identified in steps 1 to 4 to your electronic document. As you finalize your resumé, check for information that too frequently is forgotten or not presented appropriately. This is the fifth step in finalizing the information on your resumé. The top of your resumé is called the **information heading**. An information heading contains relevant contact information including name, mailing address, city, state, Zip code, contact phone, and e-mail address. Include your complete and formal name, including a middle initial if you have one. When listing your e-mail address, remove the hyperlink so the print color is consistent. If your current e-mail address is unprofessional, secure an address that is professional. Only include one contact phone number. Whatever number is listed should be active and have a professional voice-mail message. Check the spelling and numbers for accuracy. Spell out the names of streets. If you use abbreviations, check for appropriate format, capitalization, and punctuation.

Immediately after your information heading is the Career Objective or Personal Profile created in step one. Review this opening statement to ensure it introduces the reader to who you are and encourages him or her to learn more about the specific knowledge, skills, abilities, and key accomplishments.

In step three, you determined whether a functional or chronological resumé layout was appropriate for your situation. Review the respective layout for proper order and refer to the sample resumés. Confirm that your experience and education are listed chronologically (most recent first). Keep your resumé consistent in its setup including all periods or no periods at the end of each line, line spacing, alignment of dates, date format, bold/italics, upper- and lowercase words and underlines. Be consistent with word endings and the use of tense in each section (e.g., *-ing* and *-ed*). Also be consistent with the use of the postal abbreviation for your state (e.g., the state is *CA*, not *Ca*, not *C.A*). When your draft resumé is complete, spell-check and proofread the document to ensure it is free of typographical errors and inconsistencies.

As for proper resumé layout and design, underlines, bold, and italic print are acceptable for emphasis, but should not be overdone. Do not use bullets throughout your resumé; only use bullets to emphasize key skills. Use easy-to-read fonts and sizes. Times New Roman or Arial are most common. Apart from your name on the information heading of your resumé, do not use more than two different font sizes, preferably 12 to 14 points. Do not use different color fonts, highlights, or graphics on your resumé: Use only black ink. It is not appropriate to include personal information such as photographs of yourself, your birthdate, marital status, Social Security number, or hobbies. It is also no longer appropriate to list "References Available Upon Request" at the close of your resumé. Professional references should be on a separate sheet and provided only when requested. Refer to chapter 13 for proper format for a professional reference list.

Check to ensure your resumé is presented professionally, is free of errors, and does not contain unnecessary or inappropriate information. Print the resumé in black ink on 8½ × 11 inch, letter-sized, paper. Laser print is ideal. Double-sided resumés are not appropriate. If your resumé is more than one page, put your name at the top of each page. Proper resumé paper is cotton fiber, 24-pound white (not bond) paper of good quality. Using colored paper, especially dark, is both difficult to read and does not photocopy well. Do not use fancy paper stocks or binders. Do not staple your resumé or other job search documents. Since resumés are frequently photocopied, stapled resumés and other job search documents may be torn in the process.

When you have completed your resumé and believe it is ready for distribution, have several individuals whom you trust review it for clarity, consistency, punctuation, grammar, typographical errors, and other potential mistakes. Remember that complete sentences are not necessary and the words *I* or *my* should not be used. Your resumé must create a positive, professional visual image that is easy to read.

Resumé Formats

As you begin to share your completed resumé with both potential employers and members of your professional network, you may have the option of presenting your resumé on resumé paper or electronically as an attachment. Resumés printed on resumé paper are designed to be used for face-to-face job searches. Common formats for resumés are functional and chronological resumés. If you choose to share your resumé electronically as an attachment, it is best to send your resumé either as a Microsoft (MS) Word file or as a portable document file (.pdf). It is recommended you send it as a .pdf file to ensure that the resumé layout is properly

Exercise 14-5   Check for Inconsistencies

Circle the 15 inconsistency errors on the following resumé.

AMANDA J. ERIE

1100 EAST FAVOR AVENUE • POSTVILLE, PA 16722
PHONE (555) 698-2222 • E-MAIL AERIE @ PBCC.COM

OBJECTIVE

Seeking a position as an Administrative Assistant where I can utilize my office skills

SUMMARY OF QUALIFICATIONS

- Computer software skills include Microsoft Word, Excel, Outlook, Access, and PowerPoint
- Knowledge of Multi-line telephone system, filing, data entry, formatting of documents and reports, and operation of office equipment.
- Excellent interpersonal skills and polished office etiquette.
- written and oral communication skills
- Typing skills at 50 WPM
- Bilingual in English/Spanish (speaking)

EDUCATION

Reese Community College, Postville, PA Currently pursuing AA Degree in Office Occupations.
Calvin Institute of Technology, Cambridge, OH Office Technology Certificate Spring 2010

WORK AND VOLUNTEER EXPERIENCE

01/11 – Present   *Regal Entertainment Group*   Postville, CA
Usher – Responsible for ensuring payment of services. Answer customer inquiries. Collect and count ticket stubs.

11/07 – 02/09   Loblaws   Cambridge, OH
Cashier – Operated cash register, stocking, assisting customers

01/07 – 04/07   Jolene's Diner   Cambridge, OH
Server – Provided customer service by waiting tables, cleaned, and operated cash register

maintained through the file transfer. Sending your resumé as a .pdf file also ensures that those who do not use MS Word are able to read the file. Guard your personal information by only posting your resumé on reputable job search sites.

In some instances, such as large corporations, employers will request that an **electronic formatted resumé** be submitted. Electronic Formatted Resumés are resumés which are submitted in American Standard Code for Information Interchange (ASCII) format. Once the employer receives your electronic formatted resumé, the resumé is added to a specialized database/software that routinely scans resumés based on key words (qualifications/skills) for specific jobs. The resumé is used to match key words contained in your resumé with specific jobs. Therefore, on this type of resumé, list as many relevant key words as possible related to your target job.

For electronic formatted resumés, visual appeal is not an issue. Electronic formatted resumés use Times New Roman font size 10 to 14. An electronic formatted resumé should be left-justified. Avoid tabs and centering. Headings should be in all capital letters. Hard returns must be used instead of word wrap. Avoid bold, italics, underlines, graphics, percent signs, and foreign characters. Also avoid boxes, horizontal and vertical lines, solid/hallow bullets, and table and column formatting.

Content for electronic formatted resumés include having your name at the top of the page on its own line. Standard address formatting (as when addressing a letter) should be used. Use key words specific to your desired job category and/or when communicating your knowledge, skills, and abilities. Work experience dates should have beginning and ending dates on the same line. Use asterisks or dashes (no bullets or boxes of any kind) and list each telephone number on its own line (no parentheses around area codes). Date your electronic resumé. Just as with hardcopy resumés, do not include personal information of any kind, including photographs, marital status, birthdates, or your Social Security number. See figure 14-7 for an example of an electronic formatted resumé.

Electronic Resumé Example
See Figure 14-7 on page 226.

Cover Letters

A **cover letter** is often the first impression a potential employer will have of you. It serves as an introduction to your resumé. Employers use cover letters as screening tools.

When writing a cover letter, use a friendly but professional tone. Use complete sentences and proper grammar. When tailoring your cover letter, include information about the company that communicates to the employer you have conducted research on the company. Details on tailoring both your resumé and cover letter toward a target employer will be covered in the next section.

In a cover letter, communicate how your key skills, experience, and accomplishments can meet the employer's needs. This is accomplished by identifying the skills and qualifications the employer is requesting in the job announcement and/or job description and matching these needs with your key skills and qualifications. Let the employer know what you can offer the company, not what you want from the company. In the paragraph where you are communicating your key skills and experience, refer the reader to the attached resumé. Do not duplicate what is already listed on your resumé; instead, emphasize your experience and key skills. Although it is acceptable to utilize the words "I" and "my" in a cover letter be careful not to begin most of your sentences with the word *I*. Instead, focus the attention toward the employer. Attempt to begin a sentence with what the company will receive with your skills. For example:

Instead of writing, "I am proficient in Word 2007 and WordPerfect," **Write,** "*Your* company will benefit from my proficiency in Word 2007 and WordPerfect."

Address the cover letter to a specific person. This should be the person who will be making the hiring decision. Do not address your cover letter to a department, the company name, or "to whom it may concern." Call the company and ask for a specific name and title, identifying the appropriate spelling and gender. If you have conducted research and still cannot secure a specific name, use a subject line instead of a salutation. For example, instead of writing, "To Whom It May Concern" write, "Subject: Account Clerk Position." If you have talked to a specific person or with the employer, refer to the previous communication. Include the specific position you are seeking in your cover letter and how you learned about the job opening. At the end of your cover letter, request an interview (not the job). Do not write that you look forward to the employer contacting you. Display initiative by stating that you will follow up on your request for an interview within the next week. Include an enclosure notation for your resumé and close courteously.

In chapter 9, you learned how to write a business letter. Use the proper business letter format for your cover letter. Each word and paragraph in your cover letter must have a purpose. Your goal is to communicate how your knowledge, skills, abilities, and accomplishments fill a targeted company's needs and make the reader want to review your resumé. The cover letter setup in figure 14-8 and sample cover letters in figures 14-9 and 14-10 will help you create a winning cover letter.

Print your cover letter on the same type of paper used for your resumé. You may copy the information heading you created for your resumé and use it on your cover letter. This creates a consistent and professional visual appeal for your resumé package. Avoid making common mistakes including typographical or grammar errors, forgetting to including a date, or forgetting to sign the cover letter. Complete and grammatically correct sentences must be used on a cover letter. As with your resumé, have someone you trust proofread your letter before sending it to a potential employer. Any error communicates a lack of attention to detail. Even minor errors have the potential to disqualify you from securing an interview.

Cover Letter Setup
See Figure 14-8 on page 227.

Cover Letter Example 1
See Figure 14-9 on page 228.

Cover Letter Example 2
See Figure 14-10 on page 229.

Tailoring Your Resumé and Cover Letter

When you have identified a position for which you are qualified, tailor your resumé and cover letter specifically to the job and company for which you are applying. Carefully review the job announcement. If possible, secure a copy of the job description from the company's human resource department if it is not available or attached to the job posting. Identify key job skills that the position requires and highlight the company needs with your skills. As you learned in step four of creating your resumé, utilize the O'Net web site to identify key skills for your targeted position. If necessary, rearrange the order of the information presented on your resumé so that the key skills required for your target position are presented first. On your cover letter, emphasize your specific qualifications that match those required for the open position. Figure 14-11 provides an example of a resumé and cover letter tailored to a specific job announcement.

Although mentioned earlier, it cannot be stressed enough that a daytime phone number and e-mail address need to be listed on both your cover letter and resumé. Because most invitations for job interviews occur over the phone, your phone voice-mail and/or message machine need to be professional. Do not include musical introductions or any other greeting that would not make a positive first impression to a potential employer. As mentioned in chapter 13, have a professional e-mail address to use in your job search.

Tailored Package
See Figure 14-11 on page 230–283.

Cory's friend Rebecca was a practical joker. Cory enjoyed calling Rebecca because her voice-mail message started with a joke or had some strange voice and/or music. However, the last time Cory called Rebecca, Cory noticed that Rebecca's message was normal. The next time Cory saw Rebecca, Cory asked Rebecca why her voice message was suddenly so serious. Rebecca explained that she had recently applied for a job and had been selected to interview. However, she was embarrassed because when the interviewer called to arrange the appointment, the interviewer left a message and also suggested that Rebecca change her voice-mail message to a more professional message.

Tips for Ex-Offenders

If you have served time in prison and are now attempting to reenter the workforce, you are to be congratulated for wanting to move forward with your life. Others have made poor choices in their past and you have made restitution for yours. Be honest with the potential employer.

On your resumé, include all jobs you have held and skills you learned while incarcerated. List the correctional facility in place of the employer for these jobs. List all education, including degrees and courses you received while incarcerated. Include the educational institution that provided the training.

The employment application is a legal document. At the bottom of this document, applicants sign a statement that affirms that all information provided on the application is true. Therefore, you must not lie. If, after being hired, your employer discovers that you have lied on the application, you may be immediately terminated. The majority of applications ask if you have been convicted of a felony. Please note that arrests are not convictions. If you have been convicted of a felony, check "Yes." The application should also have a space to write a statement after the felony question. Do not leave this space blank. In this space, write, "Will explain in detail during interview."

Workplace Dos and Don'ts

Do keep your resumé updated with skills and accomplishments	*Don't* wait until the last minute to update your resumé
Do change your resumé format after you have had work experience	*Don't* use outdated reference names and letters
Do use the correct format for your resumé	*Don't* send out a resumé or cover letter that has not been proofread by someone you can trust
Do check your resumé and cover letter for errors before sending them to employers	*Don't* forget to sign your cover letter

YOUR NAME (16 point, bold)

Your Address (12 or 14 point, bold)

City, State ZIP

Phone Number (Include Area Code)

E-Mail Address (Remove Hyperlink)

Horizontal line optional and thickness varies

OBJECTIVE   Headings can be on the left or centered, 12- or 14-point font, and uppercase or initial cap.

Format headings the same throughout the resumé. Keep spacing equal between each section.

QUALIFICATIONS (OR SKILLS)

- Relate to target job, all job-related skills and transferable skills
- Most relative to the job are listed first
- Bullet (small round or small square only) these items to stand out

EDUCATION

You may list before qualifications

Do not list high school if you have graduated from college

Include the dates and align to the right

List schools in chronological order, most recent attended first

WORK EXPERIENCE

Include: Name of Company and City, State—No Addresses

Job title bolded, if part-time, dates employed (month, year)

List the jobs in chronological order, most recent first align dates to the right

Align dates to the right

List the duties, responsibilities, and achievements

Be consistent in your setup

Use the same tense throughout (*ed* or *ing*)

Do not use complete sentences or *I, me,* or *my*

OTHER CAPABILITIES

Optional items in this section may not be directly related to the job but may interest the employer such as honors or awards.

Emphasize skills and education. List your skills and education before any work experience.

Keep in mind

- Watch periods, punctuation
- Watch spelling
- Use a regular font, no color, 12-point font (except heading)
- Use resumé paper, no dark or bright colors
- Do not use full sentences or I, me, or my
- References are not necessary; you will have a separate sheet with references
- Do not use graphics

Figure 14-1

Functional Resumé Layout

Suzie S. Kringle

1234 Tolearn Avenue, Meadeville, PA 16335
555-555-5555
skringle05@careerssuccess.lns

OBJECTIVE

To obtain a position as a Junior Accountant with Owen Company where I can utilize my general accounting skills in a dynamic company.

SKILLS

- Knowledgeable and accurate in general ledger and journal posting
- Basic software knowledge of QuickBooks
- Knowledge of account receivables and account payables
- Experienced with Microsoft Office, including Word, Excel, Access, PowerPoint, and Outlook
- Ten-key at 150 cspm
- Type 50 wpm accurately
- Excellent English grammar, spelling, and punctuation skills
- Accurately follow oral and written instructions
- Strong attention to detail
- Positive attitude, motivated, and organized

EDUCATION

State University, Meadeville, PA   5/11
Bachelor of Science Degree in Business, Accounting

Meadeville City College, Meadeville PA   5/09
Associate in Arts Degree in Business, Certificate of Completion in Account Clerk Program

WORK EXPERIENCE

S and L Accounting   Edinboro, PA   1/09–present
Account Clerk
Assisted the Accountant by answering telephone, bookkeeping, data entry in Excel and QuickBooks, verifying totals, making copies, faxing, and other clerical duties when needed.

Bret's Hamburger Haven   Edinboro, PA   1/05–12/05
Cashier/Food Service
Worked as a team member to assist customers with food orders, cleaned, handled cash, and trained new employees.

Figure 14-2

Functional Resumé
Example with Minimal
Career Work Experience

HEIDI H. KRINGLE

1234 Tolearn Avenue, Meadeville, PA 16335
555-555-5555   hkringle02@careersuccess.lns

OBJECTIVE

To obtain a position as an Office Assistant with Austin Office Supplies that will enable me to utilize my current skills and education.

QUALIFICATIONS

- Type 50 wpm
- Experienced with Microsoft Office, including Word, Excel, Access, PowerPoint, and Outlook
- Accurately proofread and edit documents
- Knowledge of records management
- Positive telephone skills
- Excellent oral and written communications skills
- Positive attitude, motivated, and organized
- Excellent customer services skills

EDUCATION/CERTIFICATION

2009–2011   Meadeville City College   Meadeville, PA
Associate of Art Degree, Business & Technology
Clerical Administration Certificate
GPA 3.9, Dean's list

EXPERIENCE

06/2006–present   Fine Linens by Jen   Meadeville, PA
Cashier
Responsibilities include: providing customer service, cashiering, placing merchandise on the floor, helping return go backs, processing merchandise on the floor, stocking merchandise in back/stockroom, training new hires.

02/2000–05/2006   Jerry's Burger Place   Meadeville, PA
Cashier/Counter Person
Responsibilities included: assisted guests with their orders, ensured a safe and clean work environment, and assisted other team members as needed.

Figure 14-3

Functional Resumé
Example without
Career Work Experience

YOUR NAME (16 point, bold)

Your Address (12 or 14 point, bold) ■ **City, State ZIP** ■ **Phone Number** (Include Area Code)

E-Mail Address (Remove Hyperlink)

PERSONAL PROFILE:

Include key skill sets. Headings can be on the left or centered, 12- or 14-point font, and uppercase or initial cap. Format headings the same throughout the resume. Keep the spacing equal between each section.

PROFESSIONAL EXPERIENCE:

Group key skills, experience, and accomplishments under each major skill set heading.

First Skill Set Subheading

- Communicate experience, and key accomplishments relating to your first skill set subheading
- Using power words, quantify as much as possible
- Include duties, responsibilities, and achievements

Second Skill Set Subheading

- Relate statements to target job. Communicate both job-related skills or transferable skills
- Accomplishments and experience most relative to target job are listed first
- Bullet (small round or small square only) accomplishments and experience to stand out

Third Skill Set Subheading

- Be consistent in setup
- Use same tense throughout (ed or ing)
- Do not use complete sentences or I, me, or my

WORK HISTORY:

Name of Company and City, State—No Addresses—dates employed (month, year)

Job title (bold title, NOT employer)

List jobs in chronological order with most recent date first

EDUCATION:

Do not list high school

Include the years attended, areas of study, and degrees earned

List schools in chronological order, most recent attended first

PROFESSIONAL AFFILIATIONS/CERTIFICATIONS:

List professional memberships including the name of the organization, status (member, board member, etc.) and dates of membership. Also include any certifications or community service activities that are relevant to the target job.

Emphasize key skill sets and accomplishments. List work experience before education and employment history.

Keep in Mind

- Watch period, punctuation, and spelling
- Can be one or two pages. If two pages, place name on second page
- Use a regular font, no color, 12-point font (except heading)
- Do not use full sentences or I, me, or my
- Do not use graphics
- Align bullets to the right

Figure 14-4

Chronological
Resume Layout

Chapter 14 Resumé Package   221

PEARL B. KRINGLE, CPA

1234 Tolearn Avenue   ▼   Meadeville, PA 16335   ▲   555.555.5555   ▼
pbkringle@careerssuccess.lns

PROFILE:

Highly experienced, personable, and detail-oriented Certified Public Accountant with expertise and demonstrated leadership in the areas of accounting, computer information systems, and quantitative analysis.

PROFESSIONAL EXPERIENCE:

Accounting

- Audit cash, investments, payables, fixed assets, and prepaid expenses for small business enterprises, corporations, and not-for-profit organizations.
- Collect and analyze data to detect deficient controls, extravagance, fraud, or non-compliance with laws, regulations, and management policies.
- Prepare detailed reports on audit findings, report to management about asset utilization and audit results, and recommend changes in operations and financial activities.
- Inspect account books and accounting systems for efficiency, effectiveness, and use of accepted accounting procedures to record transactions.
- Examine and evaluate financial and information systems, recommending controls to ensure system reliability and data integrity.
- Confer with company officials about financial and regulatory matters.

Computer Information Systems

- Developed information resources, providing data security/control, strategic computing, and disaster recovery.
- Consulted with users, management, vendors, and technicians to assess computing needs and system requirements.
- Stayed abreast of advances in technology and forwarded research and recommendations to ensure company and respective clients were utilizing proper and most efficient tools and information systems.
- Met with department heads, managers, supervisors, vendors to solicit cooperation and resolve problems.
- Provided users with technical support for computer problems.

Quantitative Analysis

- Assembled computerized spreadsheets, draw charts, and graphs used to illustrate technical reports.
- Analyzed financial information to produce forecasts of business, industry, and economic conditions for use in making investment decisions.
- Maintained knowledge and stayed abreast of developments in the fields of industrial technology, business, finance, and economic theory.
- Interpreted data affecting investment programs, such as price, yield, stability, future trends in investment risks, and economic influences.

Figure 14-5

Chronological Résumé
Example with Degree

PEARL B. KRINGLE, CPA

Page Two

- Monitored fundamental economic, industrial, and corporate developments through the analysis of information obtained from financial publications and services, investment banking firms, government agencies, trade publications, company sources, and personal interviews.
- Recommended investments and investment timing to companies, investment firm staff, or the investing public.
- Determined the prices at which securities should be syndicated and offered to the public.
- Prepared plans of action for investment based on financial analyses.

WORK HISTORY:

Coopers & Lion, LLP, Alltown, PA   May 2007–present
Auditor

Mitchell Ho, CPA, Atlanta, GA   May 2004–April 2007
General Accountant

U.S. Department of Labor, Atlanta, GA   January 2002–February 2004
Program Assistant

Grace's Burger Palace, Riverside, GA   August 1999–December 2001
Server

EDUCATION AND LICENSE:

Masters of Computer Information Systems   August 2009
Georgia State University, Atlanta, GA

Certified Public Accountant – State of Georgia   May 2007

Bachelor of Science in Accounting   May 2004
Heather Glenn College, Heather Glenn, NC

PROFESSIONAL AFFILIATIONS:

American Institute of Certified Financial Accountants
Beta Alpha Psi Fraternity
National Association of Black Accountants

Figure 14-5

Chronological Resumé
Example with Degree page 2
(*continued*)

Steven Mark Kringle

1234 Tolearn Avenue ■ Meadeville, PA 16335 ■ 555.555.5555

smkringle@careersuccess.lns

PERSONAL PROFILE

Results and efficiency focused professional with experience in sales/vendor relations, inventory/warehousing, and management/supervision. Proven ability in relationship management with demonstrated and consistent increase in sales over a five-year period. Inventory expertise includes streamlined operations, improved productivity, and favorable inventory ratio utilization for wholesale food supplier. Management ability to create goal-driven teams, groom leaders, and facilitate the creation of a learning organization.

PROFESSIONAL EXPERIENCE

Customer Service Orientation ■ Innovative Risk Taker ■ Excellent Quantitative Skills ■ Purchasing, Inventory Planning & Control ■ Supply Chain Management ■ Warehouse Operations ■ Process Improvement ■ Cost Containment ■ Hiring, Staffing & Scheduling Safety Training ■ Excellent Computer Knowledge

Sales/Vendor Relations

- Through the establishment of vendor relationships, schedule product installations, exchanges, buy-backs or removals of equipment or other assets including supplier networks and agent contacts in order to meet customer expectations for private soda company. Have grown sales territory from two county area to tri-state contract area over four-year period.

- Source and facilitate delivery of product (e.g., beverage equipment, parts, point of sale material, return of assets) for retail suppliers. Sales complaints are consistently .05% per year, while sales volume and customer satisfaction rates are the highest of all sales team and consistently grow.

- Research and resolve issues for customers, business partners, and Company associates in order to expedite service, installations, or orders using information systems and working with supply chain partners.

- Create and maintain partnerships with customers, clients or third party service providers (e.g., contract service/installation agents, distributors) by establishing common goals, objectives, and performance target requirements in order to improve customer service and satisfaction.

- Created troubleshooting equipment process which allows retail suppliers to receive immediate response on service issues (e.g., beverage vending, dispensing) via telephone or Internet to minimize customer down time and service cost.

Figure 14-6

Chronological Resumé
Example with No Degree

Steven Mark Kringle

Page Two

Inventory/Warehousing

- Responsible for maintaining customer contact to confirm service or orders including accuracy, service follow up, equipment service confirmation, product delivery confirmation, and routine service scheduling for local foodservice broker.

- Received, recorded, and responded to customer or consumer inquiries/feedback using specially designed database which documented best practices from nationwide foodservice association in an effort to provide improved service, order accuracy, and optimized supply chain efficiency. Information was collected, analyzed, and reported to all members of the supply chain for feedback and control purposes.

- Processed orders for goods and services with food service business partners, customers, suppliers, and company associates, either through direct telephone contact or electronic means, to increase speed and accuracy of order transactions and improve loss prevention systems.

Management/Supervision

- Developed and trained team members on inventory control, customer service, and safety for local foodservice provider. Program was so successful customers within the company supply chain requested and received training. To date, over 500 individuals have received custom training.

- Supervised cross-functional team of 100 including order technicians, outside repair personnel, transportation associates, warehouse attendants, and loss prevention specialists.

- As assistant-manager for college-town restaurant, assisted in the hiring, training, scheduling, and performance evaluation of staff for small soda company and local food service supplier.

WORK HISTORY

Vendor Relations Associate
Christopher Cola Company, Susanville, NE   2005–2010

Warehouse Manager
Joshua Food Service, Pocatoe, NE   2003–2005

Assistant Restaurant Manager
Nick-Mike Ribs 'N Stuff, Pocatoe, NE   2000–2003

EDUCATION/PROFESSIONAL DEVELOPMENT

University of Nebraska, Lincoln, NE   2005–2008
Business Management/Marketing

Figure 14-6

Chronological Resumé
Example with No Degree
(continued)

AUTUMN S. KRINGLE
1234 TOLEARN AVENUE,
MEADEVILLE, PA 16335
555-555-5555
askringle@careersuccess.Ins

OBJECTIVE

Bookkeeper

KEY WORD SUMMARY

Bookkeeping skills, financial management, accounting, receivables and payroll, organized, data entry, communication skills, problem solving, responsible, team player, computer skills.

EDUCATION

City College: City, WA
2007
Associate Degree in Accounting

COURSES OF STUDY
----

* Intro to Accounting
* Intro to Business
* MS Office
* Workplace Communication
* Office Accounting
* Business Law
* Intro to Marketing

COMPUTER SKILLS
----

* Microsoft Office: Word, Excel, Access, PowerPoint
* WordPerfect
* Internet

WORK EXPERIENCE

Yang Enterprises: Fresno, CA
2007 – Present
Bookkeeping Assistant: Responsible for assisting accounting department with payroll, budgets, planning, and forecasting, purchasing, and managing accounts.

Figure 14-7

Electronic Resumé Example

Date of Letter

Employer's Name, Title
Company Name
Address
City, State Zip

Dear Mr./Ms./Dr.::

First Paragraph. Give the reason for the letter, the position for which you are applying, and how you learned of this position. Note any previous contact you may have had with the employer.

Second Paragraph. Tell why you are interested in the position, the organization, and its products or services. Indicate any research you have done on the position and/or the employer.

Third Paragraph. Refer to the attached resumé and highlight relevant aspects of your resumé. Emphasize the skills mentioned in the advertisement or on the job description. Provide specific reasons why the organization should hire you and what you can do to contribute to the organization's success.

Last Paragraph. Indicate your desire for an interview, and offer flexibility as to the time and place. Thank the employer for his or her consideration and express anticipation in meeting him or her. Include a phone number and e-mail address for contact.

Sincerely,

(Do not forget to sign your cover letter)

Your Name
Your Address
City, State Zip

Enclosure

Figure 14-8

Cover Letter Setup

September 25, 2012

Owen Corporation
Attention Brandon Owen
435 East Chesny Street
Meadeville, PA 16335

Dear Mr. Owen:

As a recent accounting graduate of State University, Meadeville, I was delighted to learn from your web site of the available Junior Accountant position. The purpose of this letter is to express a strong interest in becoming an Owen Company Accountant at your Meadeville facility. In addition to possessing a B.S. degree in Business, Accounting, I am responsible and consider myself a leader.

Owen Company sponsors a variety of community services and employee recognition programs, which I have read a great deal about. Your company has earned my respect, as it has from much of the community for your involvement in the after-school programs in Meadeville Unified School District.

As you will see on the attached resumé, Owen Company would benefit from the skills I have learned throughout college. These include: general ledger and journal posting; Microsoft Word, Excel, and Access programs; Quickbooks; and accurate ten-key (150 cspm). In addition, I also offer a superior work ethic, strong communicative abilities, attention to detail, and a keen interest in upgrading my skills.

I am confident that my skills and abilities will make me an ideal candidate for a position in this field. I would appreciate an opportunity to meet with you to discuss how my skills can meet the needs of Owen Company. I will contact you by phone within the week to discuss the possibility of an interview.

Sincerely,

Suzie Kringle

Suzie Kringle
1234 Tolearn Avenue
Meadeville, PA 16335

Enclosure

Figure 14-9

Cover Letter Example 1

HEIDI H. KRINGLE

1234 Tolearn Avenue, Meadeville, PA 16335
555-555-5555   hshore02@careersuccess.lns

September 21, 2012

Mr. Jared Bill
Austin Office Supplies
1122 Friendly Road
Meadeville, PA 93725

Dear Mr. Bill:

I recently spoke with Gene Armstrong, an employee at your company, and he recommended that I send you a copy of my resumé. Knowing the requirements for the position and that I am interested in working at this type of establishment, he felt that I would be an ideal candidate for your office assistant position.

My personal goal is to be a part of an organization such as yours that wants to excel in both growth and profit. I would welcome the opportunity to be employed at Austin's Office Supplies since this is the largest and best-known office supply company in the city. Your company has a reputation of excellent products and service.

Austin's Office Supplies would benefit from someone such as I who is accustomed to a fast-paced environment where deadlines are a priority and handling multiple jobs simultaneously is the norm. As you can see on the attached resumé, my previous jobs required me to be well organized, accurate, and friendly. I enjoy a challenge and work hard to attain my goals. Great customer skills are important in a business such as yours.

Nothing would please me more than to be a part of your team. I would like very much to discuss with you how I could contribute to your organization with my office skills and my dependability. I will contact you next week to arrange an interview. In the interim, I can be reached at 555-555-5555.

Sincerely,

Heidi H. Kringle

Heidi H. Kringle

Enclosure

Figure 14-10

Cover Letter Example 2

ACCOUNT CLERK – position #022394   full time, permanent position

The current vacancy is a full-time position at Viau Technical College.

Definition: Under direction performs a wide variety of entry-level accounting/business office work.

Compensation: Starts at $3,176 per month. Full-time permanent positions provide an attractive benefit package which include health, dental, and vision coverage for the employee and eligible dependents, as well as life insurance and disability coverage for employees.

Experience: Entry-level experience performing general accounting duties.

Education: Formal or informal education equivalent to completion of an Associate Degree in accounting.

Examples of Duties: Performs a wide variety of duties including but not limited to: basic accounting work; verifying, balancing, and posting/recording accounting information verifying and preparing invoices, checks, correspondence, and statistical information; proof-reading; and filing. Calculates, prepares, and reconciles various financial reports. Entering and retrieving data from computer system as needed. Assigning and/or reviewing the work of other employees and students. May perform other related duties as needed.

Required Knowledge and Abilities:
Knowledge of sequence of procedures in the accounting cycle, analysis, use, and interpretation of accounting and financial data; and modern office practices. Knowledge of and ability to employ proper English usage, spelling, grammar, and punctuation. Skill to make deposits, process checks, and reconcile accounts; employ mathematical and statistical techniques sufficient to maintain district records; keyboard; utilize word processing software, email, online calendaring, and data entry/retrieval from database programs; and create and utilize spreadsheets. Ability to assign, monitor, and/or review the work of others; receive and follow instructions and appropriately interact with students, staff, faculty, and the public; and learn and apply college and district policies and procedures.

Selection Process: The selection process will include screening to ensure applications are complete and meet all minimum qualifications. This process will also include a written test of knowledge and abilities (35% weight), a performance test (35% weight), and an oral appraisal board interview (30% weight). Of those candidates achieving a passing score on the first test, only the 30 highest scoring candidates, plus ties, will be invited to the performance exam. Of those candidates achieving a passing score on the performance exam, only the 15 highest scoring candidates, plus ties, will be invited to the oral appraisal board interview. Passing score is 75% out of 100% on each testing section.

FIRST EXAM IS TENTATIVELY SCHEDULED FOR SATURDAY, JUNE 20, 2012.

To move forward in the selection process, you must complete an online application through our web site at www.viaucommunitycollege.com. Resumes may also be submitted by mail, in person, or by emailing to job@viaucommunitycollege.com.

Filing Deadline: 4:30 p.m., Monday, June 1, 2012.

Figure 14-11

Tailored Package—Page 1
Job Announcement

Jolene M. Kringle

1234 Tolearn Avenue ■ Meadville, PA ■ 555.555.5555
jmkringle@careersuccess.lns

Objective

Highly motivated, responsible, and ethical individual seeks an entry-level accounting position with Viau Technical College in an effort to apply newly acquired general business and accounting skills. Experienced in basic accounting procedures, operational efficiencies, and logistics.

Key Skills & Qualifications

- Strong math and analytical skills
- Proofreading and filing
- Data entry
- Bilingual (Spanish-speak and write)

- Works well in group environments
- Excellent grammatical and English usage
- Proficient in MAS 90 and Quickbooks
- Demonstrated leadership

Education

Hill Valley Technical College, Clarkville, PA   01/08–06/10
Associate of Arts Degree, Accounting

Work Experience

El Montes Restaurant, Reedville, PA   12/00–present
Bookkeeper/Server

Perform bookkeeping functions for small family business including creation and analysis of financial statements, cash/banking functions, and communication with CPA firm. Implemented electronic accounting and inventory system which saved the company an estimated $50K. Serve as Lead Server for evening staff. In addition to exemplary customer service and cashier duties, responsibilities include inventory control, and training of new staff training in both customer service and food safety/handling for busy Mexican food restaurant.

Freshwide Marketing, Lewis, PA   05–09/06, 07, 08
Quality Control Clerk (*seasonal*)

Received and counted stock items and recorded data. Monitored fruit and produce as it arrived or was shipped from cold storage for twenty independent fruit growers. Verified inventory computations by comparing them to physical counts of stock, and investigated discrepancies or adjusted errors. Stored items in an orderly and accessible manner in cold storage and warehouse.

Starlight Produce, Lewis, PA   06/03–09/05
Shipping Manifest Clerk

As a shipping clerk for regional fruit packer, prepared, monitored, and facilitated orders for shipping to over fifty clients throughout the United States. Duties included examining contents and comparing with records, such as manifests, invoices, or orders, to verify accuracy of incoming or outgoing shipment. Prepared documents, such as work orders, bills of lading, and shipping orders to route materials. Determined shipping method for materials, using knowledge of shipping procedures, routes, and rates.

Community Service

Junior Cagers Basketball, Lewis, PA   12/02–02/05
Assistant Coach for 5–6 and 7–8 grades boys and girls

Jolene M. Kringle

1234 Tolearn Avenue ■ Meadeville, PA 16335 ■ 555.555.5555
jmkringle@careersuccess.lns

April 21, 2012

Monique Marshall, Director
Human Resource Department
Viau Community College
60157 S. Holbrook
Viau, PA 12150

RE: Account Clerk Position #022394

Dear Ms. Marshall:

It is with great excitement that I am submitting the following application package for consideration of your current full time Account Clerk Position posted on the Viau Community College web site. Viau Community College has a legacy of quality and excellence in education and nothing would please me more than to apply my newly acquired accounting education to your organization.

As you can see on the attached resumé, your company will benefit from my demonstrated leadership in the areas of general accounting, business, and computer applications. Excelling in the creation and quantitative analysis of basic financial statements, I am familiar with both the installation and utilization of common accounting software programs. At my current job, interaction with both the company owners and the company's contracted CPA firm is a weekly required activity which has greatly improved my communication and presentation skills. In my opinion, diversity is a valuable asset and I enjoy utilizing my fluency in speaking Spanish when interacting with customers. I consider myself an ethical and responsible individual with excellent verbal and written communication skills.

It would be a privilege to have the opportunity to discuss how my knowledge, skills, and professional experience can contribute to the continued success of the Viau Community College. I will contact you within the next week to follow-up on my application materials. In the interim, I can be reached at 555-555-5555 or via e-mail at jmkringle@careersuccess.lns.

Sincerely,

Jolene M. Kringle

Jolene M. Kringle

Enclosures

Figure 14-11

Tailored Package—Page 3
Cover Letter (*continued*)

Jolene M. Kringle

1234 Tolearn Avenue ■ Meadeville, PA 16335 ■ 555.555.5555
jmkringle@careersuccess.lns

Professional Reference List

Name	Relationship	Phone	E-mail	Mailing Address
Autumn Hart	Former Accounting Instructor, Hill Valley Technical College	555.555-1111	atmnhrt@hillvalley.scl	123 Hillvalley Clarkville, PA
Gloria Montes	Owner, El Montes Restaurant	555.555-1112	gloria@eatelmontes.fat	5432 Food Ct. Reedville, PA
Gary Solis	Floor Manager, Freshwide Marketing	555.555-1113	solisg@freshwide.fruit	2220 Tulare Lewis, PA
Patty Negoro	Office Manager, Starlight Produce	555.555-1114	pattyn@starlight.sun	444 Adoline Lewis, PA

Figure 14-11

Tailored Package—Page 4
Reference List (*continued*)

Concept Review and Application

Summary of Key Concepts

- A winning resumé makes it easy for potential employers to quickly and easily identify your skills and experience
- Update your resumé with new skills and accomplishments at least once a year
- Include both job-specific skills and transferable skills on your resumé
- Use the correct resumé layout for your career work experience
- A cover letter is most often an employer's first impression of you
- Check that your resumé and cover letter are free of typographical and grammatical errors
- Share your resumé electronically as a .pdf file to ensure the resumé layout is maintained

Key Terms

chronological resumé layout
electronic formatted resumé
information heading
power words
soft skills

cover letter
functional resumé layout
job-specific skills
resumé
transferable skills

If You Were the Boss

1. What would you look for first when reviewing a resumé?
2. What would your reaction be if you were reading a cover letter that had several typing and grammar errors?

Video Case Study: Resumé and Cover Letter Tips

This video presents expert advice on how to write a winning resumé and cover letter. Refer to the CD that accompanies your text, watch this video, and answer the following questions.

1. Share four common resumé mistakes and solutions.
2. Explain how to utilize a job announcement when preparing a resumé and cover letter.
3. Share four common cover letter mistakes and solutions.
4. What information should be repeated in a cover letter that is already included on a resumé?

Web Links

http://resume.monster.com
http://jobstar.org/tools/resume/index.htm
http://jobsearch.about.com/od/networking

Activities

Activity 14-1

Conduct an Internet search to identify resumé power words. List at least five new words that are not in the text.

1. _____

2. _____

3. _____

4. _____

5. _____

Activity 14-2

Using a word processing program and the steps and/or exercises from this chapter, create a resumé.

Activity 14-3

Search for a job you would like to have when you graduate and fill in the following information that will be used to tailor your resumé and create a cover letter.

Position for which you are applying	
How you learned about the job	
Any contact you have had with the employer or others about the job	
Why are you interested in this job?	
Why are you interested in this company?	
What products or services are provided?	
List reasons this company should hire you.	
List relevant skills related to the job description.	
Indicate your desire for an interview.	
Indicate your flexibility for an interview (time and place).	

Activity 14-4

Using a word processing program and the information from this chapter, create a cover letter for the job you found in activity 14-3.

Activity 14-5

Change the resumé from activity 14-2 to an electronic formatted resumé.

Sample Exam Questions

1. Update your career resumé at least _____ .

2. If you are starting a new career, create a resumé using the _____ .

3. A/An _____ resumé format emphasizes your related work experience and skills.

4. _____ skills are those that are directly related to a specific job.

5. _____ skills are transferable from one job to the next.

6. Use _____ words whenever possible in your resumé; they describe your accomplishments in a lively and specific way.

7. The _____ is an introduction to your resumé.

Interview Techniques

chapter 15

All the world's a stage.

William Shakespeare (1564–1616)

Objectives

- Conduct company specific research for interview preparation

- Prepare a *personal commercial* to sell skills and tie them to a target job

- Identify pre-interview preparation activities including creating an *interview portfolio* and practice interview questions

- Explain key areas of employee rights and how to respond to discriminatory questions

- Describe specific statements and behaviors to exhibit at the close of an interview and job offer

- Discuss salary negotiation strategies

The Targeted Job

After you have created a winning resumé, it is time to begin a targeted job search. A targeted job search leads you through the process of identifying open positions for which you are qualified, in addition to identifying companies for which you would like to work. The ultimate goal of a job search is to secure an interview and a job offer.

A targeted job search helps identify where you want to work, who you want to work for, and what position you want. If your job search is limited to your local area, you will be restricted to employers in your community, which may limit the job positions available. If you do not want to move out of your living area but are willing to commute outside of your area, determine how far you are willing to drive (both directions) on a daily basis. Finally, if you wish to move out of the area, identify what locations are most appealing and affordable.

A job search takes work, takes time, and can sometimes be frustrating. Do not get discouraged if you do not get an interview or job offer on your first try. The purpose of this chapter is to provide you the skills and confidence to secure a good job in a reasonable time period.

Company Specific Research

Prior to your interview, conduct research on the company and the specific position for which you are applying. Many candidates ignore this step thinking it is unnecessary or takes too much time. Planning better prepares you for your interview, increases your confidence, and provides you a greater advantage over the other candidates. Learn as much as you can about the company's leadership, strategy, and any current event that may have affected the company. Review the company web site if available, or conduct an Internet search. Note the key products the company produces, identify the company's key competitors, and note any recent community involvement or recognized accomplishments the company has been involved with.

In addition to the Internet, other sources for securing company information include company-produced brochures/literature, industry journals, and interviews with current employees and business leaders. Job specific information is easily gathered by conducting a quick search on the O'Net database using the position title as your key word. As mentioned in the resumé chapter, this database of occupational information provides key information by job title.

The pre-interview research will assist you during your job interview. Identify as much as you can about the company, its administrators, and the department of your target job. Not only will you have an advantage in the interview, but you will know if this company is the right fit for you and your career goals. Use the information you find when conducting company-specific research in your resumé, cover letter, and interview.

In the interview, mention specific information about the company. This shows you have conducted research. For example, a popular interview question is "Why do you want to work for this company?" If you have conducted research, be specific in your answer and respond with "this company had been green conscious in the last two years which is an area I too, believe is important" instead of saying "I have heard it is a great company."

Cory's friend, Tomasz, was excited about an interview he would be having in a week. When Tomasz was sharing his excitement with Cory, Cory asked him if he had conducted research on the company. Tomasz said he really didn't need to conduct research because the company was pretty well known. Cory explained that it was important to conduct research beyond general knowledge to make sure Tomasz stood out from the other candidates. Cory and Tomasz conducted an extensive Internet search on the target company and Tomasz discovered useful information that Tomasz was able to use throughout his interview. After a successful interview, Tomasz thanked Cory and told Cory that the research prior to his interview gave him a lot of confidence that ultimately helped him to get the job.

The Personal Commercial

Prepare a **personal commercial** that sells your skills and ties these skills to the particular job for which you are interviewing. A personal commercial is a brief career biography that conveys your career choice, knowledge, skills, strengths, abilities, and experiences that make you uniquely qualified for the position to which you are applying. Include your interest in the targeted position and use this personal commercial at the beginning or end of an interview. The purpose of the commercial is to sell your skills in a brief statement. Your goal is to sell yourself and match your skills to fit the company needs by adapting it to the requirements for each target job. Do not include personal information such as marital status, hobbies, or other private areas of your life. In chapter 13 you completed an accomplishments worksheet which assisted you in identifying your personal qualifications for your target job. This information is used to create a career objective for the resumé you built in chapter 14. Use this information in your personal commercial. When you write your personal commercial make it reflect your personality. Your personal commercial should take about two minutes to deliver. The following is an example of a personal commercial.

Personal Commercial Example

Since I can remember, I have been interested in math, numbers, and counting money. In junior high, I started myself on a budget and kept track of saving and spending. In high school I knew at that time I wanted to become an accountant.

After finishing my classes at our local community college I started working as an account clerk for a hospital. In addition to my regular duties, I was able to attend conferences and workshops where I expanded my knowledge and skills in different areas of accounting.

I am a recent college graduate from State University where I received a bachelor's of science in accounting. With the additional education, I utilized the new skills and knowledge to work with general ledgers, accounts payable, and accounts receivable. I plan to apply my abilities and improve constantly.

With my experience as an Account Clerk, I have developed soft skills including how to deal with customers and coworkers in good and bad situations. In addition to the skills I have obtained working with MAS 90, I am proficient in MS Word and Excel. I have basic skills with Access, Outlook, and PowerPoint.

My goal is to become a CPA. Your company will benefit from my work ethic, which is to give 100% of my ability to every client and provide them the confidence they need for someone handling their money. My values include integrity and innovation. I am organized, dedicated, responsible, punctual, and willing to learn. I believe I am the best candidate for this position. Since your company is committed to clients and the community I would like to be a part of your team.

Exercise 15-1   Starting a Personal Commercial

Identify key points to include in your personal commercial.

_____

_____

_____

_____

_____

_____

Use your personal commercial during your interview when asked, "Tell me about yourself." If you are not given this instruction during the interview, include your personal commercial at the end of the interview. Practice delivering your commercial in front of a mirror.

The Invitation to Interview

There is a strategy to successful interviews and it starts as soon as you receive an invitation to interview. Most interview invitations are extended via phone or electronic mail. Therefore, it is important for you to regularly check and respond to both phone and electronic mail and messages. This is also a good reminder to maintain a professional voice mail message and e-mail address. When you are invited to interview, attempt to identify with whom you will be interviewing. You may be meeting with one person or a group of individuals. Your first interview may be a prescreening interview where a human resource representative or some other representative from the company briefly meets with you to ensure you are qualified and the right fit for the job.

Ask how much time the company has scheduled for the interview. If possible, identify how many applicants are being called for interviews. Although this is a lot of information to secure, if you are friendly, respectful, and professional, most companies will share this information. Attempt to arrange your interview at a time that puts you at an advantage over the other candidates. Typically, the first and last interviews are the most memorable. If you are given a choice of times to interview, schedule your interview in the morning. People are much more alert at that time, and you will have a greater advantage of making a favorable and memorable impression. If this is not possible, try to be the last person interviewed prior to the lunch break or the first person interviewed immediately after the lunch break. Be aware that sometimes you will have no say in when your interview is scheduled. Do not make demands when scheduling your interview. Politely ask the interview scheduler if it is possible for him or her to tell you who will be conducting the interview. The goal is to secure as much information as possible prior to the interview so that you can be prepared.

The Interview Portfolio

An **interview portfolio** is a small folder containing relevant documents that are taken to an interview. Use a professional looking business portfolio or paper folder with pockets for your interview portfolio. Include copies of items pertinent to the position for which you are applying. Original documents should not be given to the employer, only photocopies. Have the following items in your interview portfolio: copies of resumé, cover letter, reference list, generic application, and personal commercial. Also, include a calendar, note paper, a pen, and personal business cards. Print copies of your resumé, cover letter, and references on resumé paper. Copies of other items such as skill or education certificates and recent performance evaluations may be included if the information is relevant to the job. Keep your interview portfolio on your lap during the interview. Place your personal commercial on the top of your portfolio for easy access. Do not read the commercial. You may glance at it if you become nervous and forget what to say. We will revisit the appropriate use and time for your interview portfolio items in an upcoming section.

Practice Interview Questions

Another activity in preparing for an interview is to practice interview questions. Table 15-1 identifies common interview questions, the purpose of each question, and an appropriate way to answer each question. Review this list and begin creating appropriate responses to each question. Whenever you are answering interview questions, be honest and provide examples of specific skills and experiences that support your answers and meet the key requirements of the target job.

Practice answering interview questions in front of a mirror, and if possible create a practice interview video of yourself answering common interview questions. Critically analyze your responses to see if you are appropriately answering the questions, selling your key skills, and projecting a professional image. Also, check for nervous gestures. Doing this will better prepare you for an interview and help increase your self-confidence.

Preinterview Practice

Prior to the day of your interview, visit the interview location, pre-plan your interview wardrobe, ensure your interview portfolio is up-to-date, and prepare post-interview thank-you notes.

Conduct a "practice day" prior to the day of your interview. If possible, drive or find transportation to the interview location. Ideally, do this on the same hour as your scheduled interview to identify potential transportation problems including traffic and parking. Once at the site, walk to the location where the interview will be held. This will enable you to become comfortable and familiar with your surroundings and let you know how much time you will need to arrive at the interview on time. Do not go into the specific office, just the general area. Make note of the nearest public restroom so you can use it the day of the interview to freshen up prior to your meeting.

Talk It Out

Identify the most difficult questions to answer and formulate appropriate responses that sell your skills.

Table 15-1   Common Interview Questions

Question	Answer	Do Not
Tell me about yourself.	Use your personal commercial modified to the job description.	Do not divulge where you were born, personal hobbies, or other personal information.
What are your strengths?	Include how your strengths meet the job requirements and how they will be an asset to the company.	Do not include strengths that are not related to the job. Do not include personal information (e.g., "I'm a good mother").
Tell me about a time you failed.	Use an example that is not too damaging. Turn it into a positive by including the lesson learned from your mistake.	Do not exclude the lesson learned. Do not place blame on why the failure occurred.
Tell me about a time you were successful.	Use an example that relates to the job for which you are applying.	Do not take full credit if the success was a team effort.
How do you handle conflict?	Use an example that is not too damaging. Include how the conflict was positively resolved. Apply the lesson from chapter 12.	Do not provide specifics on how the conflict occurred and do not use a negative example or place blame on others.
Would you rather work individually or in a team? Why?	State that you prefer one or the other and why, but relate your answer to the job requirements.	Do not state that you will not work one way or the other.
Why do you want this job?	Convey career goals and how the job supports your current skills. Include company information learned through research.	Do not state money or benefits in your response.
How do you deal with stress?	Share positive stress reducers addressed in chapter 4.	Do not state that stress does not affect you. Do not use negative examples.
What is your greatest weakness?	Use a weakness that will not damage your chance of getting the job. Explain how you are minimizing your weakness or are turning it into a strength (e.g., "I'm a perfectionist, but I don't allow it to interfere with getting my job done on time").	Do not state, "I don't have any."
Where do you want to be in five years?	Share the career goals you created in chapter 2.	Do not say you want the interviewer's job.
Tell me about a time you displayed leadership.	Use a specific example and try to relate the example to the needed job skills.	Do not appear arrogant.

Ensure that your interview attire is clean and professional prior to the day of the interview. Refer to chapter 6 to review professional dress in greater detail. Dress at a level above the position for which you are interviewing. For example, if you are interviewing for an entry-level position, dress like you are interviewing for a supervisor position. Check that your clothes are spotless and fit appropriately and your shoes are clean. Women, it is a good idea to have an extra pair of nylons available in case of snags or tears. Ensure that your hair and fingernails are professional and appropriate for an interview. If necessary, get a haircut prior to your interview. Use little or no perfume/aftershave and keep jewelry to a minimum. Remember that cleanliness is important.

Prior to the interview customize your interview portfolio for the target job. Place your portfolio in a place where you will not forget it when you leave your home.

Purchase a package of simple but professional thank-you notes. The evening before your interview, write a draft thank-you note on a blank piece of paper. Keep your thank-you note brief, three to four sentences. In the note, thank the interviewer for his or her time. State that you enjoyed learning more about the position, are very interested in the job, and look forward to hearing from the interviewer soon. This draft note will be used as a foundation for notes you will be writing immediately after your interview. Place the draft note, the package of thank-you notes, and a black pen alongside your interview portfolio to take with you.

Write a draft thank-you note.

Exercise 15-2   Thank-You Note

Write a draft thank-you note.

The Day of the Interview

Be well rested and have food in your stomach prior to leaving your home for the interview. Look in the mirror to check your appearance and clothing. Your clothes should fit properly and project a professional image. If you smoke, refrain from smoking prior to the interview. The smell may be a distraction to the interviewer.

Plan to arrive at your destination fifteen minutes early. This provides time to deal with unforeseen traffic and/or parking issues. If there is a public restroom available, go to the restroom and freshen up. Check your hair, clothing, and makeup, if applicable. Enter the specific meeting location five minutes prior to your scheduled interview. This is where your interview unofficially begins. First impressions matter and any interaction with representatives of the organization must be professional.

Immediately upon entering the interview location, introduce yourself to the receptionist. Offer a smile and a handshake, and then clearly and slowly state your name. For example, "Hi, I'm Cory Kringle, and I am here for a 9:00 A.M. interview with Mr. Wong for the accounting clerk position." If you recognize the receptionist as the same individual who arranged your interview appointment, make an additional statement thanking the individual for his or her assistance. For example, "Mrs. Jones, were you the one that I spoke with on the phone? Thank you for your help in arranging my interview." Be sincere in your conversation, and convey to the receptionist that you appreciate his or her efforts. The receptionist will most likely ask you to have a seat and wait to be called into the interview. Take a seat and relax. While you are waiting, use **positive self-talk**. Positive self-talk is a mental form of positive self-reinforcement. It helps remind you that you are qualified and deserve both the interview and the job. Mentally tell yourself that you are prepared, qualified, and ready for a successful interview. Review your personal commercial, qualifications, and the key skills you want to convey in the interview.

Cory's friend Shelby had been asked to interview with one of her target companies. Shelby really wanted the job but was afraid she was not going to do well during her interview. Cory worked with Shelby the evening before the interview by role-playing interview questions and reviewing Shelby's company research. The next day, when Shelby arrived for the interview, she arrived early, thanked the receptionist, and took a seat. As Shelby waited to be called into the interview, she began getting extremely nervous. Remembering Cory's tips, Shelby briefly closed her eyes and used positive self-talk to improve her attitude, increase her confidence, and calm her nerves. Doing this she felt more confident when called into the office to begin the interview.

The Interview

During an interview communicate confidence. Your primary message during the interview will be how your knowledge, skills, and abilities will be an asset to the company. When you are called to interview stand up and approach the individual who called your name. If it is not the receptionist who called you, extend a smile and a handshake, then clearly and slowly state your name. For example, "Hi, I'm Cory Kringle. It's nice to meet you." Listen carefully to the individual's name so you will remember it and use it during the interview. He or she will escort you to an office or conference room where the interview will take place. If you enter a room and there is someone in the room that you have not met, extend a smile and a handshake and introduce yourself. Once in the room, do not be seated until you are invited to do so. When seated, if possible, write down the names of the individuals you have just met. Inject the interviewer's name(s) during the interview. Although you may be offered something to drink, it is best to decline the offer so there is nothing to distract you from the interview.

The interview may be conducted different ways. It may only involve one person; it may involve several individuals, it may involve testing, or it may be a combination of interviewing and testing. Testing activities must be job related, such as typing tests for office work, lifting for a warehouse position, or demonstrating other skills that are included in the job requirements and/or job duties. If the interview is taking place in an office, look around the room to get a sense of the person who is conducting the interview, assuming it is his or her office. This provides useful information for conversation, should it be necessary. Depending on the time available and the skills of the interviewer(s), you may first be asked general questions such as, "Did you have trouble finding our office?" The interviewer is trying to get you to relax. During the interview, pay attention to body language—both yours and that of the individual conducting the interview. Sit up straight, sit back in your chair, and try to relax. Be calm but alert. Keep your hands folded on your lap or ready to take notes, depending on the situation. If you are seated near a desk or table, do not lean on the furniture. Make eye contact, but do not stare at the interviewer.

If you are given the opportunity to provide an opening statement, share your personal commercial. If you are not able to open with your personal commercial include it in an appropriate response or use it at the end of the interview. When asked a question, listen carefully. Take a few seconds to think and digest what information the interviewer truly wants to know about your skill sets. Formulate an answer. Interview answers should relate back to the job qualifications and/or job duties. Your goal is to convey to the interviewer how your skills will assist the company in achieving success. Keep your answers brief but complete. Sell your skills and expertise by including a specific, but short example. Whenever possible, inject information you learned about the company during your research.

Phone Interviews

In some situations your first interview may take place over the phone. Phone interviews may occur without prearrangement, while others are scheduled. During your job search consistently answer your phone in a professional manner and keep your interview portfolio within easy reach of the phone. If a company calls and asks if it is a good time to speak with you and it is not, politely respond that it is not a good time and ask if you can reschedule. Try to be as accommodating as possible to the interviewer.

Those being interviewed by phone should follow these tips:

- *Be professional and be prepared.* Conduct the interview in a quiet room. Remove all distractions including music, television, and other individuals from your quiet area. Company research, personal examples, and the use of your personal commercial are just as important to inject into the phone conversation as it is during a face-to-face interview.

- *Be concise with your communication.* Those conducting the interview are not able to see you; therefore, they are forming an impression of you by what you say and how it is stated. Speak clearly, slowly, and do not interrupt. Smile while you speak and speak with enthusiasm. Use proper grammar and beware of "ums" and other nervous verbal phrases.

- *Be polite.* Utilizing what you learned in both the etiquette and communication chapters, remember to exercise good manners. When the conversation is over, ask for the job, and thank the interviewer for his or her time. It is not appropriate to use a speaker phone when being interviewed nor is it polite to take another call. Also remember to not tend to personal matters while on a phone interview. Your attention should be completely focused on the interview.

Interview Methods and Types of Interview Questions

There are several common types of interviews. These include one-on-one interviews, group interviews, and panel interviews. **One-on-one interviews** involve a one-on-one meeting between the applicant and a company representative.

The company representative is typically someone from either the human resource department or the immediate supervisor of the department with the open position. **Group interviews** involve several applicants interviewing with each other while being observed by company representatives. The purpose of a group interview is to gauge how an individual behaves in a competitive and stressful environment. In a group interview situation, practice positive human relation and communication skills toward other applicants. Be professional, do not interrupt, and behave like a leader. Be assertive, not aggressive. **Panel interviews** involve the applicant meeting with several company employees at the same time. During a panel interview, make initial eye contact with the person asking the question. While answering the question make eye contact with the other members of the interview panel. Whenever possible, call individuals by name.

The three general types of interview questions are structured, unstructured, and behavioral. **Structured interview questions** address job-related issues where each applicant is asked the same question(s). An example of a structured question is, "How long have you worked in the retail industry?" The purpose of a structured interview question is to secure information related to a specific job. An **unstructured interview question** is a probing, open-ended question. The purpose of an unstructured interview question is to identify if the candidate can appropriately sell his or her skills. An example of an unstructured interview question is, "Tell me about yourself." When you are asked to talk about yourself, state your personal commercial. Whenever possible, pull job samples from your portfolio if you are referring to a specific skill. Relate answers back to the job for which you are applying. **Behavioral interview questions** are questions that ask candidates to share a past experience related to a workplace situation. An example of a behavioral question is: "Describe a time you motivated others." Prior to answering the question, take a moment to formulate your answer. Use an example that puts you in a positive light and utilizes key skills that are necessary for your target job.

Discrimination and Employee Rights

Title VII of the Civil Rights Act was created to protect the rights of employees. It prohibits employment discrimination based on race, color, religion, sex, or national origin. Other federal laws prohibit pay inequity and discrimination against individuals over forty years of age, individuals with disabilities, and individuals who are pregnant. This does not mean that an employer must hire you if you are a minority, pregnant, over forty, or have a disability. Employers have a legal obligation to provide every qualified candidate equal opportunity to interview. Their job is to hire the most qualified candidate. Unfortunately, some employers ask interview questions that can be discriminatory. Discriminatory questions are illegal. Table 15-2 was taken from the California Department of Fair Employment and Housing to provide examples of acceptable and unacceptable employment inquiries.

If an interviewer asks you a question that is illegal or could be discriminatory, do not directly answer the question; instead, address the issue. For example, if the interviewer states, "You look Hispanic, are you?" Your response should not be "yes" or "no." Politely smile and say, "People wonder about my ethnicity. What can I tell you about my qualifications for this job?" Also, do not accuse the interviewer of asking an illegal question or say, "I will not answer that question because it is

Table 15-2 Illegal Interview Questions

Acceptable	Subject	Unacceptable
Name	**Name**	Maiden name
Place of residence	**Residence**	Questions regarding owning or renting
Statements that employment is subject to verification if applicant meets legal age requirement	**Age**	Age Birth date Date of attendance/completion of school Questions that tend to identify applicants over forty
Statements/inquiries regarding verification of legal right to work in the United States	**Birthplace, citizenship**	Birthplace of applicant or applicant's parents, spouse, or other relatives Requirements that applicant produce naturalization or alien card prior to employment
Languages applicant reads, speaks, or writes if use of language other than English is relevant to the job for which applicant is applying	**National origin**	Questions as to nationality, lineage, ancestry, national origin, descent or parentage of applicant, applicant's spouse, parent, or relative
Statement by employer of regular days, hours, or shifts to be worked	**Religion**	Questions regarding applicant's religion Religious days observed
Name and address of parent or guardian if applicant is a minor. Statement of company policy regarding work assignment of employees who are related	**Sex, marital status, family**	Questions to indicate applicant's sex, marital status, number/ages of children or dependents Questions regarding pregnancy, child birth, or birth control Name/address of relative, spouse, or children of adult applicant
Job-related questions about convictions, except those convictions that have been sealed, expunged, or statutorily eradicated	**Arrest, criminal record**	Arrest record General questions regarding arrest record

illegal." Most employers do not realize they are asking illegal questions. However, some employers purposely ask inappropriate questions. In this case, you need to decide if you want to work for an employer who intentionally asks illegal questions. If employers are behaving inappropriately during an interview, one would wonder how they will treat the applicant after he or she is hired.

Know and protect your rights. It is inappropriate to disclose personal information about yourself during an interview. Avoid making any comment referring to your marital status, children, religion, age, or any other private issue protected by law.

Tough Questions

Life is unpredictable and sometimes results in situations that can be embarrassing or difficult to explain during a job interview. These situations may include a negative work experience with a previous employer, time gaps in a resumé, or a prior felony conviction. The following information provides the proper response to interview questions related to these difficult situations.

Unfortunately, some job seekers have had negative work-related experiences that they do not want to disclose during an interview. Disclosing such information could be potentially devastating to a job interview if it is not handled properly. Some of these experiences include being fired, having a poor performance evaluation, or knowing that a former manager will not provide a positive job reference if called. Perhaps you behaved in a negative manner prior to leaving your old job.

If you did have a difficult circumstance and are not asked about the situation, you have no need to disclose the unpleasant event. The only exception to this rule is if your current or former boss has the potential to provide a negative reference. If this is the situation, tell the interviewer that you know you will not receive a positive reference from him or her and request that the interviewer contact another manager or coworker who will provide a fair assessment of your performance.

Being honest and factual is the best answer to any difficult question. If you were fired, performed poorly, or left in a negative manner, state the facts, but do not go into great detail. Tell the interviewer that you have matured and realize that you did not handle the situation appropriately. Add what lesson you have learned. Do not speak poorly of your current or previous employer, boss, or coworker. It is also important to not place blame on who was right or wrong in your negative workplace situation.

It is common for an individual to have time gaps in a resumé as a result of staying at home to raise a young child, care for an elderly relative, or continue his or her education. Those who have gaps in their resumé may need to be prepared to explain what they did during the time gap. Identify a key skill you sharpened during your time gap and relate this experience to a key skill necessary for your target job and industry. For example, if you stayed at home to care for an elderly relative and are asked about the time gap, explain the situation without providing specific details, and then share how the experience improved your time management and organizational skills in addition to improving your awareness of diverse populations including the elderly and disabled.

If you have a felony record, you may be asked about your conviction. As with other difficult interview questions, be honest and factual in your response. Explain the situation, tell the interviewer that you are making every attempt to start anew and are committed to doing your very best. Sell your strengths and remember to communicate how your skills will help the company achieve its goals. Your self-confidence and honesty will be revealed through your body language and eye contact. Be sincere. Depending on the type and severity of your offense, it may take more attempts at securing a job than during a typical job search. You may also need to start at a lower level and/or lower pay than desired. The goal is to begin to reestablish credibility. Don't give up, each experience, be it positive or negative, is a learning experience.

Closing the Interview

After the interviewer has completed his or her questioning, you may be asked if you have any questions. Having a question prepared for the close of your interview demonstrates to your prospective employer that you have conducted research on the company. A good question refers to a current event that has occurred within the company. For example, "Mr. Wong, I read about how your company employees donated time to clean up the ABC schoolyard. Is this an annual event?" A statement such as this provides you one last opportunity to personalize the interview and demonstrate that you researched the company. This is also a good time to share any relevant information you have in your portfolio.

Do not ask questions that imply you did not research the company or that you only care about your needs. Inappropriate questions include questions regarding salary, benefits, or vacations. These questions imply that you care more about what the company can do for you than what you can do for the company. However, it is appropriate to ask what the next steps will be in the interview process, including when the hiring decision will be made.

Questions You *May* Ask the Interviewer

1. Does your company have any plans for expansion?

2. What type of formal training does your company offer?

3. What is the greatest challenge your industry is currently facing?

4. What is the next step in the interview process?

5. What are the required work days and hours of the position?

6. When will you be making a hiring decision?

Questions You *Should Not* Ask During an Interview

1. How much does this job pay?

2. How many sick days do I get?

3. What benefits will I get?

4. What does your company do?

5. How long does it take for someone to get fired for poor performance?

After the interviewer answers your general questions, make a closing interview statement. Restate your personal commercial and ask for the job. An example of a good closing statement is to restate your personal commercial and add: "Once again, thank you for your time, Mr. Wong. As I stated at the beginning of our meeting, I feel I am qualified for this job based upon my experience, knowledge, and demonstrated leadership. I would like this job and believe I will be an asset to XYZ Company." The purpose of the job interview is to sell yourself. A sale is useless if you do not close the sale.

After you make your closing statement, the interviewer will signal that the interview is over. He or she will do this either through conversation or through body language such as standing up and walking toward the door. Prior to leaving the interview, hand the interviewer your personal business card and ask the interviewer for a business card. You will use this business card for the interview follow-up. As you are handed the card, shake the interviewer's hand using a firm shake and eye contact and, thank him or her for his or her time and state that you look forward to hearing from him or her. Remember to continue communicating confidence, friendliness, and professionalism to every company employee you encounter on your way out of the building.

When you leave the building, retrieve your draft thank-you note. Modify your draft thank-you note to include information that was shared during your interview. Handwrite a personalized thank-you note to each individual who interviewed you. Use your finest handwriting and double-check your spelling and grammar. Refer to the business card(s) you collected for correct name spelling. After you have written your note, hand deliver it to the reception area and ask the receptionist to deliver the notes. Your goal is to make a positive last impression and stand out from the other candidates.

After the Interview

After delivering your thank-you notes, congratulate yourself. If you did your best, you should have no regrets. Prior to leaving the company property, make notes regarding specific information you learned about your prospective job and questions you were asked during the interview. Through the excitement of an interview, you may forget parts of your meeting if you do not immediately write notes. Write down what you did right and areas in which you would like to improve upon. This is a good time for you to evaluate your impressions of the company and determine if it is a company where you will want to work. This information will be helpful in the future.

Negotiation

Soon after your initial interview, you should hear back from the company. At that point, you may be called in for a second interview or may receive a job offer. A job offer may be contingent upon reference and background checks. This will be a good time to contact the individuals on your reference list to provide them an update on your job search and ensure your references are prepared to respond appropriately to the individual conducting your reference check.

If you are a final candidate for the job, the interviewer may ask you about your salary requirements. In order to negotiate an acceptable salary, first conduct research and compare your research to the salary range that was included in the job announcement. Check job postings and conduct online research to determine local and regional salaries. During your salary research attempt to match the job description as close as possible to that of the job for which you are applying. Depending on your experience, start a few thousand dollars higher than your desired starting salary and do not forget to consider your experience and/or lack of experience. Some companies do not offer many benefits but offer higher salaries. Other companies offer lower salaries but better benefits. Weigh these factors when determining your desired salary. Prior to stating your salary requirement, sell your skills. For example, "Mr. Wong, as I mentioned in my initial interview, I have over five years' experience working in a professional accounting office and an accounting degree; therefore, I feel I should earn between $55,000 and $65,000." If you are offered a salary that is not acceptable, use silence and wait for the interviewer to respond. This minute of silence may encourage the employer to offer a higher salary.

Cory's friend Kenny was invited to a second interview. Prior to the interview, Cory and Kenny prepared for potential questions and situations Kenny might encounter during the interview. In their practice, Cory asked Kenny about his starting salary. Kenny said he did not care; he would just be happy to get a job. Cory reminded Kenny that he needed to sell his skills and go into the interview with a desired target salary. Cory and Kenny then conducted an Internet search of both local and statewide jobs that were similar to the one Kenny wants. Kenny was surprised that starting salaries were much higher than he expected. Fortunately, the next day, when the interviewer asked Kenny about his desired starting salary, Kenny was prepared to answer.

Pre-Employment Screenings and Medical Exams

Prior to receiving a job offer or within a few weeks of being hired, an employer may conduct pre-employment screenings and medical exams. The most common pre-employment screenings include criminal checks, education verification, driver's license history, security checks, employment checks, credit checks, and reference checks. The number and type of pre-employment screenings performed will be based upon how relevant the check is to the job you will be performing. Legally, employers can require medical exams only after a job offer is made. The exam must be required for all applicants for the same job, and the exam must be job related. Employers are not allowed to ask disability questions related to pre-employment screenings and medical exams. Common medical exams include vision and strength testing. Employers may also require pre-employment drug tests.

An employer legally cannot conduct these checks without your permission. Most employers will secure your permission in writing when you complete an employment application or when you are a finalist for the position.

When You Are Not Offered the Job

As stated at the beginning of the chapter, a job search is similar to a full-time job. It takes time and can sometimes be discouraging. If you are not called in for an interview or fail to receive a job offer, do not be discouraged.

If you are not called in for an interview, evaluate your resumé and cover letter. Check for typographical or grammatical errors. Make sure you have listed important skills that reflect the needs of the job for which you are applying. Have someone who knows you and your skills—and whom you trust—review your cover letter and resumé. Many times, a fresh perspective will catch obvious errors or opportunities for improvement.

If you are invited to interviews but do not receive a job offer, do not be discouraged. Remember to make every experience a learning experience. Sit down and carefully review each step in the interview process and grade yourself. Consider your pre-interview preparation, interview day appearance, your interview answers, your ability to interject company research into each interview answer, and your overall attitude. Any area that did not receive an A grade is an area poised for improvement.

There are several steps you can take to increase the probability for success in your next interview. Consider your overall appearance. Reviewing the information in chapter 6, make sure you convey professionalism. Ensure that your clothes are clean and that they fit properly. Have a hairstyle that is flattering and well kept. Check that your fingernails and jewelry are appropriate and do not distract from your personality and job skills.

Mentally review job interview questions that were asked and the responses you provided. Every answer should communicate how your skills will assist the target company in achieving success. Review the amount of company research you conducted. Did you feel amply prepared or did you simply research the bare minimum? If you felt you did conduct the appropriate amount of research, assess whether you fully communicated your research to the interviewer.

Assess your body language and attitude. Stand in front of a mirror and practice your answers to difficult and/or illegal questions. If possible, have a friend videotape you and provide an evaluation of your appearance, attitude, and body language. Check for nervous gestures, and keep practicing until you are able to control these nervous habits.

Finally, be honest with your overall performance. Did you ask for the job? Did you immediately send a thank-you note to your interviewer(s)? Sell your skills through your mannerisms, answers, and attitude. Your goal is to stand out above the other candidates.

Workplace Dos and Don'ts

Dos	Don'ts
Do tailor your resumé and personal commercial to the needs of your targeted employer	*Don't* have unprofessional introductions on your voice-mail message
Do try to schedule your interview at a time that puts you at an advantage over the other candidates and secure information that better prepares you for the interview	*Don't* make demands with the individual scheduling the interview
Do learn as much as you can about the company, its strategy, and its competition	*Don't* forget to include your research information in your interview answers
Do practice interview questions and formulate answers that highlight your skills and experience	*Don't* show up to an interview unprepared
Do remember that your interview begins the minute you step onto company property	*Don't* let your nerves get the better of you on a job interview
Do know how to handle inappropriate questions that may be discriminatory	*Don't* answer an illegal question. Instead address the issue

Summary of Key Concepts

- Create and modify your personal commercial and adapt it to the requirements of your target job
- Review common interview questions and formulate answers as part of your interview preparation
- Conduct a pre-interview practice to ensure you are prepared the day of the interview
- During your interview, communicate how your knowledge, skills, and abilities will be assets to the company
- Understand the laws that protect employees from discrimination in the interviewing and hiring process
- Be prepared to confidently handle gaps in employment and other difficult interview questions
- Know how to sell yourself and professionally ask for the job at the close of an interview

Key Terms

behavioral interview question
interview portfolio
panel interview
positive self-talk
unstructured interview question

group interview
one-on-one interview
personal commercial
structured interview question

If You Were the Boss

1. What kind of information should you share with your current staff members as they prepare to interview a new employee?
2. How would you handle a prospective employee who disclosed inappropriate information during the job interview?

Video Case Study: Good, Bad, and Ugly

This video addresses improper and proper behavior in a job interview. Refer to the CD that accompanies your text, watch this video, and answer the following questions:

1. Of the three candidates, who was dressed appropriately for the interview and who was not?
2. Name four interview recommendations for Shawn.
3. What interview advice would you give to Kevin?
4. How did Francesca specifically use her interview portfolio and personal commercial during her interview?

Video Case Study: Interview Walk-Through

This video presents expert advice on how to prepare and what to expect the day of an interview. Refer to the CD that accompanies your text, watch this video, and answer the following questions.

1. Name three activities to perform prior to entering the specific interview location.
2. How specifically should you greet the receptionist?
3. What three activities does the expert recommend you do and what are two activities to avoid while waiting in the reception area?

Video Case Study: Preparing for a Phone Interview

This video presents a phone interview between a job applicant and a potential employer. Refer to the CD that accompanies your text, watch this video, and answer the following questions:

1. What improvements could be made to Kevin's voice mail message?
2. Did Kevin answer his phone appropriately and what kind of impression did he make on Karen Gonzales when he answered the phone?
3. Did Kevin handle the background noise appropriately? Why or why not?
4. How could Kevin have been better prepared for this phone interview?
5. If you were Karen would you call Kevin in for a second interview? Why or why not?

Video Case Study: Pre-Interview Activities

This video presents expert advice regarding activities to conduct before the day of an interview. Refer to the CD that accompanies your text, watch this video, and answer the following questions.

1. What scheduling strategy should you utilize when invited to an interview?
2. Name four specific items to be included in an interview portfolio and explain the purpose of each.
3. Name four specific activities that need to take place in preparing your interview outfit.
4. Why is it important to visit the interview site prior to the day of an interview?

Video Case Study: Tough Interview Questions

This video presents expert advice on how to respond to tough interview questions. Refer to the CD that accompanies your text, watch this video, and answer the following questions.

1. How does the expert recommend you prepare for a tough interview question?
2. What specific advice does the expert share on how to respond to a tough interview question?
3. Provide specific information the expert shared on how to deal with illegal interview questions.

Web Links

http://jobstar.org/electra/question/sal-req.cfm
http://www.collegegrad.com/intv
http://www.careercc.com/interv3.shtml
http://interview.monster.com
http://www.rileyguide.com/interview.html

Reference

State of California Department of Fair Employment and Housing. *Pre-Employment Inquiry Guidelines.* CA, DFEH-161, Sacramento, CA, 2001.

Activity 15-1

Identify a local company for which you would like to interview. Using the following table, conduct a through targeted job search on this company. Answer as many of the questions as possible.

1. Company name	
2. Company address	
3. Job title	
4. To whom should the cover letter be addressed?	
5. What are the job requirements?	
6. Is this a full-time or part-time job?	
7. What are the hours/days of work?	
8. What are the working conditions?	
9. Is there room for advancement?	
10. What kind of training is offered?	
11. What other positions at this company match my qualifications?	
12. What are the average starting salaries (benefits)?	
13. Is traveling or relocation required?	
14. Where is the business located (home office, other offices)?	
15. What are the products or services that the employer provides or manufactures?	
16. What is the mission statement?	
17. What kind of reputation does this organization have?	
18. What is the size of the employer's organization relative to the industry?	
19. What is the growth history of the organization for the past five, ten, or fifteen years?	
20. How long has the employer been in business?	
21. Who is the employer's competition?	

Activity 15-2

Write a statement to use during an invitation to an interview that will help you secure all relevant interview information.

_____

Activity 15-3

Using information obtained in your target company research (activity 15–1), write three common interview questions and answers. Integrate relevant company information in your answers.

Question	Answer
1.	
2.	
3.	

Activity 15-4

Conduct a salary search for a target job. Identify the salary range. Using your research data, write out a statement you could use to negotiate a higher salary.

Lowest Salary	Highest Salary
$	$

Write a Salary Negotiation Statement

Sample Exam Questions

1. The purpose of a/an _____ is to identify _____ and identify companies for which you would like to work.

2. In addition to finding out with whom you will be interviewing, identify how much _____ the company has scheduled and _____ are being called in to _____.

3. Prior to your interview, _____.

4. If possible, prior to the interview day, _____.

5. When asked a difficult question, be _____ and _____.

Career and Life Changes

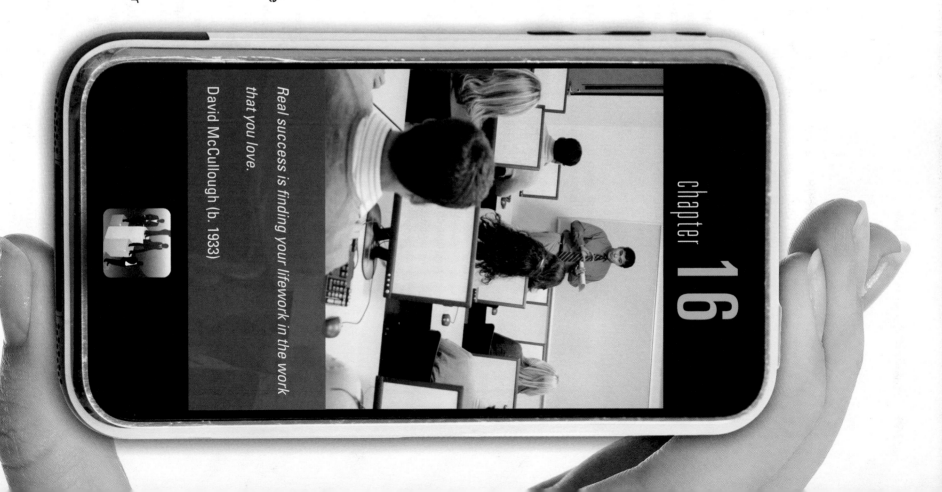

chapter 16

Real success is finding your lifework in the work that you love.

David McCullough (b. 1933)

Objectives

- Define the importance of continual *formal learning* and *informal learning*

- Explain the importance of *training* and *development*

- Know the various ways employment status can change

- Define the various types of workplace terminations

- Demonstrate how to write a *letter of resignation*

- Know the appropriate behavior to exhibit when leaving a position

- Understand the opportunities of becoming an *entrepreneur*

Training and Development

Many companies offer current and new employees **training** to learn new skills. The teaching of new skills may be used to promote employees and/or increase their responsibilities. With the increase of technology usage, employee training is important for many companies. Training is usually provided and/or paid for by the company.

In addition to learning new skills through training, make every effort to attend **development** sessions designed to enhance existing skills or increase your skills. Development sessions make employees more diverse in knowledge, skills, and abilities, which provide an advantage when promotional or other opportunities arise in the workplace. Even if you do not think a development session is in your area of expertise, continue expanding your knowledge and skills in as many areas as possible. This is especially helpful if you are considering a promotion into a management position.

As an employee who is considering a management position, learn not only the skills needed for your job but also other skills. Be aware of the key duties within other departments. The development of these skills will increase your knowledge and understanding of the company's mission and goals. When you can see beyond your job, you become more aware of what you are contributing to the company and how you are helping make it more successful.

The marketing department for Cory's company invited all employees to meet in the conference room during lunch hour to learn more about how to conduct a media interview. Cory did not know a lot about marketing and did not think media interviews were a part of Cory's job. However, Cory attended because it would be not only a good skill to learn but also a good way to meet people in other departments.

Continual Learning

In addition to training and development programs offered by a company, there are other ways to improve and increase your skills and knowledge. **Continual learning** is the ongoing process of increasing knowledge in the area of your career. This can be accomplished by formal and/or informal learning.

Formal learning involves returning to college to increase knowledge, improve skills, or receive an additional or advanced degree. This can be done while you continue working. Consider taking one or two night classes while working full time because that may stress you to a point that you will perform poorly at both work and school.

Many colleges now offer online classes which have become increasingly popular for working adults. These classes allow more freedom and flexibility. Instead of having to attend class on a certain day and at a certain time, students log on to the Internet at their convenience and complete coursework around work hours.

In addition to college, seminars and conferences are available. Some of these seminars and conferences offer college credit. Many seminars and conferences are offered by vendors or industry experts. Although you may have to pay for a conference, your company may be willing to reimburse you or share the cost with you. Conferences may last one day or may be over a period of several days.

Informal learning is increasing knowledge by reading career-related magazines, newsletters, and electronic articles associated with your job. Another means of informal learning is using the Internet to research career-related information. Informal learning is an ongoing process and can occur during informational interviews, in conversations with professionals in your career area, and by attending association meetings. Make every opportunity a learning opportunity.

Exercise 16-1   Additional Career Interests

What additional classes may be helpful to you when you start working in your new job? Name at least three classes.

1. _____

2. _____

3. _____

Changes in Employment Status

It is natural for employees to have a desire to change jobs. If and when this job change occurs depends upon many factors. Throughout this text, we have stressed the importance of personality and goal setting. As you begin meeting your stated career goals, it is time to establish new ones. Some reasons for changing jobs are:

- Acquired experience for an advanced position
- Opportunity for higher salary
- Desire for improved work hours
- Need for increased responsibility, status, and/or power
- A perceived decrease in stress
- Need for a different boss or coworker

Other times, you may be forced to change positions. It is common for employees to move within and outside of their company. Changes in employment status include promotions, voluntary terminations, involuntary terminations, lateral transfers, and retirement. This section presents and discusses these changes in employment status and provides tips on how to handle each situation in a professional manner.

New Job Searches

Depending on one's work situation some employees determine that they must find a new job immediately while other employees are constantly exploring opportunities. No matter your situation, identify when to share your desire for a new job and when to keep your job search private. If you have recently received a college certification or degree that qualifies you for a higher position, approach your supervisor or human resource department to inform the appropriate individuals of your increased qualifications and desire for additional responsibilities and/or promotion. It is also appropriate to share your need to change jobs if a situation is requiring you to move out of the area. In this instance, your employer may have contacts to assist you in securing a new job in another city. If you have had good performance evaluations and are leaving voluntarily, ask your immediate supervisor, another superior, or coworkers if they are willing to serve as references for future employers. If they agree to serve as references, secure letters of recommendation written on company letterhead. It is helpful to write and provide a draft letter for your reference that highlights your accomplishments and favorable work attitude. Finally, if you have mastered your job duties, have had good performance evaluations, and are beginning to feel bored, respectfully share your desire for increased responsibilities with your boss.

Apart from the previously mentioned circumstances, do not share your desire to change jobs with anyone at work. This includes close coworkers. Oftentimes, sharing secrets at work can be used against you. Therefore, keep your job search private. Conduct your job search during nonwork hours. Schedule job interviews before or after work.

Exercise 16-2   Your Recommendation

List at least four key points to include in a draft letter of recommendation for you. Provide an example for each key point.

Key Point (Quality)	Example
1.	
2.	
3.	
4.	

Grace and style are two key words to remember when your search for a new position is discovered by others. When confronted about your job search, be brief and positive. State that you desire a move, be it the need for additional responsibility or the need for more money, but keep your explanation simple. You do not have to share details as to why you want to move on. It is also not appropriate to share details about potential employers or the status of your job search.

Promotions

A **promotion** is when someone moves to a position higher in the organization with increased pay and responsibility. Oftentimes, an individual wants a promotion but there is not an available position. The first step in securing a future promotion within your company is to begin behaving and dressing for advancement. Secure a copy of the job description and/or research key skills necessary for your desired position. Begin acquiring work experience in the target area by volunteering for assignments that provide the needed experience. Develop new skills by taking appropriate classes, job training, and other educational experiences to increase your qualifications. Watch and learn from those who are already in the position you desire. Implement this plan and you will gain the necessary qualifications and have the experience when an advanced position does become available.

When you are promoted, thank your former boss. This can be done verbally or with a simple, handwritten thank-you note. Communicate to your former boss how he or she has helped you acquire new skills. Be sincere. Even if your former boss was incompetent or abusive, his or her poor example showed you how not to behave. Keep the note positive and professional. With your promotion, you most likely will see an increase in pay, a new title, and new responsibilities. If your promotion occurred within the same company, do not gloat; there were probably others within the company who also applied for the job. Behave in a professional manner that reinforces that your company made the right choice in selecting you for the position.

In your new job, do not try to reinvent the wheel. Become familiar with the history of your department or area. Be sensitive to the needs and adjustments of your new employees. Review files and begin networking with people who can assist you in achieving department goals. When you are new to a position, you do not know everything. Ask for and accept help from others.

With a history of favorable performance evaluations, Cory wants a promotion. Cory decided to take responsibility and began evaluating potential positions for which Cory might qualify. While conducting research, Cory created a list of additional knowledge, skills, and abilities needed for the promotion. Cory began taking classes, attending training seminars, and watching leaders within the company to prepare for a future promotion.

Voluntary Terminations

Leaving a job on your own is called a **voluntary termination.** While at times the workplace can be so unbearable that you want to quit without having another job, it is best to not quit your job unless you have another job waiting. No matter what the situation, when voluntarily leaving a job, be professional and do not burn bridges.

Resign with a formal letter of resignation. A **letter of resignation** is a written notice of your voluntary termination. Unless you are working with a contract that specifies an end date of your employment, you are technically not required to provide advance notice of your voluntary termination. It is, however, considered unprofessional to resign from work and make your last day the same day you resign. Typically, two weeks' notice is acceptable. State your last date of employment in your letter of resignation. Include a positive statement about the employer and remember to sign and date your letter. Following is a sample letter of resignation.

February 1, 2011

Susie Supervisor
ABC Company
123 Avenue 456
Anycity, USA 98765

Re: Notice of Resignation

Dear Ms. Supervisor:

While I have enjoyed working for ABC Company, I have been offered and have accepted a new position with another firm. Therefore, my last day of employment will be February 23, 2011.

In the past two years, I have had the pleasure of learning new skills and of working with extremely talented individuals. I thank you for the opportunities you have provided me and wish everyone at ABC Company continued success.

Sincerely,

Jennie New-Job

Jennie New-Job
123 North Avenue
Anycity, USA 98765

No matter how bad the boss or horrific the work environment, do not speak or behave negatively in your final days of employment. Leave in a manner that would make the company want to rehire you tomorrow. Coworkers may want to share gossip or speak poorly of others, but you must remain professional. You may also be tempted to damage or take property that belongs to the company. Do not behave unethically. Only take personal belongings and leave your work space clean and organized for whoever assumes your position. Preserve the confidentiality of your coworkers, department, and customers.

Cory had a coworker who had been looking for a job over the past few months. Cory knew this because the coworker not only told everyone but used the company equipment to update and mail her résumé. Cory often heard the coworker talking to potential employers on the telephone. On the day Cory's coworker finally landed a new job, the coworker proudly announced to everyone in the office that she was "leaving the prison" and that afternoon would be her last day at work. The coworker went on to bad-mouth the company, her boss, and several colleagues. As she was cleaning out her desk, Cory noticed that the coworker started packing items that did not belong to her. When Cory shared this observation, the coworker said she deserved the items and that the company would never miss them. A few weeks later, Cory's former coworker came by the office to say hello. Cory asked her how her new job was going. "Well . . ." said the coworker, "the job fell through." The coworker explained that she was stopping by the office to see if she could have her old position back. Unfortunately, the former coworker left in such a negative manner that the company did not rehire her.

On your last day of employment with your company, you may meet with a representative from the human resource department or with your immediate supervisor to receive your final paycheck. This paycheck should include all unpaid wages and accrued vacation. This is also when you will formally return all company property including your keys and name badge. You may receive an **exit interview**. An exit interview is when an employer meets with an employee who is voluntarily leaving a company to identify opportunities for improving the work environment. During this interview, a company representative will ask questions regarding the job you are leaving, the boss, and the work environment. The company's goal is to secure any information that provides constructive input on how to improve the company. You can share opportunities for improvement, but do not turn your comments into personal attacks. While it is sometimes tempting to provide negative information in the interview, remain positive and professional.

Involuntary Terminations

Involuntary terminations are when you lose your job against your will. Types of involuntary terminations include **firing**, which happens when you are terminated because of a performance issue; a **layoff**, which is a result of the company's financial inability to keep your position; or a **restructuring**, which is when the company has eliminated your position due to a change in strategy.

If you are fired, you have lost your job as a result of a performance issue. Unless you have done something outrageous (such as blatant theft or harassment), you should have received a poor performance warning prior to the firing. Typically, this progressive discipline includes a verbal and/or written warning prior to termination. If you are totally unaware of why you are being fired, ask for documentation to support the company's decision. Firing based on outrageous behavior will be supported by a policy, while any performance issue should be supported with prior written documentation. When you are informed of your firing, you should immediately receive your final paycheck. You will also be asked to return all company property on the spot (including keys and name badge). Do not damage company property. Doing so is not only immature but punishable by law. While you may be angry or caught off guard, do not make threats against the company or its employees. Remain calm and professional. If you think you are being wrongfully terminated, your legal recourse is to seek assistance from your state's labor commission or a private attorney.

Many people consider a layoff a form of firing. This is not true. Firing is a result of poor performance. A layoff is a result of a company's change of strat-

Talk It Out

If you were to be laid off what are the first three things you would do and why?

egy or its inability to financially support a position. While some companies lay-off employees based upon performance, most do it on seniority. Frequently, when the company's financial situation improves, employees may be recalled. A **work recall** is when employees are called back to work after being laid off. If you have been laid off, remain positive and ask your employer for a letter of reference and job search assistance. This job search assistance may include support with updating a resumé, counseling, job training, and job leads.

In today's competitive environment, it is common for companies to restructure. Restructuring involves a company changing its strategy and reorganizing resources. This commonly results in eliminating unnecessary positions. If your position is eliminated, remain positive and inquire about new positions. In a restructuring situation, it is often common for new positions to be created. Once again, do not bad-mouth anyone or openly express your anger or dissatisfaction of the situation. If you have recently acquired new skills, now is the time to communicate and demonstrate your new skills. Keep a record of your workplace accomplishments, and keep your ears open for new positions for which to apply.

Other Moves Within the Organization

In addition to promotions and terminations, there are several other methods of moving within and outside the company. These include lateral moves, demotions, and retirement. A **lateral move** is when you are transferred to another area of the organization with the same level of responsibility. Lateral moves involve only a change in department or work area. A change in pay is not involved in a lateral move. If you are moved to a different position and experience a pay increase, it is considered a promotion. If you are moved to different position and experience a pay decrease, you have been demoted. While **demotions** are rare, they can occur if one's performance is not acceptable but the employee chooses to not leave the company. Of all the changes an employee can make, a demotion is by far the most difficult. You experience not only a decrease in pay but also a decrease in job title and status. If you are demoted, remain professional and be respectful of your new boss.

The final change in employment status is called **retirement.** Retirement is when you are voluntarily leaving your employment and will no longer be working. Although this text addresses those entering the workforce, it is never too early to start planning for your retirement both mentally and financially. This can be done by establishing career goals and deadlines, in addition to contributing to a retirement fund.

Entrepreneurship

Another form of career transition is that of becoming an entrepreneur. An **entrepreneur** is someone who assumes the risk of succeeding or failing in business through owning and operating a business. While owning and operating your own business may sound glamorous, doing so involves work. Individuals become entrepreneurs for several reasons. The most common reason is when someone has identified a business opportunity he or she wants to exploit.

People also become entrepreneurs because they would rather work for themselves, want more control of their work environment, want more income, or have lost their jobs and have been unable to find another.

It is common for individuals with full-time jobs to supplement their income by running a business on the side. It is unethical to run a side business that competes with or utilizes your employer's resources or confidential information. If your current employer allows employees to run side businesses, do not allow your side business to interfere with your full-time employment. Keep the two business ventures separate. Entrepreneurship is a rewarding career option for many.

As you can see, there are several means of moving within and out of an organization. Although it is not healthy to move too frequently, those with healthy careers move and rarely stay in one position their entire career. Regardless of your plans to advance, keep your resumé updated. Doing so keeps you motivated to take on additional responsibilities and increase your knowledge, skills, and abilities. You will also be prepared, should some unforeseen opportunity come your way.

Web Quiz

Find out if entrepreneurship is for you.

http://www.sba.gov/ smallbusinessplanner/plan/ getready/SERV_ SBPLANNER_ISENTFORU .html

Workplace Dos and Don'ts

Do continually update your skills and knowledge through training and development	*Don't* assume additional skills and knowledge are not necessary for advancement
Do keep an open mind for job advancement opportunities	*Don't* openly share your dissatisfaction for your current job
Do write a formal resignation letter when leaving a company and a thank-you letter to a boss or mentor when receiving a promotion	*Don't* leave your job abruptly without providing adequate notice to your current employer
Do behave professionally when leaving a position	*Don't* take or ruin company property when leaving a position
Do provide valuable feedback and opportunities for improvement during an exit interview	*Don't* turn an exit interview into a personal attack on your former boss or coworkers

Concept Review and Application

Summary of Key Concepts

- Continue learning new skills to help reach your career potential
- Formal learning is another way to increase skills and knowledge
- Changes in employment status include promotions, voluntary terminations, involuntary terminations, lateral moves, and retirement
- Be cautious about sharing your desire for a new job
- There are two types of terminations: voluntary and involuntary
- When leaving voluntarily, submit a letter of resignation
- When leaving in an involuntary manner, do not burn bridges or behave in an unprofessional or unethical manner
- There is a difference between being fired and being laid off
- It is never too early to begin planning for your retirement
- Becoming an entrepreneur is an additional form of career transition

Key Terms

continual learning	demotion	development
entrepreneur	exit interview	firing
formal learning	informal learning	involuntary termination
lateral move	layoff	letter of resignation
promotion	restructuring	retirement
training	voluntary termination	work recall

If You Were the Boss

1. Why would it be important to encourage training and development sessions within your department?

2. You hear through the grapevine that one of your best employees is looking for another job. What should you do?

3. Management has told you that you must layoff four of your employees. How do you determine who to layoff and how best to tell them? How do you defend your decision?

Learn More

To learn more about subjects addressed in this chapter take a course in Small Business Management.

Web Links

http://agelesslearner.com/intros/informal.html
http://careerplanning.about.com/od/quittingyourjob
http://www.insiderreports.com/bizltrs/resign1.htm

Activity 16-1

Based on your career plan in chapter 2, identify additional training, development, and continual learning you will need for professional success.

Training	Development	Continual Learning

Activity 16-2

Identify your ideal job. What continual learning will you need to secure this job?

Job Move	Continual Learning

Activity 16-3

Name at least five ways you can begin to develop your work experience for a future promotion.

1. _____

2. _____

3. _____

4. _____

5. _____

Activity 16-4

Throughout this text, you have learned good human relations for the workplace. Name at least three things you can do to decrease your chances of being laid off if that becomes necessary within your company.

1. _____

2. _____

3. _____

Activity 16-5

Write a draft letter of reference for yourself.

_____

_____

_____

_____

_____

_____

_____

1. To make you more diverse in your skills attend _____.

2. The process of increasing knowledge in your career area is referred to as _____.

3. Changes in employment status include promotions, _____ terminations, involuntary _____, lateral moves, and _____.

4. If you have had positive performance evaluations and are leaving voluntarily, secure a _____.

5. A/An _____ is a written notice of your voluntary termination.

6. Your _____ should include all unpaid wages and _____.

7. Employees who are _____ are terminated due to a/an _____ issue.

8. Employees who are _____ are terminated due to the company's _____.

9. A/An _____ is when you are transferred to another area of the organization. A change in pay is not involved.

10. A/An _____ is someone who assumes the risk of _____ or _____ through owning and operating a _____.

Glossary

abusive boss: a boss who is constantly belittling or intimidating his or her employees

accommodating conflict management style: a conflict management style that allows the other party to have his or her own way without knowing there was a conflict

accountability: accepting the responsibility to perform and will report back to whoever gave the power

adjourning stage: when team members bring closure to a project

aggressive behavior: the behavior of an individual who stands up for his or her rights in a manner that violates others' rights in an offensive manner

appearance: how you look

assertive behavior: the behavior of an individual who stands up for his or her rights without violating the rights of others

assets: tangible items that you own that are worth money

attitude: a strong belief toward people, things, and situations

autocratic leaders: leaders who make decisions on their own without input from others

automatic deduction plan: when money is automatically deducted from an employee's paycheck and placed into a bank account

avoiding conflict management style: a passive conflict management style used when one does not want to deal with the conflict so the offense is ignored

behavioral interview question: interview questions that ask candidates to share a past experience related to a specific workplace situation

board of directors: a group of individuals responsible for developing the company's overall strategy and major policies

brainstorming: a problem-solving method that involves identifying alternatives that allow members to freely add ideas while other members withhold comments on the alternatives

budget: a detailed financial plan used to allocate money for a specific time period

business letter: a formal written form of communication used when a message is being sent to an individual outside of an organization

business memo: written communication sent within an organization (also called *interoffice memorandums*)

capital budget: a financial plan used for long-term investments including land and large pieces of equipment

career objective: an introductory written statement used on a resumé for individuals with little or no work experience

casual workdays: workdays when companies relax the dress code policy

charismatic power: a type of personal power that makes people attracted to you

chronological resumé layout: a resumé layout used by those with extensive career experience that emphasizes related work experience, skills, and significant accomplishments

coercive power: power that uses threats and punishment

collaborating conflict management style: a conflict management style in which both parties work together to arrive at a solution without having to give up something of value

273

communication: the process of a sender sending a message to an individual (receiver) with the purpose of creating mutual understanding

company resources: financial (fiscal), human (employees), and capital (long-term investments) resources that the company can utilize to achieve its goals

competent: knowing the product(s) a company offers

compromising conflict management style: a conflict management style that is used when both parties give up something of importance to arrive at a mutually agreeable solution to the conflict

confidential: matters that should be kept private

conflict: a disagreement or tension between two or more parties (individuals or groups)

conflict of interest: when someone influences a decision that directly or indirectly benefits him or her

connection power: based on using someone else's legitimate power

continual learning: the ongoing process of increasing knowledge in the area of your career

corporate culture (organizational culture): values, expectations, and behavior of people at work; the company's personality being reflected through employees' behavior

courtesy: exercising manners, respect, and consideration toward others

cover letter: a letter that introduces your resumé

creativity: the ability to produce something new and unique

credit report: a detailed credit history on an individual

culture: different behavior patterns of various groups

customer: an individual or business that buys a company's product (good or service)

customer service: the treatment an employee provides the customer

debt: money owed

decoding: when a receiver interprets a message

delegate: when a manager or leader assigns part or all of a project to someone else

democratic leaders: leaders who make decisions based upon input from others

demotion: when an employee is moved to a lower position with less responsibility and a decrease in pay

dental benefits: insurance coverage for teeth

department: sub area of a division that carries out specific functions respective of its division

dependable: being reliable and taking responsibility to assist a customer

development: sessions to enhance or increase existing skills

direct benefits: monetary employee benefits

directional statements: a company's mission, vision, and values statements; these statements are the foundation of a strategic plan explaining why a company exists and how it will operate

diversity statements: corporate statements that remind employees that diversity in the workplace is an asset and not a form of prejudice and stereotyping

diversity training: company training designed to teach employees how to eliminate workplace discrimination and harassment

division: how companies arrange major business functions

documentation: formal collection of items that record important events that have occurred

dress code: an organization's policy regarding appropriate workplace attire

electronic formatted resumé: resumés which are submitted in American Standard Code for Information Interchange (ASCII) format

electronic image: the image formed when someone is communicating and/or researching you through electronic means such as personal web pages and search engines

employee assistance program (EAP): an employee benefit that typically provides free and confidential psychological, financial, and legal advice

employee handbook: a formal document provided by the company that outlines an employee's agreement with the employer regarding work conditions, policies, and benefits

employee loyalty: an employee's obligation to consistently support a company and its mission

employee morale: the attitude employees have toward the company

employee orientation: a time when a company provides new employees important information including the company's purpose, its structure, major policies, procedures, benefits, and other important matters

employment-at-will: a legal term for noncontract employees that states that an employee can quit any time he or she wishes

empowerment: pushing power and decision making to the individuals who are closest to the customer in an effort to increase quality; customer satisfaction; and, ultimately, profits

encoding: identifying how a message will be sent (verbally, written, or nonverbally)

entrepreneur: someone who assumes the risk of succeeding or failing in business through owning and operating the business

ethics: a moral standard of right and wrong

ethics statement: a formal corporate policy that addresses the issue of ethical behavior and punishment should someone behave inappropriately

etiquette: a standard of social behavior

executive presence: having the attitude of an executive

executives (senior managers): typically have title of vice president Individuals who work with the president of a company in identifying and implementing the company strategy

exit interview: when an employer meets with an employee who is voluntarily leaving a company to identify opportunities to improve the work environment

expense: money going out

expert power: power that is earned by one's knowledge, experience, or expertise

extrinsic rewards: rewards that come from external sources including such things as money and praise

feedback: when a receiver responds to a sender's message based upon the receiver's interpretation of the original message

finance and accounting department: a department that is responsible for the securing, distribution, and growth of the company's financial assets

firing: when an employee is terminated because of a performance issue

fixed expenses: expenses that do not change from month to month

flexible expenses: expenses that change from month to month

forcing conflict management style: a conflict management style that deals with the issues directly

formal communication: workplace communication that occurs through memos, meetings, or lines of authority

formal learning: returning to college to increase knowledge or improve skills or receive an additional or advanced degree

formal teams: developed within the formal organizational structure and may include functional teams or cross-functional teams

forming stage: when team members first get to know each other and form initial opinions about other members

free-reign leaders: leaders who allow team members to make their own decisions without input from the leader (also known as laissez-faire leaders)

full-time employee: an employment status for employees who work forty or more hours per week

functional resumé layout: a resumé layout that emphasizes relevant skills when related work experience is lacking

glass ceiling: invisible barrier that frequently makes executive positions off limits to females and minorities, thus prohibiting them from advancing up the corporate ladder through promotions

glass wall: invisible barrier that frequently makes certain work areas such as a golf course off limits to females and minorities, thus prohibiting them from advancing up the corporate ladder through promotions

goal: a broad, long-term target

good: a tangible product produced by a company

good boss: a boss who is respectful and fair

gossip: personal information about another individual which is hurtful and inappropriate

grapevine: an informal communication network where employees talk about workplace issues of importance

grievance procedure: formal steps taken in resolving a conflict between the union and an employer

gross income: the amount of money in a paycheck before taxes or other deductions are made

group: two or more people who share a common goal and have one leader

group interview: an interview that involves several applicants interviewing with each other while being observed by company representatives

hostile behavior harassment: any behavior of a sexual nature by another employee that someone finds offensive including verbal slurs, physical contact, offensive photos, jokes, or any other offensive behavior of a sexual nature

human relations: interactions occurring with and through people

human resource department: a department responsible for hiring, training, compensation, benefits, performance evaluations, complaints, promotions, and changes in work status

human resource management: a business function that deals with recruiting, hiring, training, evaluating, compensating, promoting, and terminating employees

implied confidentiality: an obligation to not share information with individuals with whom the business is of no concern

income: money coming in

incompetent boss: a boss who does not know how to do his or her job

indirect benefits: nonmonetary employee benefits such as health care and paid vacations

informal communication: workplace communication that occurs among individuals without regard to the formal lines of authority

informal learning: reading career-related magazines, newsletters, and other articles associated with a job

informal team: group of individuals who get together outside of the formal organizational structure to accomplish a goal

information heading: a heading that contains relevant contact information including name, mailing address, city, state, Zip code, contact phone, and e-mail address

information power: power based upon an individual's ability to obtain and share information

information systems: a business function that deals with the electronic management of computer-based information within the organization

informational interview: when a job seeker meets with a business professional to learn about a specific career, company, or industry

innovation: the introduction of a new product; putting creative ideas into action

interest: the cost of borrowing money

interview portfolio: a folder to be taken on an interview that contains photocopies of documents and items pertinent to a position

intrinsic rewards: internal rewards that include such things as self-satisfaction and pride of accomplishment

introductory employee: newly hired full-time employee who has not yet successfully passed his or her introductory period

involuntary termination: when an employee loses his or her job against his or her will

job-specific skills: skills that are directly related to a specific job and interview

job search portfolio: a collection of paperwork needed for job searches and industry

job description: a document that outlines specific job duties and responsibilities for a specific position

job burnout: a form of extreme stress that results in the desire to no longer work upon past actions

labeling: when one describes an individual or group of individuals based or industry

lassez-faire leaders: leaders who allow team members to make their own decisions without input from the leader (also known as free reign leaders)

lateral move: when an employee is transferred to another area (department) of an organization with the same level of responsibility

layoff: when a company releases employees as a result of a company's inability to keep the position

leadership: a process of one person guiding one or more individuals toward a specific goal

learning style: the method of how you best take in information and/or learn new ideas

legal counsel: a function within a business that handles all legal matters relating to the company

legitimate power: the power that is given to an employee from the company

letter of recommendation: a written testimony from another person that states that a job candidate is credible

letter of resignation: a written notice of your voluntary termination

letterhead: paper that has the company logo, mailing address, and telephone numbers imprinted on quality paper

levels of ethical decisions: the first level is the law; the second level is fairness; the third level is one's conscience

liability: money that is owed

loan: a large debt that is paid in smaller amounts over a period of time and has interest added to the payment

locus of control: identifies who you believe controls your future

long-term goal: target that is anywhere from five to ten years

marketing: responsible for creating, pricing, selling, distributing, and promoting the company's product

mediator: a neutral third party whose objective is to assist two conflicting parties in coming to a mutually agreeable solution

medical benefits: insurance coverage for physician and hospital visits

meeting agenda: an outline of all topics and activities that are to be addressed during a meeting

meeting chair: the individual who is in charge of a meeting and has prepared the agenda

mentor: someone who can help an employee learn more about his or her present position, provide support, and help develop the employee's career

middle manager: typically has the title of *director* or *manager*; these individuals work on tactical issues

mission statement: a company's statement of purpose

money wasters: small expenditures that actually use up a portion of one's income

motivation: an internal drive that causes people to behave a certain way to meet a need

negative stress: an unproductive stress that affects your mental and/or physical health including becoming emotional or illogical or losing your temper

negotiation: working with another party to create a situation (resolution) that is fair to all involved parties

net income: the amount of money left after all taxes and deductions are paid

net worth: the amount of money that is yours after paying off debt

network list: a list of individuals included in a person's professional network

networking: meeting and developing relationships with individuals outside one's immediate work area; the act of creating professional relationships

noise: anything that interrupts or interferes with the communication process

nonverbal communication: what is communicated through body language

norming stage: when team members accept other members for who they are

objectives: short-term goals that are measurable and have specific time lines that occur within one year

one-on-one interview: an interview that involves a one-on-one meeting between the applicant and a company representative

open-door policy: a management philosophy, the purpose of which is to communicate to employees that management and the human resource department are always available to listen should the employees have a concern or complaint

operational budget: a financial plan used for short-term items including payroll and the day-to-day costs associated with running a business

operational issue: issue that occurs on a daily basis and/or no longer than one year

operations: a business function that deals with the production and distribution of a company's product

operations manager: first-line manager who is typically called a *supervisor* or *assistant manager*

organizational chart: a graphic visual display of how a company organizes its resources; identifies key functions within the company and shows the formal lines of authority for employees

organizational structure: the way a company is organized

panel interview: an interview that involves the applicant meeting with several company employees at the same time

part-time employee: an employment status for employees who work fewer than forty hours a week

passive behavior: the behavior exhibited when an individual does not stand up for his or her rights by consistently allowing others to have their way

perception: one's understanding or interpretation of reality

performance evaluation: a formal appraisal that measures an employee's work performance

performing stage: when team members begin working on their task

personal commercial: a brief career biography that conveys one's career choice, knowledge, skills, strengths, abilities, and experiences

personal financial management: the process of controlling one's income and expenses

personal profile: an introductory written statement used on a resumé for individuals with professional experience related to their target career

personality: a stable set of traits that assist in explaining and predicting an individual's behavior

physiological needs: an individual's need for basic wages to obtain food, shelter, and other basic needs

politics: obtaining and utilizing power

positive self-talk: a mental form of positive self-reinforcement that helps remind you that you are qualified and deserve both the interview and the job

positive stress: productive stress that provides strength to accomplish a task

power: one's ability to influence another's behavior

power words: action verbs that describe your accomplishments in a lively and specific way

prejudice: a favorable or unfavorable judgment or opinion toward an individual or group based on one's perception (or understanding) of a group, individual, or situation

president or chief executive officer (CEO): the individual responsible for operating the company; this individual takes his or her direction from the board of directors

priorities: determines what needs to be done and in what order

product: what is produced by a company

productivity: to perform a function that adds value to a company

profit: revenue (money coming in from sales) minus expenses (the costs involved in running the business)

projection: the way you feel about yourself is reflected in how you treat others

promotion: moving to a position higher in the organization with increased pay and responsibility

quality: a predetermined standard that defines how a good is to be produced or a service is to be provided

quid pro quo harassment: a form of sexual harassing behavior that is construed as reciprocity or payback for a sexual favor

race: a group of individuals with certain physical traits

reciprocity: creating debts and obligations for doing something

respect: holding someone in high regard

responsibility: accepting the power that is being given and the obligation to perform

responsive: being aware of a customer's needs often before the customer

restructuring: when a company eliminates a position due to a change in corporate strategy

resumé: a formal written profile that presents a person's knowledge, skills, and abilities to potential employers

retirement: when an employee voluntarily leaves the company and will no longer work

retirement plan: a savings plan for retirement purposes

reward power: the ability to influence someone with something of value

right to revise: a statement contained in many employee handbooks that provides an employer the opportunity to change or revise existing policies

Robert's Rules of Order: a guide to running meetings, oftentimes referred to as parliamentary procedure

safety needs: an individual's need for a safe working environment and job security

self-actualization: when an employee has successfully had his or her needs met and desires to assist others in meeting their needs

self-discovery: the process of identifying key interests and skills built upon career goals

self-esteem: how you view yourself

self-esteem needs: an individual's need for workplace titles, degrees, and awards

self-image: how an individual thinks others view him or her

sender: an individual wanting to convey a message

senior managers or executives: individuals who work with the president in identifying and implementing the company strategy

service: an intangible product produced by a company that one cannot touch or see

sexual harassment: unwanted advances of a sexual nature

shop steward: a coworker who assists others with union-related issues and procedures

short-term goals: goals that can be reached within a year's time (also called *objectives*)

slang: an informal language used among a particular group

social needs: an individual's need for positive workplace relationships

soft skills: people skills that are necessary when working with others in the workplace

stereotyping: making a generalized image of a particular group or situation

storming stage: when team members have conflict with each other

strategic issues: major company goals that typically range from three to five years or more

strategic plan: a formal document that is developed by senior management; the strategic plan identifies how the company secures, organizes, utilizes, and monitors its resources

strategy: a company's road map for success that outlines major goals and objectives

stress: a body's reaction to tense situations

structured interview question: a type of interview question that addresses job-related issues where each applicant is asked the same question

supervisor: first-level manager that concerns him- or herself with operational issues

synergy: extra excitement that occurs when people are truly working together as a team

tactical issues: business issues that identify how to link the corporate strategy into the reality of day-to-day operations; the time line for tactical issues is one to three years

team: two or more people who share a common goal and share responsibility and leadership

temporary employee: an employee who is hired only for a specified period of time, typically to assist with busy work periods or to temporarily replace an employee on leave

time management: how you manage your time

trade-off: giving up one thing to do something else

training: the process of learning new job skills for the purpose of an employee promotion and/or increased responsibility

transferable skills: skills that can be transferred from one job to another

union: a third-party organization that protects the rights of employees and represents employee interests to an employer

union contract: the formal document that addresses specific employment issues including the handling of grievances, holidays, vacations, and other issues

unstructured interview question: a probing, open-ended interview question intended to identify if the candidate can appropriately sell his or her skills

value: getting a good deal for the price paid for a product

values: ideas that are important to an individual

values statement: part of a company strategic plan that defines what is important to (or what the priorities are for) the company

verbal communication: the process of using words to send a message

vision benefits: insurance coverage for vision (eye) care

vision statement: part of a company's strategic plan that describes the company's viable view of the future

voluntary termination: leaving a job on your own

work recall: when employees are called back to work after a layoff

work wardrobe: clothes that are primarily worn only to work and work-related functions

workplace bullies: employees who are intentionally rude and unprofessional to coworkers

workplace discrimination: acting negatively toward someone based on race, age, gender, religion, disability, or other areas

workplace diversity: differences among coworkers including culture, race, age, gender, economic status, and religion among other things

written communication: a form of business communication that is either printed, handwritten, or sent electronically

Appendix A:
Creating Your Career Portfolio

If you could have anything in your life, what would you want? This is the place where you begin to evaluate your work philosophy and establish goals. This chapter will provide you with the mechanics and several tools for generating the pieces you need in your portfolio. You analyze current and yet-to-be acquired skills. This is where you design your career. Keep in mind your career is more than a job—it's the paths those jobs take.

This is a process you do when you are looking for a job, and where you should go three to four months into the job to connect with the corporate culture and company goals.

Designing Your Career

You've got to have a goal. If you don't, your career will be one reaction after another. With a plan in place from your master design, you're able to maintain your focus. You may encounter opportunities or career shifts or additional training. With your career goals in mind, you can determine which opportunities to accept and which to decline. This is the part of the process where you get a master plan. Be sure you hold a higher vision of your potential when you do it.

Work Philosophy

A work philosophy is a statement of your beliefs about yourself, people, and your outlook on life in your industry. Your work philosophy is often used by an interviewer to see if you match a company's corporate culture. After reading this statement, a potential employer should know whether you would fit the "style" of the organization.

Try This with a Friend...

Have both your friend and yourself list five adjectives that describe who you are and how you want to be seen in the workplace. Use a friend to react to your list. Do they agree? Use these adjectives to guide your work philosophy statement, serving as the core thoughts and keywords.

Make sure you have a friend to assist you when you're ready to develop your work philosophy. Your friend can help you take your beliefs and the ideas that you have internalized and verbalize them on paper. Many people know in their hearts what they believe, but they've never put it into words. Your work philosophy might also be called a management philosophy.

What you need to know about your philosophy...

- **Think about it**—Don't expect to "whip out" a work philosophy or personal mission statement in 10 or 20 minutes. It usually takes a few days worth of thought and reflection before the "final draft" is ready.

- **Place your most important belief first**—Your work philosophy should be unique to you, communicate who you are and what makes you different from others who may want the same position.

- **Length**—Your work philosophy should be one to four sentences in length, and should address your beliefs and your outlook on people.

- **Use bullets**—Consider using bullet points for added clarity.

- **Have a friend review it for clarity**—After you have it on paper, ask a few friends to read it for clarity—not for approval. Remember, your work philosophy is never right or wrong; it represents your key beliefs and values.

Here's the work philosophy of one graduating student:

Work Philosophy

- The customer always comes first.
- Financial and operational controls must be clear to all members of the company.
- Technology will be critical in reaching the guests and communicating within the company.
- I want to be part of a winning team.

Template

Use the **Work Philosophy and Goals.doc** file on the companion disk as a starting point for developing your own portfolio.

Goals

Your goals set a direction for your career and are general in nature. The goals in your portfolio should focus on the professional achievements, skills, and knowledge you want to acquire over the next several years. Companies use these goals to anticipate your developmental needs and interests. They also show management and recruiters that you do indeed have a plan for your future.

Here again, a friend can help you develop your goals. He or she can ask questions that make you think about your goals and can help make sure your goals make sense.

Making Your Goals Work

- **Plan your goals for two to five years from now**—When writing goals, think ahead several years. What do you want to be doing in two years? What do you want to have accomplished four years from today? Goals written for one year or less are often too narrow in focus, and usually concentrate on learning a new position rather than planning for the future. You should also make sure your goals are not so specific as to imply only a narrow interest in the industry or in a specific job. If you are starting in an entry-level position, think about the job you want to be doing in two to three years. Goals can help share your vision for where you will fit in the organization in the future.

- **Make your goals measurable**—Your goals should be specific enough that you will know when you've achieved them. We measure goals in terms of time, money, and resources.

Too broad:
"To expand my technical knowledge."

Good:
"To develop my database skills by attending a class on Microsoft Access by May 2001."

- **Goals are different from career objectives**—Career objectives are broad and set a direction for your career. Goals are more specific; they include shorter-range objectives that are measurable.

- **Write three to five goals**—If you only write one or two goals, you may appear unfocused and give the impression you're not really interested in advancing your career.

- **Don't make your goals too personal**—Goals such as losing weight or winning a marathon can alienate your interviewer; it may give the person more information than he/she may want to know about sensitive topics. Keep your goals professional and related to your career.

Here is a sample of goals that are appropriate for individuals just starting their careers:

Two-Year Goals

- To hold a leadership role in my department

- To hold at least one active professional membership

- To further develop my computer application skills as they apply to controlling costs

- To earn the customer service award

- To apply my creativity to develop new menus.

Template

Use the **Work Philosophy and Goals.doc** file on the companion disk as a starting point for developing your own goals and your philosophy.

Your Career Plan

OK... by now you have already dealt with your work philosophy and flushed out at least a couple of years' worth of goals. What happens next? You have spent your time on the "big picture" — NOW you need an action plan. The first step is to take an in-depth look at your skills, interests, and abilities from the professional and personal perspective. Understanding and identifying the different skills you have can help you be better prepared for a job or keep you on track for a promotion. Knowing what you have to offer an employer is important, and you may have more going for you than you think! Once you know where you're going, you can use some techniques to help you develop your action plan.

Identifying Your Skills

When you're in school you are constantly learning new skills. At the beginning of every new class, your teachers usually start by reviewing the goals and objectives for the class. You know what you will be learning and what skills you should have by the time you finish the class. Whether you're taking an accounting class or psychology, you are gaining skills in that area. Skills are often broken down by the type of skill you are learning. **Hard skills** relate to practical skills, like working with computers or operating equipment and machinery. When you follow steps to complete a task, whether it's operating a forklift, keyboarding a report, doing an experiment to produce a reaction, or maintaining an engine on a car, you are doing a hard skill. Most classes are geared to learning a set of hard skills.

Soft skills consist of a broader range of skills related to your personality and attitudes. Examples of soft skills include self-confidence, communication skills, teamwork skills, tolerance, discipline, management, etc. Working on a team project, problem solving a process, leading a meeting, and being able to make decisions are some of the soft skills you can gain from a class without knowing it. They are often thought of as hidden skills, but they are some of the most important skills you can have. Employers are always looking for people with a certain set of hard skills, but when they have good soft skills to go with them, they can be a powerful combination in a good employee. Take a look at the following list to see just what kinds of skills employers are looking for. You can use your portfolio to promote many of these soft skills.

Soft Skills Employers Look For

Teamwork

Being a good team member means:

- Putting the good of the team ahead of yourself
- Respecting others' opinions
- Hearing people out
- Involving everyone in finding solutions to problems.

Presentation skills

- Leading a meeting
- Promoting an idea to the boss
- Giving your thoughts in a union meeting.

Communication skills

- Answering the phone
- Writing e-mails
- Putting together a proposal
- Interacting with co-workers and customers
- Being a good listener
- Giving and receiving feedback.

Attitude

- Enthusiastic, high energy
- Flexible, open-minded
- Dependable.

Leadership

- Heading up a project
- Training others
- Delegating
- Negotiating
- Managing conflict
- Planning
- Setting priorities
- Organizing skills.

Other Soft Skills

- Problem solving
- Multi-tasking
- Thinking quickly
- Ability to make decisions
- Customer service
- Courtesy
- Ability to work with people from different cultures
- Work ethic
- Self-discipline.

Ask the Expert

Identifying the skills I need

Q. How do I know what skills I need to prove?

A. A good way to identify what skills you may need to prove is by reviewing job postings for the entry-level position and future positions you may seek. Most potential employers will indicate what skills they value in their job advertisement or job description. Usually, after reviewing a variety of job postings, you will see a pattern of skills desired by potential employers.

Transferable Skills

Transferable skills are the skills you've gathered through various jobs, volunteer work, hobbies, sports, or other life experiences that can be used in your next job or new career. Transferable skills are important to those who are facing a layoff or looking for a different job, new graduates who are looking for their first jobs, and those re-entering the work force after an extended absence. Transferable skills are skills you can use in a variety of industries and settings. A person with management skills can transition from a career in banking to a career in insurance. Good computer skills can be used to develop spreadsheets for a restaurant or track medical records in an office. Begin to identify your skills and how they can be used in different ways. What else can you bring to the table in terms of expertise? Are you a subject matter expert in any fields? The ability to speak a second language could be the asset that sets you apart from other candidates and gets you the job.

Transferable skills can be hard or soft skills. If you can drive a semi truck, a hard skill, you can also drive a delivery van. If you can coach a softball team, you have soft skills that can be used when training people on the job. Take a look at the following list of transferable skills that employers like to see. Notice how many of the skills listed are soft skills.

Transferable Skills

Verbal communication	Leadership
Nonverbal communication	Management
Plan and organize	Financial
Counsel and serve	Administrative
Create and innovate	Analyze
Written communication	Construct and operate
Train/consult	Research
Interpersonal relations	

Assembling the Portfolio

OK, you have all your stuff in piles and files—now what? This Appendix will take you from the pieces to the whole finished product. You won't be ready to assemble until you first gather, sort, secure, and update your materials. We'll also take a look at special tips for assembling a Performance Portfolio for use in job reviews or promotion interviews.

Here are the five major steps to assembling your portfolio:

Step 1: Gather your supplies and documents.
Step 2: Sort and organize your work samples.
Step 3: Put them all together.
Step 4: Develop support materials.
Step 5: Check it out—proof it, test it.

Step 1 . . . Things to Gather

Know what your goals and objectives are and how you plan to use your portfolio. Next, bring to one central location all your collected materials—consciously collect:

- Portfolio supplies
- Your resumé
- Your work philosophy
- Your professional goals
- Your box of work samples... (Are there any old papers or projects that you can find or copy?)
- Certifications
- Degrees or diplomas
- Thank you letters or letters of recommendation
- Skill sets with signatures
- Faculty/employer bios
- Academic plans of study
- Professional membership cards and service samples
- Certification checklists
- Community service accommodations or service samples
- List of references
- And don't forget—your best friend.

Step #1 - Gather your materials ... and a friend

Assemble Your Portfolio BEFORE You Need It!

With all the work involved in creating a portfolio, it's easy to put it off until another day. Even the authors of this book have had to choose between sleep and finishing a portfolio. Be prepared to clean off a big section of the floor for the assembly. If the floor cramps your style, use a table or large desk—just be prepared to find some space on a flat surface.

Step 2 . . . . Sorting and Organizing Work Samples

Set Up Your Tabbed Areas

Use the job description, classified ad, and any other knowledge you have of the company or the position to prioritize the skills you will emphasize in your portfolio. Begin by selecting three to five main skill areas you want to emphasize and create a tab for each. Select categories which you can support with work samples. If you are a business major, for example, your tabs might be Management, Finance, and Communication. Now is the time to decide what other tabbed areas beyond work samples you want to use.

Step 2 - Select tabs that represent you.

Remember, this is your portfolio. You need to select the tabbed areas that best represent you. If you don't have any community service experiences, don't create a tab for it and then leave it blank. Don't struggle to find some activity or event to include just so you can write up two lines on a page. If you don't have it, don't include it! Play to your strengths. If you have only one sample for an area, consider grouping it with another sample from a different area and make a tab to reflect this. If you've been on the job for 10 years, you probably don't need to include a tab for Academic Plan of Study. If you can only come up with two really good tabbed areas, don't struggle to find a third and then include marginal samples. You are designing this portfolio to show off your strengths. Choose your tabbed areas to reflect this.

Select Samples

How do you decide which samples to use? Consider first the needs of the employer and look at the job ad to see what samples would be most effective. When sorting work and service samples, ask yourself:

- Which skills is the organization looking for in this position?
- What is your best work?
- Which samples show the most skills and competencies?
- Which work samples are the most interesting to you?
- Which work samples use more than text as an exhibit? Do any include pictures?
- Can you talk about your sample?

Bright Idea!

Remember to select your best samples!

Consider using some of the following items as demonstrations of your skills and competency:

- Class projects
- Projects or reports demonstrating organization and professionalism
- Writing samples
- Computing samples
- Team efforts
- Certificates from workshops

- Performance appraisals (include internships/co-ops)
- Certifications
- Handouts
- Presentations
- Letters itemizing what you have accomplished.

Remember the Friend

Having a friend there to help you during assembly can be extremely important. Your friend is there to ask the "right" questions and to look at your portfolio from a "different angle." You may find that your friendship will be tested, especially if he or she does his/her job! Your friend's job is, of course, to ask you the really hard questions that push you to be your best. Your friend is also here to role play possible answers you may give the interviewer. Don't take things personally; give that friend honest answers even if they are not your best answers. You'll improve with practice.

Once you have organized your work samples you are then ready to develop the support materials that give your portfolio flow.

Step 3 ... Putting It Together

Now that you have everything gathered, go ahead and put everything you've prepared into page protectors and into the 3-ring notebook. Organize your information into appropriate tabbed areas. Remember, we've included several documents on the accompanying disk that can give you a starting point for creating your documents.

- Begin with your **work philosophy** and **career goals.**
- Put your résumé in another page protector behind the work philosophy/goals page.
- Insert **skill sets** if used.
- Insert **letters of recommendation** where appropriate.
- Order your **work samples** and put them into page protectors. You may want to use connected page protectors to keep samples together. Order the work samples with your best examples first.
- Insert copies of **certifications, diplomas,** and **degrees.**
- Insert **community service samples.**
- Insert **professional membership** certificates and service samples.
- Insert **academic plan of study** and **faculty/employer bios.**
- Insert **references.**

Step 4 ... Developing Support Materials

Now that you have the key elements inserted into the portfolio, it's time to create a few support materials.

Statement of Originality and Confidentiality

This one-page sheet should be placed at the beginning of your portfolio. It states that the portfolio is your work and indicates if certain portions of the portfolio should not be copied.

Statement of Originality and Confidentiality

This portfolio is the work of James Cook. Please do not copy without permission. Some of the exhibits, work samples, and/or service samples are the proprietary property of the organization whose name appears on the document. Each has granted permission for this product to be used as a demonstration of my work.

Sample Statement of Originality and Confidentiality

Template

Use the document on the accompanying disk to create your own page. **(stmt of originality.doc)**

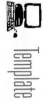

Work Sample Overview Cards

A work sample overview card is a small card (the size of a business card) that contains a brief description of the work sample. Use sheets of blank business cards to print descriptive information about each sample you have within your portfolio. If you have electronic copies of a work sample, you may want to edit the file and insert a text box directly into the work sample to act as your overview card. This way, your overview card remains with the sample at all times.

You may encounter a situation where an electronic work sample does not fill an entire page. In these cases it is appropriate to add headers to the page (in addition to the overview card) briefly describing what the work sample represents. Whether you choose to print separate overview cards using business cards or insert electronic overview cards, each overview card should include certain details about the work sample:

- Title
- Purpose
- Date developed
- Names of team members who developed it
- Demonstrated skills in keyword format—use words that are emphasized on your résumé and heading.

Fund-Raising Brochure

Designed and produced brochure for
fund-raising marketing piece
- raised $125,000 - Spring 2004

Skills - Graphic Design, Color Printing,
Fund-Raising, Writing

Work Sample Overview Card

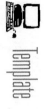

Template

Use the template on the enclosed disk to create your own work sample overview cards. **(Work Sample Overview Cards.doc)**

Allow for Your Style

You are creating a document that represents you and your career to the world. Be sure it feels like you and is a tool you feel comfortable using. Some people make title pages for each section of their portfolios. You can use clip art, photos, and graphics to give the portfolio your own style. Just be sure the end result looks professional.

General Rules to Follow

- Put all papers into the page protectors using both the front and back
- Use colored paper to draw attention to special work or service samples
- Use the same type of paper on your resumé and references (prepare two extra sets of these documents to hand out during the interview)
- Proofread everything at least three times
- NEVER USE YOUR ORIGINALS.

Step 5 . . . Check It Out

We hope this was not an emergency assembly of your portfolio and that you have at least 12 hours to proof and let the portfolio cool. Here are a few items you should check and recheck:

- Read for typos, spelling, grammar, and format. If you are not good at this, have a friend do it.
- Talk through the sections of your portfolio with a friend, thinking about which parts you will elaborate on in an interview.
- When in doubt, take it out... if you are not sure or are not pleased with an item—leave it out.
- If you have assembled this portfolio for a particular interview, make sure you have selected work samples that meet the needs of the organization.

Assembling an On-the-Job Portfolio

When you have a job, your portfolio can help you keep it and get a pay increase or promotion. The overall organization of the portfolio is the same, except that work/service samples are organized in chronological order and your professional goals may be organized by your previous year's professional goals and objectives (or the time since your last appraisal).

- **Check your calendar**—Get in the habit of writing down the start dates, benchmarks, and completion dates of projects. Write down in your calendar any letters of acknowledgment or awards received. Months from now you will have a road map ready to read and secure your documentation for the portfolio.

- **Once a month make two lists of what you have accomplished, planned and unplanned**—If you can't do it once a month, then take 30 minutes once every 90 days and think about your career. Make the appointment with yourself right now; map out the appointments and keep them.

- **Set up a file box or file drawer**—At the end of each project, make a second copy of it and put it in your file. At the very least, save it on a disk. Remember that setting aside a copy of your work needs to become reflex; it will save you a lot of chasing when you put together your actual portfolio.

- **Review the job description for your position**—As far in advance of the review as possible, reread the job description of your position. It is good to strategically consider your level of skill in each of the position statements. Use the job description to guide your quest for work samples and skill set documentation. You may even want to consider seeking out certifications that will document and help you recover from any deficits. If you don't have a specific job description for your position (and many people don't), the solution is simple. Write one now. Give a copy of your job description to your supervisor and seek his or her input. It is helpful and strategic to establish the criteria of your position before your review.

- **Review the performance appraisal standards before the actual review**—It seems simple, but be sure you understand the "rules of the game" at the beginning of the performance period. This may or may not be possible. Some organizations have very general standards or criteria. It is especially necessary in these cases that you develop your career portfolio and utilize it for the review. Now that you know the specifics, keep them in the back of your mind as you make decisions on your work samples and career activities.

- **Concentrate on your skill sets, your work samples, and professional activities**—The other parts of the portfolio, such as your work philosophy, goals, resumé, awards, and certificates, should appear in your portfolio but not be emphasized. The other sections serve as background and quite often serve as subtle support to refresh the reviewer's knowledge of you.

- **Write documentation for other people the way you would like to receive it**—Remember the key elements of good documentation: timeframe, skills demonstrated, people on the team, attitude of the individual, and suggestions for future projects based on this work.

- **Put it all together**—Put together this year's work in chronological order or into the major areas set up in your job description. Then be sure to explain to the person reviewing you that you have put together a self-review. Set your supervisor up to utilize your career portfolio. Never simply walk in the door with your portfolio; it could be perceived as a threat.

Congratulations—You Have a Career Portfolio!

Whew!! Assembly is a lot of work. If you've gotten to this point and have a finished portfolio in hand, congratulate yourself. You've taken a huge step toward understanding yourself and you're ready to take your portfolio to the marketplace. You have taken time to examine your beliefs and goals and had the opportunity to evaluate your work, your skills, your strengths and weaknesses. You've searched through and found the best examples of your work and you now have a tool for tracking your career.

In the next chapter, we'll look at how you can adapt your portfolio into an electronic portfolio. If you want to explore the new frontier of Internet websites and find ways to create new opportunities, read on.

Congratulations on Your Portfolio!

The finished portfolio involves a lot of hard work!

Technology "Levels the Playing Field"

What exactly is an electronic career portfolio? It is a personalized, career-oriented website that you use to get a job or to make your skills known. It can be accessed from the Internet, or you can control access to the portfolio by putting it on a disk or CD-ROM. The electronic career portfolio contains the same information as your "hard copy" portfolio, but it is organized and accessed differently. Consider this... one is linear, like a newspaper which is read one page after the other—the hardcopy one; and one is nonlinear, or organized in such a way that you can mix up the order and still make sense, like a website— the electronic career portfolio.

Why Would I Want an Electronic Portfolio?

"It takes long enough to develop a hard copy portfolio, why would I want to spend all my time developing a website to do the same thing?" You're asking the right question. The beauty of the Electronic Portfolio is its ability to:

- **Cluster ideas that are related**—Consider using the same work sample but showing your link in two or more skill sets. For example, you may have a report you generated which demonstrates your leadership ability, knowledge of technology, and training skills. If you have separate pages for leadership, technology, and training, you can reference the same sample from each page. You are able to dial in the user to the exact parts of the work sample with the electronic portfolio.

- **Search by keywords using buttons or frames**—Employers like to scan quickly and get a lot of information.

- **Add more of yourself**—as your voice or a video clip. Short sound bites allow you to "show yourself in action." Keep in mind that these files can be big and work fine on a CD but may be too big or take too long for access on a web connection.

- **Follow up your interview with support material**—It is appropriate to leave a "copy" of your career portfolio in electronic form for an interviewer to review at a later time.

- **Provide new and different work samples that supplement your hard copy portfolio**—You can include more work samples in the electronic portfolio that support your paper portfolio.

So... Do I Even Need a Paper Career Portfolio?

Oh, yes! The hard copy and the electronic portfolio include the same elements, but people process, view, and explore the information differently. The paper (hard copy) portfolio and the electronic portfolio work differently in the career market.

Hard Copy Portfolios

- Hard copies work better in interviews. They are more flexible and easier to manage in an interview setting. They allow you to interact with the interviewer in a personal way.
- Some people may not have access or be comfortable using a computer.
- It is usually faster to make changes to a hard copy portfolio by switching out work samples to meet the needs of an interview. It takes more time to adjust the contents of an electronic portfolio.

When Does the Electronic Portfolio Become Attractive?

- As follow up after a successful interview—so others who did not get time to spend with you can be SOLD on you
- When they want more time with you after the interview to learn even more about you
- It is something they can view without time restrictions
- It is a perk that you have some technology literacy
- It is a support vehicle—it is not the primary source.

 # Ask the Expert

When to use an electronic portfolio

Q. Is it appropriate to use an electronic portfolio during an interview?
A. Typically you do not use an electronic portfolio during an interview unless you are interviewing for a position in the tech field. The paper portfolio lends itself best to the needs of an interview. There are three ways a paper portfolio is used in an interview:

1. Offer your portfolio at the beginning of an interview for the interviewer to review
2. Use your portfolio to answer a question during your interview
3. Use your portfolio as a summary or review at the end of the interview.

An electronic portfolio is best used during the pre-interview process by noting on your cover letter that you have a portfolio available for preview . It can also be an effective tool after an interview as a summery.

Some things to keep in mind regarding your electronic portfolio include:

- Make it easy to navigate, set it up to automatically execute
- Be sure to attach the directions for launching the electronic portfolio
- Common platforms for an electronic portfolio include using Power Point slides or HTML (web page) formats.

Electronic Portfolios Work Differently

Electronic portfolios are used differently than printed ones—you can't expect the person to whom you are showing it to run and get his/her laptop. You can, however, use it as the copy you leave with the interviewer to support your printed copy. People process information differently, and tabbed work samples and statements support what you say. With the electronic portfolio and the nonlinear approach, you can never be sure in what order people will view your info—so it becomes more important that it be able to stand alone and is organized into chunks.

No Coding!!!

Wait! I'm not a "Techno-Wizard" — How Can I Do This?

If you're feeling a little intimidated right now, thinking you don't have the skills or ability to design a website or something really technical.... relax. There are several ways to get this accomplished and it doesn't have to cost a lot. You are either going to design this website yourself or you're going to get someone to help you. There are actually many easy-to-use programs for designing websites where you don't have to know any "code" or "HTML" stuff, and some are even free.

Stay focused on your goal. If you have problems "coding" or getting something to work like a graphic or a table or a form, call in your "tech" buddies or friends for help. Don't let the technology manage you. Don't give up. Local universities have plenty of places with lab assistance. Check out job boards and find a person who is looking for a way to get more web development experience for their portfolio!

> **Students! Check your computer lab resources to see what programs are already available! Microsoft FrontPage is an easy-to-use program for creating web pages. You can also create web pages in Microsoft Publisher and Microsoft Word.**

Getting It All Together

- **What do you already have on disk?**—Find projects, reports, presentations, budgets, etc., that you already have in electronic format.

- **Get the rest of your documents into electronic format**—(Take your tote box to a friend with a scanner!) This can take some time, so allow half a day or so for this task.

- **Get yourself an electronic suitcase**—Find a way to store all these files. You can put files on several disks, a Zip disk, a writable/rewritable CD-ROM disk, or have someone burn a CD-ROM disk for you with all your samples.

- **Get the software you will use to develop the web page and figure out how to use it**—(or get your techno friend to help).

- **Not all work samples belong on your electronic portfolio**—Prioritize and choose your best samples. You may need to customize your electronic portfolio for a potential employer, so scan all of your work samples.

- **Now you're ready to design your site!**

Designing the Electronic Career Portfolio

- Start with a solid, working hard copy career portfolio.
- Consider your style and your "look," including
  - Fonts
  - White space
  - Graphics and photos.
- Decide how you will structure the items to be used including Work Samples, Work Philosophy, Goals, Resumé, References, Certificates, etc. Will they go on separate pages, or will some of them be together?
- Use templates and wizards where possible.
- Choose the work samples—remember that you can organize them in a nonlinear way.
- Storyboard the electronic portfolio; that is to say, take a large sheet of paper and colored markers or pencils and draw pictures of what you want where and what links or references you want on the contained pages. If you have access to a classroom or boardroom, use the chalk or white board. Take a good look here at how much information you want to give in the "big" picture. How much information do you want to have connected and how do you want the people to navigate or move through your portfolio? Consider using basic web HTML editors.
- Design the site on your computer.
- Test it to make sure it works. Pull in a few friends and have them take a look. Revise the site as needed.
- Write the instructions for executing the files. Attach them to the holder of your disk or the cover letter with your website.
- Then go for it—electronically produce the portfolio, date, and make copies. If you have to acquire a new skill, consider how it will support you in your career. In today's world most people are used to navigating a website and understand how they work.
- Once you've developed a website on your computer you need to get it from your computer to the Internet. Keep in mind that when it's on the Internet, everyone can access it unless you know how to password protect it. You need to find a host for your website. There are a lot of free or inexpensive ways. First, check with your Internet service provider (ISP) to see

if you can put up a free personal website—many ISPs include a "personal" site as part of your monthly fee. You can also get space on other sites. Many colleges and universities offer free web space for every student.

How do I put it on the Internet?

- Get an ISP—find a spot on the web to "host" your website
- Create your web pages on your computer
- Upload or FTP the files to the Internet site.

Upload Your Files

- Once you've got a place to put your site, you need to "upload" your files from the computer to the web. This process is called FTPing, or publishing your files.

- You will be given a user name and password that will allow you to upload the files to a specific location on the website. To update the site you make changes to the pages on your computer and then upload the files to the web. If you know how to copy and paste files between directories on a computer, you can update your site. If you need assistance, find a friend to help.

Maintaining Your Site

- Put up current work samples as you create them.

- Don't forget to take it down. When you get the job or achieve the goal it may be time to take down your site. You don't want to generate "business" if you're unable to accept it.

Bright Idea!

Don't forget to include your web address in your hard copy portfolio!

Ask the Expert

Publicizing your site

Q. **Should I include the web address in my résumé?**

A. It depends on how well dialed in you are to this particular employer. It's very tempting on the electronic portfolio to put more there than you need. You still need to strategically design the website to meet the needs of the employer.

Making the Most of Your Electronic Portfolio

In all cases, electronic or paper, the career portfolio is a tool for demonstrating who you are and what knowledge and skills you have—use the portfolio to help people learn about you and your attitude. The mental process of developing a career portfolio is the same for a paper hard copy and an electronic portfolio. The real benefit of the electronic portfolio is the ability to give people more time to access your portfolio. For examples of electronic portfolios visit our website **http://learnovation.com.**

The following pages show pages from a student electronic portfolio. This site was created in Macromedia's Dreamweaver, but you can easily create web pages in Microsoft Publisher, Microsoft Word, and Microsoft FrontPage. You can see this student website online at **http://learnovation.com/egportfolio/default.htm.**

Note: Portions of this electronic portfolio sample have been modified or edited for learning purposes.

Template

The enclosed disk contains a directory called **e_portfolio.** It contains nine HTML pages you can use to create and customize your own career portfolio. The following pages are included: home/opening page, work philosophy and goals, resumé, four blank skill area pages that can be customized to your specific skill areas, awards, and community service. The style of the pages is similar to the examples on the next few pages. Feel free to change the layout, colors, and information included to create your own unique portfolio.

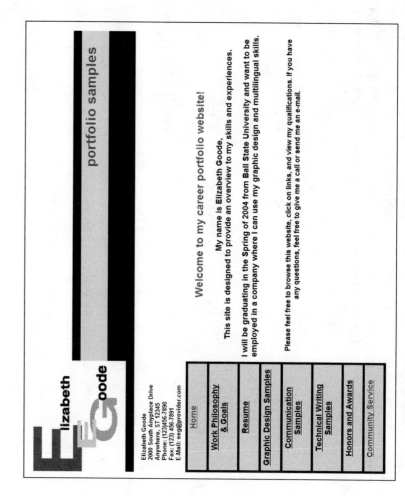

Elizabeth Goode
2000 South Anyplace Drive
Anywhere, ST 12345
Phone: (123)456-7890
Fax: (123) 456-7891
E-Mail: eeg@provider.com

- Home
- Work Philosophy & Goals
- Resume
- Graphic Design Samples
- Communication Samples
- Technical Writing Samples
- Honors and Awards
- Community Service

Welcome to my career portfolio website!

My name is Elizabeth Goode,

This site is designed to provide an overview to my skills and experiences.

I will be graduating in the Spring of 2004 from Ball State University and want to be employed in a company where I can use my graphic design and multilingual skills.

Please feel free to browse this website, click on links, and view my qualifications. If you have any questions, feel free to give me a call or send me an e-mail.

Home page

The Home page of your website serves as a starting point for the electronic portfolio. It introduces who you are and serves to orient the viewer to your website. Navigation buttons help the viewer easily go between the pages in the website. Underlined text are links to additional pages. The user can click on the text to go to a related page. It is a good idea to put your contact information on the home page, or on a separate contact page.

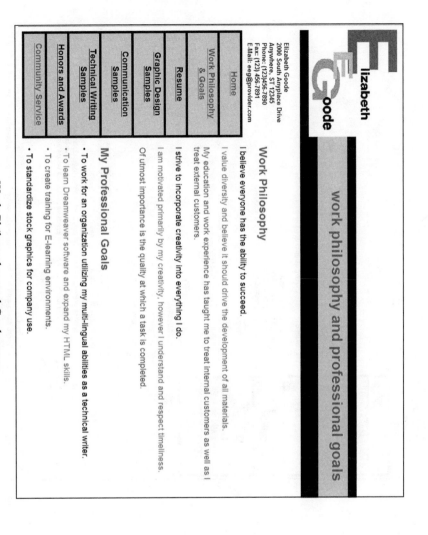

Work Philosophy and Goals page

This page lists Elizabeth's work philosophy and goals. This should be one of the first things a person sees when viewing your electronic portfolio. You may choose to list the work philosophy and goals on your home page. You might also decide to add some simple clip art to make a page more interesting. Be sure any clip art you use is related to the items on the page.

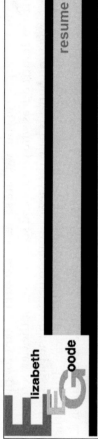

resume

Elizabeth Goode
2000 South Anyplace Drive
Anywhere, ST 12345
Phone: (123)456-7890
Fax: (123) 456-7891
E-Mail: eeg@provider.com

Home

Work Philosophy & Goals

Resume

Graphic Design Samples

Communication Samples

Technical Writing Samples

Honors and Awards

Community Service

Print a copy (PDF)

Elizabeth Goode

2000 South Anyplace Drive • Anywhere, ST 12345
Phone: (123) 456-7890• Fax: (123) 456-7891 • E-Mail: eeg@provider.com

Skills and Qualities

- **Self-motivated, creative, problem solver with a "can-do" attitude**
- **Flexible in ability to participate in, or lead on long- and short-term projects**
- **Skilled in both PC and Macintosh environments**
- **Able to quickly learn and adapt to new software**
- **Skilled in the following applications and languages:**

Windows '98 & 2000 & XP • Adobe Illustrator • QuarkXPress • Adobe InDesign
Adobe PhotoShop • Adobe Acrobat Exchange • Xerox Elixir Software Suite • MS Word
MS Excel • MS PowerPoint • MS Access • Word Perfect • FrontPage • HTML
Lotus 1-2-3 • Internet Explorer • Netscape Navigator • Hotmail • Groupwise • MS Outlook

Education

Bachelor of Arts - Ball State University, Muncie, IN
Major: English and Japanese • Minor: Business Operating Systems
Anticipated Graduation – May 2004

Associates of Arts: May 2002 - IUPUI Herron School of Art, Indianapolis, IN
Visual Communications – major

Employment

Electronic Publisher (part-time)
USA Group/Sallie Mae - 2001 – Present

- **Created original art pieces** for use in intranet pages and internal communications
- **Designed** posters, flyers, invitations, **postcards, brochures, slide shows, envelopes,** letterheads, manuals, **and business** cards for internal clients
- **Designed paper, electronic, and mainframe-compatible forms** in a full print production environment; preparing artwork and print specifications to vendors to meet clients needs
- **Performed client** outreach presentations detailing departmental capabilities
- **Initiated an electronic, paperless process to reduce waste and cost.**

Quality Control Coordinator
USA Group 2001

- **Tracked and coordinated all department jobs** from request through approval and delivery
- **Coordinated with purchasing and external vendors** to fill customer orders in a timely and cost effective manner
- **Proofread and edited all forms** for style and compliance to Corporate Communication Guidelines.

Tutor of Reading and Study Skills
Ball State University 2000 - 2001

- **Performed desktop** publishing duties: creating flyers, posters, worksheets, and data reports
- Tutored ESL clients in reading English, composition, conversational skills, and related tasks.
- Edited and reviewed book drafts and documents geared to ESL learners.

Retail Salesperson
Educational Materials Kelso's/Education Galore 1998 - 1999

- Created original and unique displays for seasonal stock
- Self supervising, key-holding sales person responsible for opening, closing, preparing back deposits, scheduling, intra-company communication and fielding customer complaints.

Résumé - (continued)

Administrative Assistant
Simmon's Real Estate 1997 - 1998

- Operated one-person office for real estate and rental agency
- Prepared real estate documents and maintained full charge bookkeeping for small business.

Honors & Memberships

- USA Group August 2002 Employee of the Month – selected out of 2,500 national employees
- Member MSD United Way Committee – 1998 – 2000
- Member MSD Diversity Implementation Team
- Alpha Lambda Delta Gold Key/National Honor Society
- Dean's list 6 semesters at Ball State University
- LCSA Board Representative 1999

The résumé page looks very similar to Elizabeth's hard copy résumé. She has added colored headings and included links to work samples in other areas of the electronic portfolio. If you click on the invitations link under the job title Electronic Publisher, you will go to the graphic design samples page.

The formatting of the online résumé takes up more space and if you print the web page, you may lose some of the information from the printed page. Elizabeth has included a graphic of a printer that is linked to a PDF copy of her one-page résumé. When you click the printer, a new browser window will open and display a printable version of her portfolio in Acrobat Reader. The person viewing the electronic portfolio must have Acrobat Reader installed on their machine in order to view the printable résumé. Acrobat Reader is available for free from Adobe. Most new computers come with Acrobat Reader already installed. In order to make a PDF file, you need to have a copy of the complete Adobe Acrobat on your computer.

The next several pages of the electronic portfolio are Elizabeth's key skill areas. These are the skills she is trying to promote to potential employers. She has grouped work samples by area. She has included smaller graphics (sometimes called thumbnails) of her work samples on each page. If the viewer wants to see a larger copy, they can click on the sample, or on the underlined link, and a new window will open with a larger version of the sample.

As with a hard copy portfolio, you should put your most important and best work samples first. You should also organize your key areas, so your strongest area is the first in the site navigation.

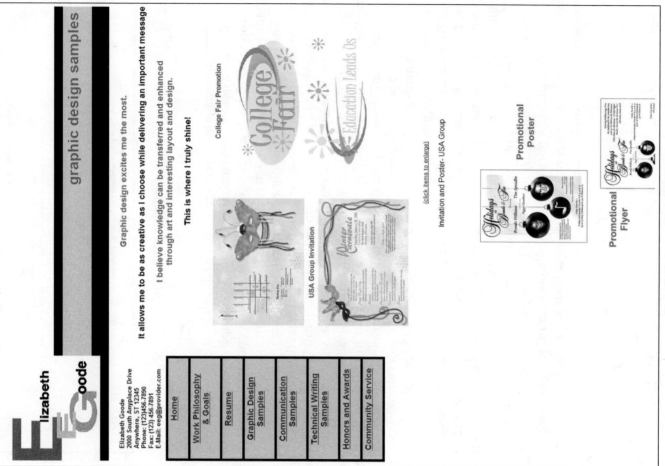

Key Skill Area - Graphic Design

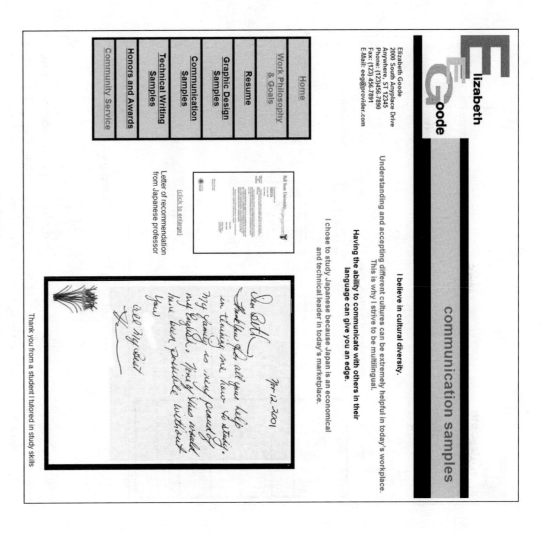

Key Skill Area - Communication

Additional work samples could include reports, project summaries, slides, and presentations. Remember that the web is a more graphic environment. People get bored very easily with loads of heavy text. Use graphics and clip art to make your site more appealing.

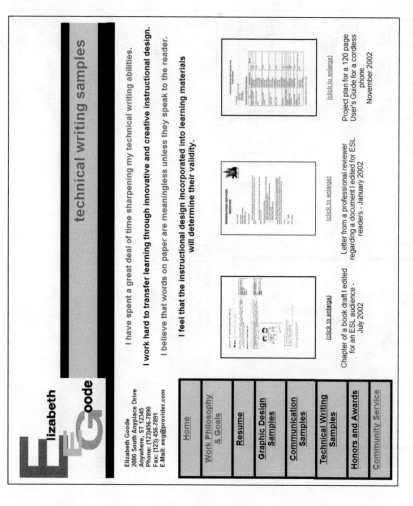

Key Skill Area - Technical Writing

When you click on any of these work samples, a new browser window will open and a PDF version of the file will display. Using smaller versions of a graphic saves space and browsing time for the viewer.

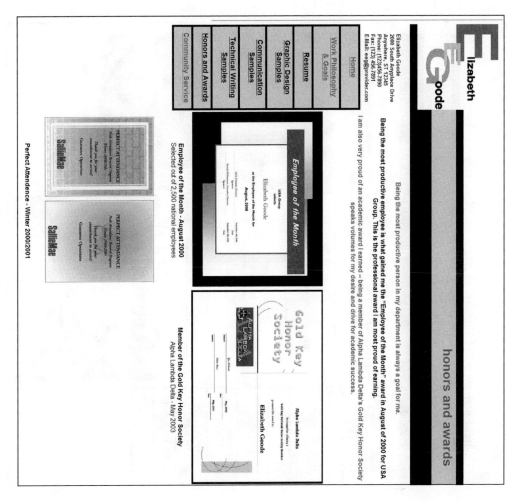

Honors and Awards

Don't forget to include graphics or photos of honors and awards you've received. Remember, the goal is to show the viewer what sets you apart from others.

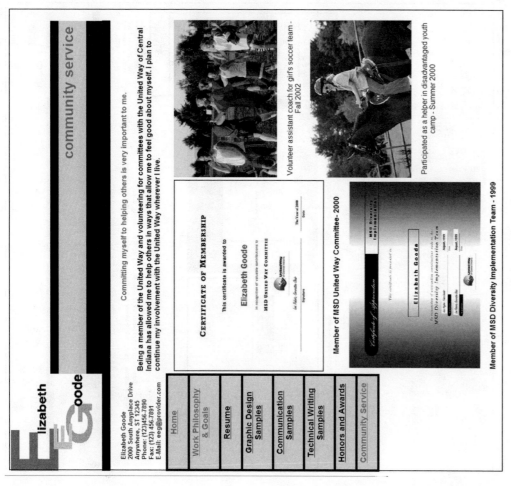

Community Service

Community service is a great place to include certificates and photos of people in action. Don't forget to include graphics and pictures when you can. It makes the electronic portfolio more interesting and draws the viewer into the portfolio.

If you've taken the time to create an electronic portfolio, give youself a pat on the back—you deserve it! Electronic portfolios give you more flexibility and more opportunities to show your skills and talents, but it takes time and effort to produce an electronic portfolio.

Don't forget that electronic portfolios are often used to give an employer another look at your skills, or to emphasize something you forgot you had. It may be just that extra effort and initiative that gets you into the job you want.

Appendix B:
Interviewing Made *Almost* Easy

Interviewing Made *Almost* Easy

Of all the phases of job searching, from writing your resumé to the time you say "yes" to a job offer, the one most traumatizing to job seekers is the interview. No wonder: The interview is the most critical part of the job search. The *interview is where you are hired or not hired.* It's the zero hour, and you must be prepared to be scrutinized. During the interview, you are the "bug under the glass," to put it bluntly.

What can you do to minimize the fears, the anxiety, the sweaty palms? How can you get through the interviewing process with your self-confidence intact and get the job you want? That's what this appendix is about: helping you take the fear out of interviewing and showing you that you *can* have the job you desire. No matter what your age is or what field you're in, there are certain strategies and techniques you can use that will help you handle this phase of the job search with more confidence and less stress. Knowing how companies conduct interviews, what their expectations are of you as a prospective employee, what subjective assumptions are made in 75 to 80 percent of all interviews, and how to evaluate your performance are just a few of the things that can make interviewing *almost easy.*

How *Not* to Interview

Some of the most common mistakes that will keep you from being hired are:

- Not conducting the necessary research on the company and the industry.
- Not practicing (role-playing) for interviews.
- Not knowing the job requirements.
- Improper dress or sloppy appearance.
- Giving inappropriate or untruthful answers to interview questions.
- Not having questions to ask the interviewer other than "What are the salary and benefits?"
- Poor communication skills and body language that "give you away."
- Criticizing former employers or supervisors.
- Not selling yourself, being too passive, lacking enthusiasm.
- Not knowing salary ranges and your worth.
- Lack of career direction and goals.
- Not knowing how to close the interview.
- Overemphasizing money.
- Being late to the interview.
- Sharing a marked dislike for school work.
- Failing to follow up after the interview.

Would you like to hear about just a few of the outrageous reasons that applicants didn't get hired? Vice presidents and personnel directors from 100 of the largest corporations were asked to describe their most unusual experience interviewing prospective employees. Here are a few of the incidents they reported:[1]

- A job applicant challenged the interviewer to an arm wrestle.
- The candidate fell and broke an arm during the interview.
- The candidate announced that she hadn't had lunch and proceeded to eat a hamburger and fries in the interviewer's office.
- One candidate brought a large dog to the interview.
- The applicant interrupted the interview to phone her therapist for advice on how to answer specific interview questions.

In this appendix you will learn how to avoid the common pitfalls. You will learn how employers conduct interviews and what they are really looking for, what is the necessary preparation, how to find out about salary ranges, and how to sell yourself. In addition, this appendix will give you some advice about what to do between interviews, how to deal with rejection, how to negotiate for the best salary, and how to evaluate a job offer.

Interviewing is not as difficult as most people think. Yes, it does make you feel very vulnerable. After all, the interviewer could say, "Sorry, you don't measure up; you're not what we're looking for." And that hurts! It is not an attack on your self-worth, and you can save yourself a lot of agony if you prepare for your interviews properly and know how to present yourself to a prospective employer confidently and professionally. You will have a much greater chance of getting the job of your choice, and to deal with rejections effectively.

I can promise you this: If you do your "homework," follow the suggestions in this appendix, and remember to believe in yourself, interviewing will be less fearful than it has ever been. Who knows . . . you might even consider it an exciting challenge.

Successful Interview Preparation

Preparation, the first step to successful interviewing, is the most neglected. People searching for work usually do not have the vaguest idea how to prepare for an interview correctly. And not being prepared creates about 75 percent of your fear. You simply cannot expect to make a favorable impression on the employer who is interviewing you if you do not prepare yourself beforehand. First, you must know something about the company to which you are applying. If you go into the interview with no idea what this company does, you are asking for rejection. It is an insult to them that you didn't care enough to find out what they're all about, and the last thing you want to do is to ask them about their company in the interview.

What Does the Company Do?

It's actually quite easy to research companies. Now is the time to put your library and Internet techniques to use. Learn as much as you can about the company to which you are applying. Interviewers try to determine not only your interest in obtaining the job, but also why you wish to work for them as opposed to other companies. Two questions they may ask are "What do you know about our company?" and "What contribution can you make to our organization?" In order to answer these questions knowledgeably, you must have done your research. The more information you have on the company, the better qualified you will be to answer their questions about your ability to contribute to their growth and prosperity—which is, by the way, the most important thing to them. Below are lists of library and Internet sources to assist you in your search for information on companies, the latter taken from the *Cyberspace Job Search Kit*.

Library Research Sources

- *New York Times Index.* Twice monthly index of newspaper articles in the *New York Times*, according to subject matter, dates, etc.

- *Applied Science & Technology Index.* Index of articles from magazines devoted to aeronautics, automation, chemistry, construction, metallurgy, transportation, and other related subjects.
- *Facts on File.* Weekly 8- to 10-page news digest that gives unbiased coverage of significant news events of each day, indexed for easy location.
- *Information Please Almanac.* In addition to statistical information, it features brief articles summarizing developments in various fields during the previous year.
- *World Almanac.* One-volume, yearly publication that presents statistics on business, education, industries, governments, population, sports, foreign countries, etc.
- *Business Periodicals Index.* Indexes more than 100 magazines in accounting, advertising, banking, business, insurance, labor, and other related fields.

Libraries also provide access to CD-ROMs such as InfoTrac and ProQuest, which are collections of magazine articles, and microfiche copies of newspapers and journal articles.

Internet Sites for Employer Information[2]

- *EDGAR.* The Electronic Data Gathering, Analysis, and Retrieval system. Contains the publicly available filings submitted to the Securities and Exchange Commission (SEC). At this site, you can find a public company's annual report, or 10-K, which describes the company's overall direction and includes financial data, information on research projects in development, and other plans. www.sec.gov/edgar.shtml
- *Hoover's Online.* Contains "company capsules" on every U.S. company traded on a major stock exchange, as well as some 2,000 private companies, that offer information on recent reports, brief financial data, and links to each company's website. www.hoovers.com
- *Forbes 500 Largest Private Companies.* Includes a brief company description, number of employees, sales rank, and a link to the company's website. www.forbes.com/private500
- *Companies Online.* A joint project of Lycos and Dun & Bradstreet that includes private companies. www.companiesonline.com
- *Fortune.* *Fortune* magazine's 100 Best Companies to Work for in America. www.fortune.com/fortune/bestcompanies/index.html
- *Fortune.* The magazine's ranking of the most admired companies. www.fortune.com/fortune/mostadmired/index.html
- *Women's Wire.* *Women's Wire's* list of the best companies in the United States for women, based on salary, benefits, and opportunities for advancement. www.womenswire.com (bottom of page, key in city, state, ZIP for localized search)
- *Working Woman.* Contains the magazine's list of the top 500 women-owned companies. www.workingwomanmag.com
- *The Hispanic Business 500 Directory.* www.hispanicbusiness.com/research/companies/default.asp

Where Is the Company Located?

Another vital step in preparing for a successful interview is to make certain that you know exactly where the company is located and how to get there. Don't make the grave error of thinking you know approximately where it is and then end up walking in late for the interview because you didn't know for sure. When you schedule the interview, ask for directions. If you forget to ask, call and find out. Ask about parking: Is there a special lot or space for visitors? Is it controlled by security? Find out if there is more than one building, and if so, which one are you to go to. Next, if at all possible, take a trial run to the business so that you are prepared for any detours, street repairs, etc. By doing this, you will also know how long it takes to get there. Take into account the hour of the day when you will be interviewing. Is it during the rush hour? If so, be sure to allow sufficient extra time, depending on the distance.

What *Is* Professional Dress?

This question usually brings up a lot of discussion and a lot of different ideas about what is or is not professional dress. Unfortunately, there is no one simple way to describe, for everyone, what it is. A few years ago, the concept of what is professional dress in the workplace underwent a dramatic change. In many companies, suits and ties were replaced with the "Dockers look" and "casual Friday" became a common trend. According to Kim Johnson Gross, coauthor of *Work Clothes: Casual Dress for Serious Work*, this change reflected what people were wearing outside the workplace to what they wear to church and the theater.[3] It appears that the concept of professional dress changes with the values of society as it has now in the twenty-first century. I am now hearing from some employers that the casual Friday dress code is being abandoned because their employees were abusing the privilege and coming to work in sloppy apparel; however, one thing remains constant: We definitely have a good idea of what is not professional. Also, what is appropriate for one industry or person may not be for another. Standards differ from profession to profession and industry to industry. For example, an automotive technician probably would not wear a pin-striped suit complete with vest and tie to apply for a job; likewise, a senior networking administrator or human resources manager would most certainly not show up for an interview in blue jeans. What is needed here are some general guidelines to use in determining what you should wear so that you are seen as a professional in your field and so that you make a good first impression.

First impressions stay with an interviewer, and like it or not, the clothes you wear create an image and play a major part in how you are perceived. Nemnich and Jandt say "The amount of care you take in dressing appropriately for your job interview equates in an employer's mind with how much respect you have for the profered job."[4] Consequently, if you wish to be treated as a professional, you must create a professional image, and that is determined, in a large part, by how you dress.

Color

One of the important aspects of your dress is the color you choose. Some colors convey a message of power or energy, some are interpreted negatively, and some convey a positive impression. The most desirable for an interview would, quite obviously, be colors that emphasize the positive.

Many people assume dark colors are always safe, but this is not always true. Black is a power color, and wearing a completely black outfit could intimidate your interviewer. Think about it: Who is always dressed in black? Judges, ministers, and, of course, people in mourning wear black. If black is your very best color, and it is the only thing you have to wear, then add a brightly colored accessory to offset that authoritative tone. Blues are always safe colors, especially navy blue. Blues convey serenity and a sense of balance. Greys and burgundy are also considered to be good choices as they represent dignity. Brown is a very somber color and can project a mood of despondency, so again, if it is the only thing you have, give it a spot of cheer by adding another color. Pastels such as yellow, pink, and light blue do nicely as a contrast color, but not as a total look.

Other colors that could convey the wrong message are green and yellow—studies show that green and yellow are the least-liked colors of executives. In general, wear a color that looks good on you and one that isn't going to shock the person with whom you're interviewing.

Style

The second aspect of being professionally dressed is the style of clothes you wear. *Conservative* is the key. For women, it is especially important to convey the image of someone who is serious about her career. Avoid frilly blouses, see-through materials, or "little girl" clothes. If you want to be taken seriously, you must dress seriously. Authors Greenleaf and Schaefer say, "While looking good is important, leave your sex appeal at home. The key is to be attractive through class and attention to detail, not through revealing clothing."[5] A simple suit or skirt and jacket is always a good choice. Women should wear closed shoes with medium-height heels and flesh-colored nylons. Men should avoid casual sportswear, faddish apparel, and sneakers. Your socks should be the same color, or a close match, to your suit or pants and jacket.

Jewelry should be worn sparingly and should be either gold, silver, or good-quality costume jewelry. Anything that dangles and is heavy makes you look as if you're going out for the evening. We see many men today wearing a single gold or diamond earring in one ear. Even though this is more common and much more accepted than it was a decade ago, conservative companies still frown on this practice and do not view it as professional. Wearing an earring is certainly your decision, but you should be aware of the consequences. Obviously, multiple body piercings can be viewed as unacceptable when employees are required to greet and work with the public. Makeup and perfume can be inadvertently overdone, so moderation is essential. Remember that you are going to an interview, not on a date. Anything that could be labeled as "far out" can distract your interviewer and give him or her the opportunity to make assumptions that could hurt your chances of being offered the job.

An equally important factor in achieving a professional appearance is to choose apparel appropriate to the current season. Don't wear linens and light-weight fabrics in the winter or heavy woolens in the spring or summer. Cotton for shirts and blouses is a good selection year-round and always looks professional. White shoes, in most parts of the country, are not considered to be in good taste from September through April. The part of the country you live in has a definite bearing on what is appropriate. If you are new to the area and not sure what to wear, talk to a sales clerk in a well-known clothing store; he or she can usually give you some sound advice.

Don't observe what the employees of the company for which you are interviewing are wearing and use that as a guideline. It could be very misleading. They already have their jobs, so they are sometimes not concerned with what they wear on a day-to-day basis. Besides, everyone has "bad hair days" when they do not look their best. If it is a Friday, the employees might be wearing casual apparel if that is a custom at the company. Interviewers want to know that you know how to dress professionally. After you get the job, you can wear what the others are wearing. Even then, if you are interested in being promoted, you might want to dress "up," that is, dress as if you already have that position. How you present yourself is one of the criteria on which many promotions are awarded.

Whether you're an automotive technician, a chief financial officer, or a graduate with a degree in Business Administration, the same rules apply: The employer is judging you as to how you would fit in as a potential representative of the company image.

I INTERVIEW DAY CHECKLIST

Use the checklist below on the day of your interview.

○ 1. I have prepared a list of appropriate questions to ask the interviewer.

○ 2. I have my list of references ready should it be requested.

○ 3. I have reviewed my benefit statements and am prepared to sell myself to get the job.

○ 4. I have done the necessary research on the company with which I'm interviewing.

○ 5. My hair is cut, washed, combed, and styled in a professional manner.

○ 6. I have bathed and used deodorant.

○ 7. My makeup, jewelry, and perfume or after-shave lotion are not excessive.

○ 8. My fingernails are trimmed, clean, and if polished, have been freshly done.

○ 9. My teeth are clean, and I have used a mouthwash for fresh breath.

○ 10. My shoes are clean, neat, and unscuffed.

○ 11. My clothes are clean, pressed, and styled appropriately for the job for which I'm interviewing. I feel comfortable in them.

○ 12. I promise myself that I will not fuss with or rearrange my clothing, hair, etc. once I arrive.

○ 13. I promise that I will be myself whatever the circumstances of the interview.

○ 14. I will take extra copies of resumes, transcripts, and portfolios with me in case they ask for these.

○ 15. I have all the necessary tools to correctly and neatly complete the application form should I be asked to fill one out.

How Interviews Are Conducted

One of the factors that makes interviews stressful is that you really can't be sure of what to expect. What questions will be asked? How are you going to be treated? Are you going to get the opportunity to sell yourself? What can you do about a question you don't understand or feel you can't answer? Are you going to be tested? And on and on and on. It is always the unknown that is so scary. This is why doctors and hospitals usually "walk a patient through" a surgery before the actual operation takes place. They have discovered that if the patient knows what to expect, a lot of fear can be eliminated. Being interviewed is a little like being operated on, wouldn't you agree? So if knowing what to expect can minimize the fear of surgery, then it should work as well for interviewing. What then, can you generally expect to happen in an interview?

Before the Interview

In most instances, you will be asked to complete an application form before interviewing. This is a very good reason to be early for the interview. If your interview time is set for 10:00, be there at least by 9:45. Also, your interviewer will love you for this, especially if he or she has finished with the one before you a little early. Interviewers are always eager to get on with the next one, and there you are, all ready to go! Being early also gives you time to check your notes and your appearance one last time before you meet your interviewer. It allows you to enter the interview relaxed and ready.

Many employers prefer to test an applicant before the interview, particularly in technical fields. Positions in electronics, mechanics, computer programming and networking, drafting, graphics, and word processing require levels of dexterity and accuracy that can be measured by performance tests or paper-and-pencil tests. Some employers evaluate prospective applicants through psychological testing (such as general intellectual ability and personality tests).

According to Caroline Hsu in *The Testing of America*, "Personality tests are increasingly a part of American life . . . and they are big business. The tests are being used in hiring, promotions, and professional development by a third of U.S. businesses. . . . In the last three months, the online testing website *Tickle* administered 10 million personality tests."[6] The objective of psychological assessment is to obtain as pure an estimate as possible of characteristics such as intelligence, leadership potential, creativity, and so on. However, the downside of these tests is that they are highly controversial and widely criticized, are not regulated by state and federal agencies, and are very costly to the employer. However, as quoted by Ms. Hsu, John Putzier, a performance consultant and author of the new book *Weirdos in the Workplace*, "argues that personality testing can be enormously valuable, precisely because often what is revealed as a weakness may actually be a strength."[7]

Whatever the type of testing the employer uses, you should make every attempt to find out if you are going to be tested before the interview; the best way is simply to ask. You don't need any surprises the day of your interview; your anxiety level will be high enough.

Types of Interviews

There are as many kinds of interviews as there are companies and interviewers because everyone does things a little differently. How an employer decides to administer the interview could vary from a personal face-to-face interview to videotaping an applicant to possibly a lunch or phone interview. Still, interviews can generally be categorized in four basic types: the *group* or *committee/panel* interview, the *unstructured* (discussion) interview, the *structured* (direct) interview, and the *stress interview*.

The kind of interview you will have is sometimes determined by the size of the company. The larger the company, the more structured and extensive your interview is likely to be. Larger companies have personnel and extensive your interview is likely to be. Larger companies have personnel staff who are usually skillful and experienced at conducting interviews, whereas smaller companies usually lack personnel staff, and managers and supervisors conduct all interviews. When you interview with a manager or supervisor, you might find that you know more about interviewing than the person sitting behind the desk. Whatever you encounter, it is best that you leave the control of the interview in the hands of the interviewer. If you are too aggressive or come across as a "know it all," you could be seen as a usurper, a person who likes to infringe on others' authority.

Group or committee interview.

In a *group interview*, several people ask questions of the applicant; the interviewers could include those who will be your peers if you are hired. Sometimes, applicants are interviewed more than one at a time and are asked to react to one another rather than to the interviewer(s) so they can determine how well you function in a group or team setting. You should make eye contact with, and speak to, each individual.

In a *committee/panel interview*, generally used for hiring for high-level positions, one candidate is interviewed by several interviewers. Group or committee/panel interviews can be somewhat intimidating, but they needn't be. Do expect that you will have less time to think about your answers, but take your time answering and try to establish a degree of rapport with everyone in the group. Do not feel pressured to be totally spontaneous. Keep your answers short and direct. You might want to ask yourself why you are being interviewed in this way. Does it mean you are going to have more than one boss?

Unstructured interview.

The *unstructured interview* is rather informal. The person interviewing you will expect you to do most of the talking by asking broad questions and may respond only with "Yes?" or "Is that so?" This type of interview usually yields more information about the applicant's opinions and reactions. In this kind of interview, job seekers often talk themselves right out of a job offer. Remember to stay focused on facts about your ability to fill the position, your qualifications, and what you can do for the company. Don't let nervousness sidetrack you into talking about irrelevant topics or personal trivia.

Structured interview.

The *structured interview* is the most commonly used and involves a predetermined pattern of questions that will be asked. It is considered to be the most valid for employee selection, as the questions are usually drawn directly from the job description. The drawback to this type of interview is that it does not allow you to exhibit your personality, communication skills, or other attributes.

Stress interview. The fourth kind of interview is the *stress interview*. It is designed intentionally to put you under stress so that your behavior and your responses and reactions can be observed. It is not often used, and when it is, the reason is usually because the position for which you are applying is a high-stress one. The reason could be merely that you are being interviewed by someone who enjoys watching others in the "hot seat." If you find yourself in a stress interview, you must stay calm, cool, and collected. The interviewer may deliberately and frequently interrupt you, remain silent for long periods of time, or ask stressful and intimidating questions. Try not to take anything personally. Just answer as well as you can and keep in mind that you are being tested to see if you can handle stress.

If you are applying for a job in another city and cannot meet with the interviewer in person, you could be asked to do a videotaped interview via a third party such as a career service agency. To prepare for facing a video camera, you might want to practice beforehand. Your nonverbal communication (discussed later) is especially critical in this type of interview because the camera picks up and clearly records your body language more than an interviewer might in a face-to-face interview. You should speak slowly and clearly and show enthusiasm, but don't overdo it. An employer might also require a phone interview either because an in-person interview is not possible or because the person interviewing you wants to see how you respond to questions over the phone. It is very important to prepare for this interview just as you would for a one-on-one.

Lunch interviews are usually more casual than interviews done in the office, but don't forget it is still an interview. Follow the person doing the interview in whatever manner he or she sets. Whether it is casual or professional, don't order messy foods or alcohol. Also, even where it is still allowed, it is wise not to smoke.

For all types of interviews, always do your homework beforehand, show self-confidence, and trust yourself to manage anything that comes up tactfully and professionally. Then, no matter how *they* rate you, *you* will know that you did your very best.

How Employers Evaluate You

The one thing you can be sure of in any interview is that you will be evaluated. During the interview, an unconscious evaluation is taking place, and after the interview, a formal evaluation is done.

There are no standardized evaluation or rating forms that all employers use. Each company evaluates its applicants differently, according to the needs of the company or the division for which you would be working. The following list will give you an idea of some of the things that employers say they observe when interviewing a prospective employee.

- Attitude
- Personal appearance
- Ability to communicate, orally and in writing
- Skills, ability to perform the job
- Self-confidence, poise
- Enthusiasm for the job and the company
- Criticism of past employers, coworkers

- Goals, self-motivation
- Willingness to do whatever is asked (overtime, additional training)
- School grades/attendance
- Educational requirements of the job
- Pre-employment testing
- Leadership potential

Overall, your level of self-confidence will be measured by the way in which you present yourself to the interviewer. How you dress and speak, your mannerisms, and the validity and content of your answers to questions will all influence the employer's evaluation. A study done at UCLA a few years ago revealed that the impact of a performance was based 7 percent on the words used, 38 percent on voice quality, and 55 percent on nonverbal communication. So—do your research, prepare your answers to possible questions, and maintain a positive attitude; this will carry you through most interviews with a good rating.

What Employers Are *Really* Looking For

Aside from the technical, administrative, or management skills that are called for in the job description, what kinds of personal and interpersonal skills do employers look for? Frequently, applicants who have the best skills, education, and abilities are not hired. Quite often, the applicant who gets the job is the one who doesn't have quite all of the required experience or education. Wondering why this is the case, I began to question employers about their reasons for choosing one applicant over another. What would be the strongest selling points for their choice?

I discovered that there is much more to winning the approval of the interviewer and getting the job than skills and education. Being chosen over other applicants has everything to do with your interpersonal skills, your personality, and how you conduct yourself in the interview. Employers are looking for the applicant who "fits" with the company and its culture. Many interviewers told me that they hired the person with whom they felt the most comfortable, the one that they believed would be a good "match" for their employees. Of course, this person also had to have most of the qualifications for the job to even get the interview, but the candidate was hired because he or she was *liked*.

By the time you're in the interview, the employer usually knows about your employment background, education, and skill level. Now the interviewer will try to determine if you are compatible with the company. This is one time when the old saying "Opposites attract" does not apply: employers are looking for someone who is *like* them. The decision to hire or not hire becomes very subjective, so the more you understand about what takes place in the interviewer's mind, the more you're looking for or feeling about you, the better chance you have of getting the job. An excellent way to do this is to practice "reading" people so that you can respond accordingly. What kinds of cues is the interviewer giving you? What kinds of body language is he or she exhibiting?

Interpersonal Skills

The employer is interested in the occupational skills you have (such as typing 65 words per minute, programming, networking, repairing computers, designing a building, or doing a blood analysis) but he wants to know other things about you as well. Can you take criticism and direction? Can you follow instructions? Are you a good team player? Are you flexible and adaptable? Can you communicate clearly? Can you handle change and conflict? Are you reliable, dependable, and responsible? Do you have initiative? Can you "hit the ground running?" Can you take on additional responsibilities? Can you demonstrate uncompromising integrity, professional ethics, and morals? Over the past few years, we have observed the flagrant abuse of authority and the complete lack of integrity by many of our nation's top senior-level executives, so employers are screening applicants for these most important traits. Most important, over and above performing the duties of the position, are you going to get along well with your coworkers and your supervisors? Are you able to work with others who have different values, work habits, and cultures than you? Research shows that approximately 78 percent of all terminations take place not because the employee didn't perform the job well but because he or she had difficulty with coworker/supervisor relationships.

Personality

The employer's subjective evaluation also includes a determination on the kind of personality you have. In order to learn how to respond to the needs of the interviewer, you need to learn more about yourself. Gaining an in-depth understanding of your personality style has enormous value in your career, and learning how to use this knowledge will make you more successful in your job search. How perceptive or creative are you? Do you have warmth and diplomacy? Are you self-confident? Depending on the culture (personality) of the company, how closely does your personality match that of the company's current and most valued employees? If the company is filled with outgoing and gregarious people, you might not be a good choice if you are generally quiet and reserved—and vice versa. The other side of this coin is that *you* probably would not be happy working there.

You may disagree with judgments of this kind, thinking that it shouldn't matter what your personality is as long as you can do the job. But it does matter. In today's world of committees, teams, quality circles, and participative management, you must blend in and be cohesive with your coworkers and management. If you don't, you will not only be very uncomfortable and dissatisfied, you will not be a productive worker—and neither will the people who must work with you. Also, it is highly probable that you will not stay long at the job. Enlightened management knows this, and so to avoid constant and expensive turnover of employees, they do everything they can to hire the "right" employee.

Are You a "Match"?

How does the company determine if you are a "match"? Do employers have a crystal ball? No, they just practice a little detective work. From your answers to the questions they ask, they can learn a lot about your personality and character. Questions such as the following can uncover things that your resumé and cover letter don't tell them:

- Tell me about yourself.
- What kinds of things do you do for relaxation?
- What are the qualities that you consider necessary in a good supervisor?
- If you've ever had a disagreement with a former coworker or supervisor, how did you deal with it?

In addition, if your answers are in any way negative or derogatory, this might indicate that you have difficulty in relating to others or that you may not function well as a team member. Likewise, if you are not prepared with well-thought-out answers, the interviewer could draw a negative conclusion about your reliability. Maybe you can't be relied on to be prepared in the workplace either.

Conduct in the Interview

General Guidelines

Some basic rules of behavior and appropriate conduct should be observed during an interview. Remember, everything you do and say is observed by the interviewer and is important. These guidelines may seem trivial, but whether you follow them or not can determine the success—or failure—of the interview.

- Do not take notes during the interview unless the interviewer asks you to do so or you ask permission to do so. (*Do* make notes immediately afterward while it is still fresh in your mind.) It is sometimes intimidating for the interviewer to see you taking down what she is saying. If the company does not hire you, they could fear being accused of discrimination based on some innocuous statement made in the interview.

- Remember your interviewer's name and use it when speaking to her during the interview. Refer to the person as Mr. or Ms. unless invited to use their first name.

- When introductions are made, do offer to shake hands, whether the interviewer is male or female, and make it a firm handshake. Be careful of "bone crushers"! If your hands are prone to perspire, either use a moisture-absorbing powder or run them under cold water for a few minutes just before you go in to the interview. There is nothing more "dampening" to the interview than a wet, limp handshake.

- Do not smoke, chew gum, or drink anything in the interview. Even if a beverage or cigarette is offered, you are probably better off turning it down. Today, smoking is prohibited in most offices, chewing gum is very unprofessional, and trying to balance a drink while being interviewed is risky. The last thing you need is to spill something on yourself, or worse, the carpet.

- Wait for the interviewer to offer you a chair before you sit down.

- Present yourself as an honest person. Do not try to hide anything, and above all, *never, never lie!* It will only come back to haunt you later. A lie that you "get away with" during an interview could come up after you're hired and cause you to be dismissed.

- Sell yourself! Your job as an interviewee is to sell your assets to the interviewer. If you wait expectantly for questions and dutifully answer them, you have done absolutely nothing to distinguish yourself from the other applicants.

- Bring the necessary paperwork that may be required: an extra resume, college credentials or transcripts, work portfolios, and a reference sheet. Do not, however, load yourself down with unnecessary props.

- Show enthusiasm and sincerity.

- Close the interview using the suggestions given in the section "How to Close the Interview."

Body Language

A very important part of your conduct in the interview is your body language. Sometimes it's not what you say in an interview but what you do that reveals many things to the interviewer. Volumes have been written about **body language:** the nonverbal messages that your facial expressions, physical stance, and gestures convey to a listener. Evidence shows that body language plays a vital part in communication. Experts estimate that as much as 65 percent of communication is nonverbal. Some common types of body language, such as the position of the body, hand gestures, and facial expressions, can enhance or even contradict what you actually say.

Facial expressions.   Eye contact is extremely important during the interview. Continually averting your eyes could be interpreted as a sign of guilt, lack of self-confidence, or even dishonesty. You don't want to stare either, so just glance away from time to time. Your mouth also is a major silent communicator. Smiling too much conveys an unnatural message, and pursed lips can be a signal of disapproval or a sour personality. You can gauge what is too much or too little by watching your interviewer and responding accordingly. Avoid touching any part of your face or hair during the interview. It can indicate nervousness or insecurity.

Body gestures.   Crossed arms can mean defensiveness, dissatisfaction, or simply that you've found a comfortable place for your hands. Since the meaning is ambiguous, it is best to keep your hands in your lap. The head tilted far up indicates superiority; if it's tilted down most of the time, you are giving a message of submission. A ramrod straight posture can signal inflexibility, and the other extreme, slouching in the chair, could be viewed as an indication of laziness or disinterest. The physical distance that you put between yourself and the interviewer is very important. Everyone has his or her "space," and you should not invade it. Don't lean on the desk or get too close when you are speaking with the interviewer. You will know if you've crossed that boundary by watching the person's eyes and stance. If you are too close to someone, she will usually move backward in an attempt to gain her space again.

Hand gestures.   Try to keep from gesturing too much with your hands, as it can be distracting or irritating to the interviewer. Avoid clenched hands—the "white knuckle" look—as it can reveal anxiety or fear. If at all possible, keep your hands in your lap and certainly not in your pockets. Keep them away from your face, hair, and clothing. Straightening your clothing or hair can be viewed as sign that you are unsure of yourself.

Questions You Could Be Asked and How to Answer

There is no guaranteed way to determine exactly what questions are going to be used. All companies have specific needs and will ask questions related to those needs. Some questions, however, are very likely to be asked and are worth taking the time to prepare for. Some questions can be very difficult to answer extemporaneously. If you are not prepared with appropriate answers, you could be eliminated.

There is a story about a young man who applied for a job that involved operating a small train station along a remote section of the track. The personnel officer of the train company interviewed him carefully to find out his qualifications. Then the officer said, "Well, it looks like you have the basic qualifications for the job, but we need somebody who can think on his feet and solve problems if they come up. Can you do that?" The young man replied, "Well, I think so." The personnel officer then said, "Okay, I'll give you a hypothetical problem concerning train operations, and you tell me how you'd solve it. Suppose you find out one day that there's a southbound train headed down the only track that runs by your station. You also find out that there's a northbound train coming up the same track. The engineers of the two trains don't know about each other. What would you do?"

The applicant replied, "I'd get on the telephone and call all the stations down the track to notify them of the problem." Said the interviewer, "What would you do if you found out the telephone didn't work?" "Well," said the young man, "I'd use the telegraph." "Suppose the telegraph didn't work either?" "In that case," said the young man, "I'd run outside and throw the switch so that one of the trains would be shunted off onto the spur." The personnel officer said, "And what would you do if the switch was jammed?"

"Well, in that case I'd run home and fetch my brother." This left the interviewer somewhat puzzled, so he asked, "Why would you go home and get your brother?" To this, the young man replied, "Because he ain't never seen a train wreck before."

All joking aside, you do need to be prepared before tackling the interview process. The following 26 questions are likely to arise in interviews. Rehearse the questions and become very familiar with your qualifications so that you can show the employer how you can benefit the company.

1. *Tell me about yourself.* What does the interviewer want to know? That you took lessons in knitting or home improvement? Hardly. He is not looking for personal information. Don't begin by saying that you are single or married, that you have X number of children, or that you are looking for a job with security. Take this opportunity to present your key qualities and your interest in and understanding of the company; focus on the needs of the company and its people, not what *you* want in a job. Don't be tempted to rattle off your employment history. This is the opportune time to sell yourself.

2. *What do you see yourself doing three (or five) years from now?* This question helps the interviewer determine if you plan ahead or just live from day to day. She wants to know if you have goals. If you have never before set goals and written them out, now is the time to do so. Preferably, your answer should relate to a possible career with their company. This is also the perfect opportunity to ask what the career path for this

position is. If you've done your research, you should have a pretty good idea of where you want to go with your career. Do not say you want to be in management without stating exactly what kind of management. So many people say this, thinking that it shows planning for the future; believe me, it does not. It just puts you in a category with those who have not done their homework.

3.   *Which is more important to you, the money or the type of job you do?*   With this question the interviewer attempts to find out whether you are "paycheck oriented." Be honest; explain that you, like everyone else, have to be concerned with the salary you receive because you have to support yourself (and your family, if that is the case), but that you also want a job that you enjoy doing. Some applicants make the mistake of answering this question by saying that money is not important to them. Usually, this will only lead the employer to believe that you will take a low salary.

4.   *How would you describe yourself?*   This is a tricky question, so be careful how you answer it. The interviewer is asking you to describe yourself in terms other than "I'm 28 years old; I have a degree in Business Administration," etc. She is looking for information about your personality, your character, and what kind of worker you are. This is a good place to mention your functional skills, flexibility, communication, and responsibility.

5.   *What is your greatest weakness (or strength)?*   Most job seekers are completely stumped by this question as they have never taken the time to consider what their weaknesses or strengths are. Also, some people find it very difficult to talk about themselves. As with all questions, avoid giving answers of a personal nature. An appropriate answer would be to mention one of your work-related weaknesses or strengths. Are you a workaholic, or too detail-oriented? Does your strength lie in the fact that you get along well with coworkers, or that you have excellent communication skills? These are the kinds of things interviewers look for. If you describe a weakness, mention as well that you are aware of the weakness and are working on correcting it.

6.   *What motivates you to put forth your greatest effort?*   Employers know that in order to obtain the most productivity from their employees, they must offer motivation. When the employer knows what motivates you, she can provide you with greater job satisfaction, and in turn will have a more productive worker. Are you motivated by money, rewards, recognition, responsibility, self-satisfaction? Think about this before you interview and prepare an answer in case you are asked.

7.   *Why should I hire you?*   If you are unable to sell yourself because you don't know the answer to this question, you could lose the job offer. Your research should have given you some information about the company and what they are looking for in an employee. Remember that all companies are looking for people who can help them make a profit. Show the employer that you have qualities that can help to save time and make money, and you have just provided a reason to hire you. Use your benefit statements and be specific. Can you increase productivity, cut expenses, and build good customer relations?

8. *Why are you leaving your present job?   Why did you leave your last job?* Stress reasons that put you in the best light, such as that you need more room for growth and advancement. Above all, *do not criticize your present or past supervisor or employer.*

9. *How do you feel about relocating?* Unless you absolutely do not want to relocate, or can't because of personal reasons, you can say that you are open to discussing relocating at the appropriate time. Things change, and it's always a possibility that, at a later date, you might want to relocate.

10. *What salary do you expect?* In the first interview, try to avoid this subject and do not ask about salary yourself. James E. Challenger, president of Challenger, Gray & Christmas, Inc., an outplacement firm, advises applicants not to bring up the subject of money in the first interview because it sends a message that you are more interested in yourself than in the job. However, if it is asked, you need to be prepared with an answer. If you are pressed for an answer, never give a single figure; always give a salary range and add that you are willing to negotiate.

11. *Do you smoke, drink, or use drugs?* If at all possible, avoid any emotional reaction to this question. Whether you do, have, or never have, it almost always gets an emotional reaction. To some interviewers, this could signal guilt. An employer can legally ask questions of this nature and require pre-employment drug and alcohol testing as long as the reason is to determine whether an applicant can regularly and successfully perform the job for which the employer is hiring. If this question is asked, do not try to avoid answering. Just be prepared to give an honest answer.

12. *What do you do to reward yourself after a difficult and stressful day or week?* Employers are interested in whether you are able to relax and to lead a balanced life. Since they cannot ask this directly because it is of a personal nature, they get the information by asking the above question. They also want to know if you are pursuing additional education or training, or are an active, industrious person. Let's face it, you might be considered a not-too-motivated person if you sit in front of the television set from Friday through Sunday.

13. *I see you're not married. Do you live with a man (or woman)? Do you plan to have children? Do you have adequate child care?* It is illegal for an interviewer to ask any of these questions. As with all illegal questions, you should ask politely if this has a bearing in any way on your ability to perform the job. Or you could reply that you are willing to answer any questions about your skills and qualifications to perform the job and ask if this is required information for the job. You also might ask yourself at this time whether you would want to work for a firm that is so insensitive and ignorant as to permit questions of this nature. As to reporting them, go ahead if you want to, but remember the burden of proof is on you. It will be your word against the interviewer's, and the EEOC requires proof to prosecute.

14. *Have you ever been fired or asked to resign?* This is a legitimate question, but a very sensitive one, and how you answer could mean the difference between getting and not getting a job offer. If you have been fired, the most appropriate answer is, "Yes, I have, and as I look back on it, I realize that I could have done things differently. I learned a lot about myself from that experience." Then stop, and don't say any more unless you are asked for details. I've found that 95 percent of the time, you won't be. You probably have given the needed information, that *you take responsibility for your role in that termination.* One thing you must never do is bad-mouth a former employer or supervisor. You will not be hired if you do. No one wants to deal with an employee who is insubordinate, blames others for what happens, and does not accept responsibility for his or her actions.

15. *Why do you want to work for us?* "I don't know" or "I need a job" are not exactly the best answers. Your goal should be to convince the interviewer that this company is the one you really want to work for. You can do this by saying that you are sold on the company's product or service, or that from your research, you found that the company is employee oriented and offers opportunities for growth and advancement. Of course, you must do your research so that you have a factual answer, not a glib statement.

16. *How good is your health?* The interviewer is treading on thin ice with this question (see the section on legal and illegal questions below). You can answer it by saying that there is nothing about your health that will prevent you from doing the job for which you are applying.

17. *I don't believe you have enough experience for this position.* Now is the best time to sell your functional skills, and if it is possible for you to do so, offer to begin at a little lower salary with the opportunity to prove yourself in a given period of time. You might want to ask for more information about the job: "What would a typical day in this position require? What would I be doing?" Get specifics and then use this information to show that your skills are appropriate. Most important, do not be defensive or argumentative; be agreeable, but sell yourself *with other qualities.* The objective is to persuade the interviewer that you can do the job and that you are able to learn quickly. If you've just graduated from college, stress the fact that in school you had hands-on or practical experience in the skills, if your college did provide you with a self-paced, work-simulated environment to prepare you for the actual workplace. You can add that since you just came from a learning environment, you can be trained quickly, thereby saving the company time and money. Point out that you are perfectly capable of learning from a manual if one is available.

18. *I see you've been out of the job market for several years; do you believe your skills are still up to date?* This question is usually directed to people returning from parental leaves, schooling, or sabbaticals. Focus on the knowledge and experience you gained through home study or research, volunteer work, schooling, and home projects. Inform the interviewer that although you were not employed for a salary, you have been continually learning and improving your skills. Stress that you learn quickly and that you would be willing to take whatever courses or training is needed to upgrade your skills. As with the previous question, suggest that you

are capable of learning from an instruction manual or tutorial, which saves time and money.

19. *Have you met your military obligations? Are you currently serving in the National Guard?* The first question is illegal and is not relevant unless a draft is in place. The second one is legal, and if you are in the National Guard, just assure the interviewer that your service is not going to interfere with your ability to perform the job.

20. *Of all the jobs you've held, which one did you like the most? The least? Why?* Interviewers ask questions like this to determine if the work environment is suitable for you. Be careful not to mention reasons that would conflict with the environment or the duties of the job. Formulate your answer around general work-related responsibilities and avoid specifics.

21. *If you are hired, how long do you plan to stay with our company?* I've heard a lot of career counselors tell job seekers to answer "Forever." Now, both you and the interviewer know that this is very unlikely to be true, so don't say it. An appropriate and honest answer is simply to say that you will stay as long as it's mutually beneficial. According to research by Walker Information Global Network, a workplace consulting firm, and Hudson, a think tank, the average employee has 12 to 15 jobs during his or her lifetime and stays with a job an average of 3.6 years. [8]

22. *Can you work under pressure or deadlines?* If you can and are willing to do so, give examples from your background that demonstrate your ability to handle stress, pressure, etc. Be sure to include how *you* handled it.

23. *How do you feel about working for a female (male) boss?* Caution! This is a loaded question and could put a noose around your neck. The only correct answer is to say that either would be fine, that gender is not an issue but that it is the management or supervisory ability of the person that matters.

24. *What immediate contribution can you make to our company?* The keyword in this question is "immediate"; very few employees make an immediate contribution to any company. New employees always have some "down time": time to train and just to get familiar with the company. So, be honest and say this, but add that after this period, you will contribute to the company by being an industrious and reliable employee. Illustrate this with one of your benefit statements.

25. *Do you have any questions?* This is usually the last question of the interview, and unless the interviewer had completely covered everything, you should have some relevant questions to ask. Remember, *don't ask about salary, benefits, or things of this nature.* You're probably dying to know so you can decide if this job is for you, right? But, unless you have been made an offer, you don't have a decision to make at this time.

26. *Are you interviewing with anyone else?* This is not exactly a professional question because the interviewer is asking for information that he really has no right to. However, since you don't want to ignore it or not answer, you could say, "Yes, I am. I realized when I began my job search that I should market my skills to as many companies as I could. This would enable me to choose the one that is best suited to my job goals."

Behavioral Screening Questions

Over the past few years, behavioral interviewing has become a popular method with many companies for selecting candidates. The idea behind behavioral interviewing is that the candidate's past performance is the most accurate for determining future performance. Some interviewers use a method called **behavioral screening**—asking questions that deal with actual past experiences in specific situations. When an interviewer asks this kind of question, she is looking for a brief description of a specific problem or situation, what you did about it, and what were the results. The interviewer does not want to hear your opinion or how you deal with things in general. Do not respond to the questions in the future tense, that is, what you *would do* if faced with a particular situation. Before you respond to this kind of question, take your time to think about your answer. You don't have to answer immediately. This kind of question gives you the opportunity to sell yourself, so take advantage of it. Consider preparing some answers in advance about previous experiences when you, for example, dealt effectively with stress, showed initiative in your job, worked cooperatively and successfully in a team, or demonstrated proficient customer service skills. A few examples of behavioral screening questions are:

1. Give me an example of a time when you needed to adjust to a situation quickly. What did you do, and how did it turn out?
2. Tell me about a situation when you had to stand up for a decision you made even though it was unpopular.
3. What has been your experience in working with conflicting, delayed, or ambiguous information? What did you do to make the most of the situation?
4. Solving a problem often necessitates evaluation of alternate solutions. Give me an example of a time when you actively defined several solutions to a single problem. Did you use any tools such as research or brainstorming?
5. The correct understanding of differences in personality can affect work decisions such as work assignments, employee motivation, and conflict management. Tell how your knowledge of personality differences has benefited your effectiveness.

Dealing with Difficult Questions

Sometimes in an interview, you are asked questions for which you may not feel you have an answer. To deal with these, first be sure that you clearly understand what the question is. Ask the interviewer to repeat or rephrase it for you, or ask for examples. Encourage the interviewer to tell you more by asking specific questions. If you still are not sure how to answer, ask for a few minutes to think it over, or ask if you can come back to it. If you simply do not know the answer, say so. It is far better to admit not knowing than to give an answer that makes a fool of you. Some interviewers will ask questions that they are pretty certain you would not know the answer to in order to see if you will try to bluff your way through them. This could indicate to them that you would do the same on the job, which could cause accidents, poor-quality workmanship, and unhappy customers. Remember, no one has all the answers.

Additional Interview Questions

Following are more questions you might encounter during interviews. To prepare, think about how you would answer them.

1. How do you feel about your present job?
2. How many hours do you feel a person should devote to a job?
3. What are some of the things about which you and your former supervisor(s) have disagreed?
4. What kind of people do you like working with? What kind do you find difficult to work with?
5. What are some of the things you would like to avoid in a job? Why?
6. How would you describe a good supervisor?
7. Which one of your accomplishments has given you the most satisfaction?
8. Do you have reliable transportation to and from work?
9. What one thing do others need to know about you in order to work effectively with you?
10. How do you define success?
11. What was your most rewarding experience in college?
12. Why did you choose this career?
13. What have you learned from your mistakes?
14. Are you planning to continue your education?
15. Are you willing to spend three to six months as a trainee?
16. Do you work better in a team or by yourself?
17. Have you changed careers in the past year?
18. If you were hiring a person for this position, what skills and abilities would you look for?

Your Turn to Question

You can demonstrate your interest in the company and prior research by asking pertinent and intelligent questions of your interviewer. Answers to these questions will give you a clearer picture of how the company's objectives relate to your interests and assist you in making a decision about a job offer. Beware, however, of asking too many questions, and watch your interviewer for signals (such as looking at a watch) that the interview is over. Below are suggestions for questions you could ask.

1. Can I answer any questions about my qualifications for this position?
2. Would you please describe the job duties for me? Do you have a copy of the job description I could see?
3. Do you have a formal training program? How long is it? Please describe it.
4. Is this a newly created position?
5. What type of education and experience do you most like to find in persons filling this position?
6. Was the person who previously held this job promoted?
7. Will I be responsible for supervising other staff? If so, how many?
8. How do you evaluate your employees? How often?

9. Could you describe a typical career pathway in your organization for an employee in this position?
10. How does today's economic environment affect your organization?
11. Do you have plans for expansion in terms of product development, services, new branch offices, etc.?
12. From your experience, what would you say are the company's greatest strengths?
13. How do you rate your competition?
14. What is your employee turnover rate?
15. Would you say that your company follows a chain-of-command-type management policy or one of a less structured, participative nature similar to MacGregor's Theory Y? (You may not want to use this question unless you have some basic understanding of management theories.)
16. How much involvement do your employees have in making decisions or setting policies and procedures?
17. How long have you been with this company, and what about it do you like best?
18. Will there be any further testing?
19. Will I be required to take a physical examination?
20. When will you be making your decision as to whom you're going to hire? May I call you on _____?

Questions Not to Ask

1. *Is this a union shop?* You should already know this from your research. It can also be a very threatening question to the interviewer if the company is not. You might be suspected of being a union organizer.
2. *What happened to the person who had this job before?* You are asking for personal information, and the question could sound antagonizing. Instead, rephrase it. See questions 4 and 6 in the list above.
3. *Will I have to work much overtime?* The interviewer will see you as a time-clock puncher.
4. *How much job security do you offer?* Job security is a myth—don't even mention it. Helen Keller said, "Security is mostly a superstition. It does not exist in nature, nor do the children of men, as a whole, experience it." This has never been more true than it is today with mergers, takeovers, outsourcing, and the total reorganization of many companies. Your security comes from within you.
5. *When will I get my first salary raise?* This question is totally inappropriate until you have been offered the position and have accepted.
6. *What is it that you people do at this company?* Believe it or not, applicants actually ask this question. Obviously, if you have to ask this, you are not in the running for the position. Do your homework so you know this before the interview.
7. *Can you afford me?* This question conveys a message of arrogance and over-confidence. It could be very insulting to the interviewer.
8. *What kind of benefits do you offer?* Any question related to salary or compensation, including benefits, is not appropriate until you have been made a job offer.

9. *If I'm asked to relocate, will the company pay for it?* You're assuming that you're going to get the job, so it is a premature question.

10. *How many people are you interviewing?* The answer to this question should really not be of concern to you. It might lead the interviewer to think that you are insecure or just plain "nosey."

Legal and Illegal Pre-Employment Questions

The Equal Employment Opportunity Commission and two federal laws, the Civil Rights Act of 1991 and the employment provisions of the Americans with Disabilities Act of 1990, govern the questions that may be asked on application forms and in interviews. Employers who ask questions of an illegal nature leave themselves open to charges of bias and lawsuits. Read the following list to be aware of questions you do not have to answer.

- *Name:* It is legal to ask, for access purposes, whether the applicant's work records are under another name. It's illegal to ask if a woman is Miss, Ms., or Mrs. and to request the applicant to give a maiden name or any other name he or she has used. (Legislation: Title VII as amended by Equal Employment Opportunity Title IX.)

- *Address/housing:* It's legal to request a current address and phone number and how the applicant can be contacted if a phone number is not available. It is illegal to ask for past residences, length of residence at a particular address, and whether applicant owns or rents. (Legislation: Title VII.)

- *Age:* It is legal to ask age *only* if it is needed to show that applicant is old enough to work or serve alcohol. It's illegal to request a birth certificate or similar records showing age. (Legislation: Age Discrimination Act of 1967.)

- *Race/color:* Any inquiry about color or race is illegal unless it is done under the Affirmative Action program. (Legislation: Title VII.)

- *Sex:* Again, inquiries may be made only under an Affirmative Action program. The question is legal when it is job related, e.g., when hiring locker room or restroom attendants. (Legislation: Title VII and IX.)

- *Religion/creed:* There are no legal questions about religion or creed, religious customs, or holidays. (Legislation: Title VII.)

- *Marital/parental status:* Employers may ask these questions only after hiring and only for insurance purposes. It is illegal to ask questions of any nature regarding children, who cares for them, or if the applicant plans to have them. (Legislation: Title IX and VII.)

- *Relatives:* After hiring, employers may ask for the name, relationship, and address or phone number of a person to be notified in case of an emergency. Nepotism policies that have a disparate impact on one sex are illegal. (Legislation: Title IX.)

- *Military service:* It is legal to inquire about job-related experience in the U.S. Armed Forces, but illegal to request information on the type of discharge or for military service records.

- *Education:* Employers can ask about job-related education and English language skills only if they are required for the work to be performed.

Questions about nationality, racial, or religious affiliation of schools attended are illegal, as are inquiries as to how a foreign language ability was acquired. (Legislation: Title VII.)

- *Criminal records*: It is illegal to ask for arrest records involving no subsequent conviction. (Legislation: Title VII.)

- *Organizations*: It is legal to ask about organizational and professional affiliations that are job related so long as the information is not used to discriminate on the basis of race, color, etc. (Legislation: Title VII.)

- *Photographs*: After hiring, it is legal to request photos for identification or security purposes. (Legislation: Title VII.)

- *Work schedules*: It is legal to ask about willingness to work required schedules, but not to work specific religious holiday(s). (Legislation: Title VII.)

- *Physical data*: It is illegal to require applicants to give height and weight or other non-specified, non-job-related physical data. It is legal to ask applicants to prove their ability to do manual labor, lifting, and other physical requirements for the safe performance of the job. (Legislation: Title VII.)

- *Handicap(s)*: It is legal to inquire about physical handicaps for the purpose of determining the applicant's capability to perform the job. (The burden of proof lies with the employer for non-discrimination.) It is illegal to exclude handicapped applicants on the basis of their type of handicap. (Each case must be determined on an individual basis by law.) (Legislation: Americans with Disabilities Act, Handicap Discrimination Guidelines of the Revised Code, Chapter 4112.)

- *National origin/citizenship*: All employers are required to have applicants (after hiring) complete the Employment Eligibility Verification (Form I-9), which is proof of citizenship or "intending citizen" (an alien who has been lawfully admitted to the United States). (Legislation: IRCA of 1986, EEOC, Title VII.)

Other questions that employers are advised to avoid are:

- Graduation date from grade school, high school, or college.
- Diseases or major illnesses for which the applicant has been treated.
- Hospitalization history, including mental health treatment.
- Prescription drugs being taken.
- Past treatment for drug addiction or alcoholism.
- Workers' compensation history.
- Whether applicant has ever filed for bankruptcy.
- Past garnishment of wages.

How to Close the Interview

When you are being interviewed, you let the person doing the interview take charge—up until the close, that is. During the interview, you do not interrupt, disagree with, or contradict your interviewer (even if it appears that he is inexperienced and is handling the interview rather badly). You can, however, influence how you are judged by the way you answer the questions, by being aware of your body language, and by the questions you ask. At the close of the interview, it is especially important that you get the information you need, so you should subtly and professionally exercise some control.

When you are asked if you have any questions, that's a signal that the interview is winding down. After you have asked your questions, you have the opportunity to make some important points. First, be sure to reiterate your strong points for the position; then ask if the interviewer has any questions about your qualifications. Finally, ask: When will a decision be made? Will you be contacted, or would it be appropriate for you to contact the interviewer? When would be the best time to call? Will there be second or third interviews? Will you be tested? The interviewer may not remember to tell you all these things, so ask now.

Always end the interview by asking for the job and thanking the interviewer for taking the time to consider you for the position. Many employers say that they hire the person who asks for the job. Reaffirm your interest in the company and the position.

Follow-Up After the Interview

When the interview is over, you wipe your brow, breathe a sigh of relief, and head for the nearest bar for a beer, right? Of course not! One of the first things you do is to find a quiet place and make some notes about the interview. How did you feel during the interview? Did you promise to provide more information if it was needed? If so, when? Did you forget to tell them something you felt would reinforce your credibility to do the job? Make a reminder to include it in your thank-you letter. Did you forget to ask something? Make yourself a note to ask when you call. Keeping records of and evaluating all interviews will help you to remember what took place, and later, to be able to make a sound decision as to an offer if one is made. You should also evaluate your performance. Take the time to reexamine your qualifications and your weak points. This time to recap is so important because after many interviews, the facts and your feelings will tend to blur. Don't trust your memory; jot it down.

After you've made your notes and done your evaluation, the last but most important follow-up to all interviews is to send a thank-you letter. A thank-you letter is a brief, well-written reminder that you are the best person for the job. Whether you want the job or not, and regardless of how the interview went, you should always send a thank-you to your interviewer(s). Send separate ones to each of your interviewers if there were more than one. Some hiring decisions have been made on this point alone.

One final note about follow-up: Even if you don't get the job, you should follow the rejection with a response. You can either call or write a short letter expressing your appreciation for the time spent with you and asking that you be considered for future openings when they arise. Sending a letter is best because job seekers do not often do it, so it sets you apart from your competition. Applicants who were turned down for the first position have often been called for a second one. In addition, if you were offered the job but turned it down, you should write a polite letter thanking the company for offering you the position and give valid reasons for declining. You want to keep your options open for future opportunities.

What to Do Between Interviews

When you are looking for employment, you need to devote as much time to it as is possible. If you are unemployed, you should treat job hunting as though it were your job, giving it eight hours a day and no less than five days a week. If you are looking while you are holding a full-time job, you need to use all available time you have before and after work, during lunch hours, and on Saturdays. Many employers will meet with you on their lunch hour, after work, or on Saturday if you've given them good reason to do so—that is, if you've created a desire in them to consider you for a position they have open. The only way to acquire the job you want is to pursue it with all the energy, commitment, and determination you can muster. That means that you continue to search out job leads and openings and to arrange for interviews when you are between interviews. You do not sit by the phone waiting to hear from an interviewer who "almost promised" you the job.

Job seekers very often come back from an interview absolutely *positive* that they had the job because "the interviewer just the same as said so." Well, many times they didn't have it. Most interviewers are very positive during the interview and will give you strong indications that you are "the one." This may be because they do have an interest in you, and they want you to hold your options open for them *in case* they decide to offer you the job. Interviewers are also sometimes very inept at rejecting applicants face to face. Or it may be that at the time you were interviewed, you were the best applicant, but a subsequent interview may have produced another applicant who was better qualified.

So don't sit around waiting for a call. If you don't get the job, you are back to square one. You will have to get your momentum and morale up and your feelings of rejection down. So don't waste time sitting by the phone and checking the mailbox when you could be generating new job leads and interviews. The strongest argument in favor of keeping busy with your job search while you wait to hear is that your feelings of rejection will be minimized if you have another interview or offer pending when you get the "Sorry" call or letter.

Dealing with Rejection

Realistically, you usually do not get the first job for which you interview. You need to prepare yourself to accept the fact that you will have to deal with some rejection. Everyone has difficulty dealing with rejection. We often assume that there is something wrong with us, when in fact, there isn't. Ninety-nine percent of the time, rejection says nothing about you but more about the person who is doing the rejecting. In a job search, being rejected can be devastating unless you prepare yourself to handle it in a constructive manner. Here are some tips to help you.

Above all, don't take it personally. Rejection has nothing to do with you as a person. The chances are, you didn't get the job because you didn't "fit" with the company because of some minor detail. If the employer didn't feel that you would fit in with the other employees, you probably *wouldn't* have. This can be a blessing in disguise because had you gotten the job, the possibility is very strong that you would not have felt comfortable and would have quit soon after taking it. That just wasn't the right job for you; yours is still out there waiting for you.

Find others who are job searching.   Either join a job search support group or establish one of your own. The employment section of your local newspaper publishes lists of activities, workshops, and support groups for all kinds of people looking for work. There is a lot to be gained from getting and giving help and support to others who are facing the same situation as you. You can give each other moral support and encouragement and exchange ideas about what works or doesn't work. You may even get job leads—all job seekers, when they are searching, uncover positions that do not apply to them.

Don't get sidetracked.   This is not the time to clean the garage or the hall closet, or to change the oil in your car. Devote your energy to finding a job.

Do your own footwork.   Don't sign up with an agency unless you have exhausted all possibilities. Even then, be very cautious because you are very vulnerable at this time and may be tempted to take a job that is not right for you. Besides, you have all the techniques right in this book that agencies use to find jobs, and maybe even more. Make more cold calls and get more information on what you are qualified to do and for which companies. The more you know about what employers are looking for in your field, the better you can sell yourself to them. Also, you could reap a double reward from this: In the process of getting information, you could acquire viable job leads.

Don't turn down any interview.   Even if the job looks like one that you wouldn't be particularly interested in, you just never know what might turn up. Also, the more you interview, the better you become at selling yourself.

Look at your job search as a positive, learning experience.   Every time you interview, get turned down, or talk to an employer about a job, you learn more about yourself and your capabilities.

Job searching is sometimes simply a "numbers game."   According to the law of averages, after so many calls, interviews, and "no's," you are bound to get a "yes." So just keep going!

Evaluating the Job Offer and Negotiating Salary

I received a phone call one day from a former student I had placed in an excellent position with a prestigious company. Julie said that it was a very good job, the employer was very good to her, and she was making more than an adequate salary, but she just wasn't happy. She said, "Carolyn, I need to come talk to you; this job is just not what I want. There is no challenge, and I'm not using the talents that I know I have. I guess I just didn't look at the job closely enough before I took it." Sound familiar?

This happens to many people. If you don't take the time to evaluate the job and the company in relation to your abilities and goals, you may become like the workers that Fredrick Herzberg, noted psychologist and professor at Case Western Reserve University, speaks of in his book *Work and the Nature of Man*. He says that most workers are in a sort of neutral world, neither satisfied nor dissatisfied. Do you doubt this? I challenge you—survey offices in any city in the United States and observe how many workers display signs, posters, or pictures that say "Hang in there, it's only Monday," "I'd rather be fishing/camping/ skiing," or "T.G.I.F. (Thank God It's Friday!)." Robert G. Allen, author of *Creating Wealth*, echoes the bumper sticker that reads "I owe, I owe, so it's off to work I go!" when he says that 20 million people go off to work each day to jobs they can't stand because they value security more than satisfaction.

How can you avoid being one of those 20 million? Evaluating a job offer is the final step in successful job searching and the key to job satisfaction. Many applicants accept jobs that are not right for them. After all, you've worked hard at doing all the "right" things to get interviews, and now you finally have an offer. Shouldn't you eagerly accept it? You can usually think of a thousand reasons why you should take it, but unfortunately, you probably haven't considered the reasons why perhaps you shouldn't. Often the only thing job searchers consider when given a job offer is the salary, and even then they usually accept less than what they are worth.

Only when you have matched the job offer to your self-assessment can you be certain that it is the right job for you. The "ideal job" is a match of several factors, not just the salary and benefits. If those factors are present, *then* it's appropriate to examine the salary and benefits.

Negotiating Your Salary

Before you attempt to negotiate with an employer for a salary, you must be certain that a solid job offer has been made. Once this has been established and you've decided you want the job, the next step—*before* you speak with the employer—is to learn as much as you can about how companies set salaries. Many factors determine the salary a company offers a prospective employee. A company may use the Job Worth system (sometimes called the Factor Comparison Method), the Market Worth system, the salaries of other employees within the company, the company's ability to pay, market demand, and sometimes, your last or current salary.

In the Job Worth system, each job in the company is assigned a point value. Points are awarded on the basis of the following criteria:

- Job responsibilities
- Minimum experience and training required
- Mental skill and knowledge
- Physical requirements
- Problem-solving skills
- Accountability

Everyone who fills this position will be paid exactly the same; in other words, the job has a certain salary value, and anyone occupying that position draws that salary.

If a Market Worth system is used, the salary will be commensurate with what the competition (the market) is paying, based on industry standards. Small- to medium-sized companies generally use this system. The market, and therefore the salary, will differ in different geographical areas, because it costs a lot more to live in cities such as New York City and Los Angeles than to live in, say, a small town in central Kansas.

The company's ability to pay is, of course, also a crucial factor in salary determination. Small and brand-new companies may not have the revenue of larger, more established companies so will offer non-monetary benefits instead of higher salaries. These benefits could vary from a free parking space to days off to flextime scheduling.

The company may use your last or current salary as a factor in their offer, but it is not always a fair judge of how much you're worth. You may have added educational and skill levels that were not required in that job.

Demand (as in market demand) is another possible factor. If the demand is high, meaning that there are too few qualified applicants to fill available positions, employers are more likely to offer higher salaries. The opposite may be true when the market is saturated with applicants.

You're probably wondering what to do with all this information. How is this going to help you with negotiating when you receive an offer? Now that you know the factors that determine salary, you can personalize your package for negotiation. To do this, you need information on the range of salaries in your geographical area, the skills required for the position, the market demand, and the "scoop" on the company. Guess what? You are going to do more research. Where? Here are a few places you can obtain salary surveys that contain comparative information on average wages across different occupations, regions of the country, and levels of experience:

- Annual State Occupational Guides.
- Publications such as your local newspapers and news and trade magazines (*U.S. News & World Report* is excellent).
- College placement offices.
- Peers and people you know who are in the field.
- Are You Paid What You're Worth? by Michael O'Malley, Broadway Books, New York.
- Recruiters and headhunters.

The Internet offers salary surveys at the following websites:

- www.careers.wsj.com
- www.bls.gov
- www.yahoo.com/society and www.yahoo.com/culture/organizations/professional www.yahoo.com/business and www.yahoo.com/economy/ organizations/trade associations
- www.careersoncommand.com
- www.salary.com
- www.wageweb.com
- www.newslink.org
- www.dbm.com/jobguide
- www.careerbuilder.com (advice and resources)

When you know the salary ranges for your area, the skills required, the market demand, and the "scoop" on the company that has made you an offer, you're ready to assess your market value: what *you* are worth. Complete the forms on the next three pages and use them as a guide to help you determine the wage you can ask for.

D ETERMING YOUR PRICE TAG

Position Being Considered:
_____

What are the skills and qualifications for this position?

_____
_____
_____
_____
_____
_____
_____

What did I find is the average salary for this type of job?

What are my skills and qualifications as compared to the average worker in this position?

_____
_____
_____
_____
_____
_____

Based on the information above, I believe that I am worth $_____

in annual (monthly, hourly) salary; therefore, I will request wages in the

range of $_____ to $_____ .

![Y] OUR BOTTOM LINE

What do you think you are worth? What is the job worth? Earlier, you evaluated the things that you value. Now is the time to determine if the job really offers the things you value—or the salary level you require. In the Needs/Interest area, you answered some questions titled "What Do I Want?" You can now evaluate the job offer to see if the job offer provides those things.

YOUR BOTTOM LINE _____!

SALARY

_____ Hourly Wage

_____ Monthly Salary

_____ Annual Salary

BENEFITS

_____ Full Medical—Employer Paid

_____ Full Medical—with Copay

_____ Family Medical—Employer Paid

_____ Family Medical—with Copay

_____ Dental

_____ Vision

_____ Prescriptions

_____ Uniform Allowance

_____ Travel Allowance

_____ Cafeteria Plan

_____ Life Insurance

_____ Disability Insurance

_____ Pay for Time Not Worked/Overtime

_____ Retirement Plan

_____ Tuition Reimbursement

_____ Higher Salary if Some Benefits Waived

QUALITY OF WORK LIFE

_____ Respect

_____ Scope of Responsibilities

_____ Professional Environment

_____ Coworker Compatibility

_____ Management Compatibility

_____ Advancement Opportunity or Career Path

_____ Time Off (Leisure Time)

_____

_____

_____

_____

_____

_____

_____

Y OUR NEGOTIATING LINE

What will make you very happy? (Realistically)

Negotiating Line _____ !

SALARY

____ **Hourly Wage**

____ **Monthly Salary**

____ **Annual Salary**

QUALITY OF WORK LIFE

_____
_____
_____
_____
_____
_____
_____
_____
_____
_____

BENEFITS

_____
_____
_____
_____
_____
_____
_____
_____
_____
_____

Negotiating Your Benefits

Your compensation package includes benefits as well as salary. These, too, can be negotiated, so you should be prepared and not always accept what is offered if the benefits do not meet your needs. When deciding whether to reject or accept an offer, remember that money isn't everything, and that you can sometimes actually make *more* money with things like bonuses and stock options—anywhere from 30 to 60 percent of your base salary—than by receiving a higher salary. Some benefits, such as Social Security, unemployment, and workers' compensation, are mandated (all employers must offer them by law) and some are voluntary. Employers are realizing that in this day and age, they must change their thinking about what constitutes a benefits package. According to James E. Challenger, "companies are offering 'soft benefits' that are designed to give employees more time to work and enjoy life." Employees now enjoy perks such as car washes at lunch and in-house dry cleaning. Some companies even adjust work schedules to allow early quitting times on Fridays during the summer. Other benefits that could be offered are relocation assistance, vacation time, stock options, club memberships, commissions, or even company cars. So before you negotiate with an employer for a benefit package, be aware of what you need and what is available to you. To begin, use the Benefit Checklist on pages 350 and 351. Your objective is to negotiate the maximum benefit package possible. Keep in mind that benefits can cost the employer anywhere from 15 to 40 percent of your salary, so it is in the company's best interest to keep those costs to a minimum.

Negotiating the Offer

Once you've established your worth and have the compensation package that you believe you deserve firmly in mind, the next step is negotiating with the employer. This step requires that you know what benefits you can bring to the company and are prepared to sell them. Why should an employer agree to give you the compensation for which you are asking? What are you offering in return? Why are you worth the figure you're asking? If you've done your research, you will know what the company's needs are and how you can help to fill those needs. Your job is to convince *them* you can fill their needs. Assure the employer that you are as interested in meeting the company's goals as well as your own. Keep your negotiation focused, and don't get sidetracked into talking only about your needs. You are paid a salary, not because you need a new computer, car, or house or because your kid needs braces, but because of your worth to the company. Do not under any circumstances let the negotiation become an adversarial (me against you) relationship by becoming argumentative or emotional. Your objective is a win/win solution.

Negotiating Tips

Ask for what you want (and negotiate if your request is declined).   If you don't ask, you may never get what you want, and more likely, you will get your bottom line (or lower). Be comfortable with silence. The person with the least tolerance of silence will attempt to fill the void by speaking—many times by offering to compromise.

If the proposed salary is too low, try to negotiate other ways to achieve both your goals and those of the prospective employer.   Be flexible: Introduce ways besides salary that will achieve both your goals and those of the prospective employer. You might want to negotiate the benefit package. For example, if you don't need the medical insurance and it costs the company $200 per month, decline coverage and ask for half of the premium to be added to your salary—a $100 increase for you and a $100 savings for the company. You might propose that the employer enlarge the job to give you more latitude in salary range. If you are going to do more than the current job description, a higher salary is appropriate.

Don't let the employer negotiate your salary down with non-monetary perks.   Accept this only if the perks are ones that you place a high value on and would be happy with.

Avoid providing a specific salary figure, if possible, until the full negotiation of the position and other factors have been resolved.   Don't be the first to give a definitive figure; ask for the salary range of that position. If pressed, say that you believe your qualifications probably place you somewhere between the midpoint and maximum salary range and resell your best features again at this time. Understanding that there is a "going rate" range for similar personnel in the workforce and knowing what that range is lets you state a figure at the midpoint or higher level.

If asked, discuss your current salary honestly.   Sometime during the negotiating process, you may be asked a question about your current or most recent salary. How you answer this question could be a strong deciding factor in the salary offered you by the interviewer. Be truthful when you give them a figure, of course, and be sure to include your non-monetary compensation in addition to your base salary.

Know the benefits available in the workplace.   For example, some companies offer six paid holidays a year, and others may offer eight or more. Some offer one week of vacation with pay after one year, others may offer two weeks after a year. Some offer only a maximum of two weeks of vacation no matter how long you work for the company, while others allow you to take additional weeks of paid vacation per year after a certain number of years of employment. Not all health plans cover what you need. For example, some require you to use the plan's doctors, others allow you to use the plan's doctors at one rate (plan pays 100 percent) or to use doctors outside the plan at another rate (60/40—the plan pays 60 percent, you pay 40 percent). Keep in mind the benefits you want, including what kind of flexibility you want in a medical plan.

Read about employee benefits at the library. I recommend *The Handbook of Employee Benefits* by Jerry S. Rosenbloom. While you're there, also see Michael O'Malley's book *Are You Paid What You're Worth?* for some excellent tips on negotiating salaries, benefits, bonuses, and raises.

Negotiate from a position of strength and with enthusiasm.   How do you do this? Simple: Sell the employer on the idea that you are the best solution to the company's problems. If the employer has offered you the job, it has made the decision that you are the number one choice. Having selected you as number one, the employer will negotiate, to a point, to hire you rather than settle for their second or third choice. This gives you an advantage and a strong negotiating position. If you express your enthusiasm for the position and resell your abilities to meet the employer's needs, you will indeed be negotiating from a position of some power.

Have your completed Bottom Line and Negotiating Line checklists available when negotiating.   With this information readily available to you, you can usually make an immediate decision to accept the position or not. If you are not completely sure, the alternative is to say "I very much appreciate this offer, I believe it is an exciting opportunity for me, and I would like to think it over. If it's acceptable to you, may I call you tomorrow with my answer?" If the offer is too low, you can renegotiate by saying something such as "I am really thrilled with your offer and am highly motivated to work for your company; I know I can do an excellent job for you. However, I would have difficulty meeting my financial needs at the proposed salary. With school loans and other financial obligations, I need a salary of around $_____. Would it be possible to meet again and take another look at the salary to see if we can somehow reach a position where I could help you to meet your needs and, at the same time, still meet my financial obligations?"

Be gracious. Allow the employer to feel that he or she has won some compromises. "You've got to live with these people after you join them," says Scott Kingdom, managing director of the Chicago office of Korn/Ferry, the nation's biggest headhunting firm.[10]

Additional Considerations

In addition to the salary and benefits, a few other things warrant your attention. Are the company itself, the physical environment, and the personnel what you are looking for in a job?

- *The company:* Is it large or small, new to the community or an older, respected and reliable organization? Is the company progressive? Is the industry that it's in expanding or receding? Does the company have a policy manual (or written statements) regarding its policies on employee vacations, terminations, and working conditions?

- *The physical environment:* Where is the company located? Is it in a "better" part of town or in an inconvenient or even dangerous area? What do the buildings, furnishings, and equipment reflect: pride or indifference? Where will you be working: in the back of the building away from everyone, or up front where the action is? Where would you like to be?

- *The people:* What kind of people work for this company? Are they primarily of one age group, and is it yours? Who is going to be your immediate supervisor? Have you met this person and does your intuition tell you that you could work comfortably with him or her? In your interactions with this company during pre-interview and interview visits, how were you treated? Were you made to feel at ease and welcome? How did the employees interact with each other? How would you describe the company and the people, and will you be happy and productive working with these people?

- *The job:* How is this job going to affect your personal life? Is it going to require that you be away from home frequently, possibly on weekends, limiting your time with your family and friends? Do you know exactly what you will be doing during the day? Where does this position lead? What are your chances for promotion, transferring to other departments, and learning new skills?

Make the decision to accept or not accept a job offer based on all of the foregoing items. This decision is a vital one that will affect your life, your happiness, and your well-being. You should not make it hastily without carefully considering all the ramifications. If you've prepared an error-free resume and cover letter, have studied the tips on how to interview effectively, and have matched the job to your personal assessment of values and needs, you are well on your way to getting your ideal job with an ideal compensation package. The bottom line is, only *you* can decide whether or not the job is right for you.

E MPLOYEE BENEFIT CHECKLIST

○ **Health Plan**

_____ Employee Only—Company Paid

_____ Copay Premium for Employee

_____ Family

_____ Type _____ PPO _____ HMO _____ Other

_____ Dental

_____ Vision

_____ Rx Plan

_____ Wellness (Physical Exams)

○ **Life Insurance**

_____ Times _____ Year's Salary

_____ Additional Coverage Available

○ _____ Disability Income Plan

○ _____ Dependent Card—Child Care Assistance

○ _____ Employee Assistance Programs (EAPs)

○ **Payment for Time Not Worked/Overtime**

_____ Vacation Policy

_____ Paid Holidays

_____ Comp Time

_____ Overtime Compensation

_____ Personal Leave of Absence (w/o pay)

_____ Funeral Leave

_____ Jury Duty

_____ Military Leave

_____ Inclement Weather Absences (office closed down)

_____ Sick Leave

○ **Retirement Plans**

_____ Profit Sharing Plans

_____ 401(k) Plans

(continued)

EMPLOYEE BENEFIT CHECKLIST Continued

⊘ —— SEP (Simplified Employee Pension)

—— Keogh Plans

—— Employee Stock Option Plans (ESOPs)

⊘ Pay Raises —— Annual —— Other —— Merit —— Negotiated

⊘ Cafeteria Plan

—— Pretax Savings of Medical Premiums/Child Care/Adult Care

⊘ Pay Status

—— Exempt Only basis for exemption from being paid overtime is if you are classified as:

—— Executive (Managers)

—— Administrative (for those who carry out the policies of the company)

—— Outside Sales

—— Computer Related (primarily programmers and systems analysts)

—— Professional (requires advanced degrees—teachers, lawyers, artistic endeavors)

⊘ Pay Periods

—— Monthly

—— Biweekly

—— Twice a Month

Salary/Wages

$—— Hourly

$—— Biweekly/Twice a Month

$—— Monthly

$—— Annually

Travel

—— If you have to travel on behalf of your employer, are you compensated for using your car? (approximately 36 cents per mile)

⊘ Tuition Assistance (for job-related courses)

⊘ Other Benefits

——

——

Notes

1. Todd E. Van Hoosear, April 14, 1995, [online]. Available e-mail: vanhoose@gdl.msu.edu.

2. Mary B. Nemnich and Fred E. Jandt, *Cyberspace Job Search Kit 2001–2002 Edition, The Complete Guide to Online Job Seeking and Career Information* (Indianapolis, IN: JIST Publishing, 2001), 74–76. Reprinted by permission.

3. Kim Johnson Gross, *Work Clothes: Casual Dress for Serious Work* (New York: Knopf, 1996).

4. Nemnich and Jandt, p. 215.

5. Clinton T. Greenleaf III and Stefani Schaefer, *Attention to Detail: A Woman's Guide to Professional Appearance and Conduct* (Chesterland, OH: Greenleaf Enterprises, 2000), p. 12.

6. Caroline Hsu, The Testing of America, *U.S. News & World Report* (September 20, 2004): 67.

7. Caroline Hsu, Science & Society, *U.S. News & World Report* (September 20, 2004): 68.

8. Charting Your Own Course, *U.S. News & World Report*, Career Guide 2001 (November 6, 2000): 56.

9. James E. Challenger, Job Decision Isn't Just About the Money, January 16, 2000 [online]. Available: www.suntimes.com/output/challenger/chat.

10. How to Negotiate, *U.S. News & World Report* (November 1, 1999): 92.